DOODLEBUG DAYS

DOODLEBUG DAYS

An American Family's
Ups and Downs as
Middle-Class Migrants
in the California of the 1930s

Nancy L. Gallop
Dorothy L Bristol

NANCY LOCKARD GALLOP
AND
DOROTHY LOCKARD BRISTOL

To order additional copies of this book, contact:
Xlibris Corporation
1-888-7-XLIBRIS
www.Xlibris.com
Orders@Xlibris.com

CONTENTS

DEDICATION

To our parents,
who somehow managed
to make hard times
seem like good times.

INTRODUCTION

We tend to put books, like people, into categories. A book labeled "memoir," especially one written by two women who were school children sixty years ago, suggests family tales recalled over tea in hushed voices.

Doodlebug Days does not fit in that category any more than the authors fit the stereotype that burdens many older women.

Doodlebug Days, rather, is a slice of women's history peppered with humor and salted with authenticity.

While photographer Dorothea Lange gave us a picture of the Great Depression that seared the despair on one migrant woman's face onto pages of nearly every account of those years, the sisters have widened what we know about the 1930s by focusing on what those times meant to the women of one middle-class family. What's more, they have made it fun to read.

At the National Women's History Project, we celebrate a song written for us called "A Fine and Long Tradition." We also call it "Our Song." The chorus, which has caused more than one of us to shed tears while singing, describes women's experiences as a woven tapestry with ". . . Woman after woman making choices just like me. . . ."

In *Doodlebug Days*, the Lockard sisters make the hard choice to leave the security of their hometown and follow their father, a civil engineer on an oil exploration party, into the heat, tule fog and prejudice against migrants of California's San Joaquin Valley. Again, words from "Our Song" ring true: ". . . They challenged their own times. . . ."

I feel it's significant that Sunny and Nancy's parents allowed them to make this choice, especially their mother, Dorothy, who, while not exactly ". . . Sacrificing willingly . . ."—again from "Our Song"—bore the brunt of the hardships.

It's also significant that the sisters confided to me that, in planning the book and reliving those two years, they began to come to terms with their feelings for their mother. They admitted that most of their lives they had been critical of her, focusing their love and admiration on their father.

And, as the book developed, chapter by chapter, the sisters' feelings deepened. "Look what Mother had to contend with!" they agreed. "Being uprooted from her home, parents and friends. Cooking three meals a day in 100 degree heat and moving on a few days notice. Looking for rentals, cajoling landlords, settling us children in ever-new schools! No wonder she was often out of sorts."

As their resentment diminished, their admiration for their mother grew, and feelings that had long been troublesome mellowed. Again, words from "Our Song" say it: ". . . Some were great and some were good, some did as they could. . . ."

I feel ". . . *did as they could* . . ." is key. During the Great Depression, many families simply did the best they could. In *Doodlebug Days* we hear the voices of two plucky girls doing their best. And, quoting "Our Song" once more, ". . . It's there to find between the lines . . ."—the strength of their mother as well as their father.

Molly Murphy MacGregor, Executive Director, National Women's History Project

PREFACE

What possesses two sisters in their seventies to sit down at their PCs and write a book?

Our ages and our lifelong close relationship led to many discussions about our childhood, which was lived in California against a background of the Great Depression while the conflicts that led to WWII were brewing elsewhere in the world.

The more we talked, mostly on walks among the redwoods or on the blustery Northern California beaches, the more we saw a period of our lives, from 1935 to 1937, as very special—and perhaps worth the telling. We felt it could even be called unique since our parents allowed us to decide whether or not to travel with our father, a civil engineer, on a geophysical survey crew that would move every few months in search of oil primarily in California's San Joaquin Valley.

The San Joaquin Valley, some 250 miles long and up to 75 miles wide, lies within California's Great Central Valley, which grows one quarter of the table food produced in the United States. Summers are hot, and winters can bring oppressive, low-lying tule fog. The Sierra Nevadas tower to the east, and to the west lie the Coast Ranges. It is generally agreed that the San Joaquin Valley, *our* Valley, reaches south from the confluence of the Sacramento and San Joaquin rivers to the Tehachapi Mountains. The first direct passage between the Valley and Los Angeles, the old Ridge Route, twisted precipitously through the lower Tehachapis.

In 1933 some of the twists of "the most dangerous highway in the U.S." were modified, but a trip over the Ridge was still an adventure.

Between 1900 and 1936 California led the nation in petroleum production. Oil companies, certain that great reserves of oil still lay hidden, sent exploration crews—called doodlebug parties—out to find them.

By setting explosives off in a series of holes, doodlebuggers would measure the echoes and make a seismic record that might indicate the presence of oil. Because of the competition among oil companies, doodlebuggers, such as our father, were pledged to keep the nature of their jobs and their movements secret.

Twenty percent of the country's labor force was unemployed in 1935, and more than a million of the jobless rode freight trains and hitchhiked across the country seeking work. Conditions in the Dust Bowl drove additional thousands to abandon their homes and look for farm work in California. Our father felt fortunate to be holding a job, even one that worked a hardship on his wife and children.

Yet, as we left our home in Southern California and headed north over the Ridge Route, towing our possessions behind our 1935 Oldsmobile in a small canvas-covered trailer, the security of our family unit buffered us against these hardships. In small towns up and down the Valley, our parents pulled their kitchen chairs close to their radio to listen to President Roosevelt's fireside chats, their faces showing quiet concern as FDR discussed the social turbulence that marked the era. We children dealt with the more pressing matter of always being the new kids at school.

Life in the mid-thirties was different. Radios, not televisions, were prominently enshrined in each living room. We played Hearts or Monopoly, read the Oz Books and kept a jigsaw puzzle on the coffee table alongside the *National Geographic*. Our family, along with friends and relatives, talked and *talked* as we sipped giant glasses of iced tea, and the ordinarily socially taboo subjects of religion and politics were favorite topics—along with the meaning of life. We children were never left out. We had our say then sat on our front porches and watched shooting stars while our father pointed out the Big Dipper and the North Star.

One suitcase apiece held our clothes and treasured keepsakes. One pair of brown oxfords, half-soled until we outgrew them, did for all occasions. If a trip to the Fred Astaire, Ginger Rogers movie, *Top Hat*, was suggested, the whole family poured loose change onto the dining room table and counted it to see if it was enough.

Rose water and glycerin soothed chapped hands, and mustard plasters treated chest colds. Doctors, of course, made house calls, and most men could fix the family car on a Saturday afternoon. Migrant workers, who earned 15 cents an hour picking potatoes or 50 cents for 100 pounds of cotton, could buy a meal of soup and bread for a nickel. For the more fortunate, Sunday dinner was a well-done rump roast, mashed potatoes and gravy, pineapple and cottage cheese salad, and glasses of whole milk followed by Jell-O and whipped cream. Yes, the thirties were different. One day, walking along Doran Beach near Bodega Bay, we decided our story *was* worth telling. We call it *Doodlebug Days*.

Dorothy Lockard Bristol
Nancy Lockard Gallop

CHAPTER 1

Let the Girls Decide

Spring 1935, Lynwood, California

> *"Never marry a civil engineer," Mother told her two daughters repeatedly, "especially one on an oil exploration crew. He'll never be home."*
>
> *Her oldest daughter, Sunny, was 12 1/2, and her youngest, Nancy, had just turned 10. Their brother, Skippy, was nearly four.*

Sunny and Nancy

We girls had no immediate plans for marriage.

Daddy had been away for seven months working on a geophysical survey—or "doodlebug"—party, in the San Joaquin Valley. His job was to obtain permits to work on private land and survey the lines along which a series of holes would be drilled. Dynamite exploded in these holes provided a seismic record for interpretation by geophysicists. Because of the fierce competition among oil companies to discover new sources of oil, the party moved on little notice and kept as low a profile as possible.

While Daddy was far away with the seismic crew Mother was left in Lynwood to cope single-handed with a growing

---

37-GALL

family. Understandably, Daddy's home visits were infrequent. Mother missed him and we children missed him even more. Mother often reassured us by saying, "Girls, one of these days your father will be working closer to home, I'm sure!"

One Friday night in April when Daddy arrived home for a weekend visit, our parents, a serious young couple anxious to do the best for their children, had it out. We imagine it went something like this:

"Bruce, can you be serious? Following you wherever your job takes you would be such a hardship on the girls! They like their schools, they're getting good grades, and I'd planned to start them with music lessons. I'm certain they won't want to leave their friends. This house we're renting is in a good neighborhood. The girls like it here and they have suitable playmates."

Mother's lips set in a thin line as she reinforced her case. "We don't know anything about the schools in the Valley. All those farmers, and you know what kind of people farm work attracts. No. As much as we miss you, it just doesn't seem right. Children need stability, continuity." Mother took a sock out of her basket of mending and started darning the hole in the toe. Daddy was silent for a while, then he spoke.

"I know how you feel, Hon, but children are more adaptable than we think. The fact that they're good students means that they could adjust to any school, and there's nothing wrong with the schools in the San Joaquin Valley. Also, there would be advantages."

"Advantages? Such as?"

"For one thing," Daddy answered, "I'd be home every night. On weekends we could go to the Sierra Nevada Mountains. The girls and Skippy would love trips to Sequoia National Park. In the Valley they'd meet different kinds of people and have new experiences. They'd see more of California and learn about its geography and diversity. I think it would be very educational for them."

Mother's mouth tightened into an unconvinced pucker. "The children have advantages, as you call them, right here. And what would we do with our furniture? Put it in storage, or sell it? How often would we have to move?"

"I don't know," Daddy replied with characteristic honesty. "We could be in one place for weeks, even months. I just can't say with any certainty. It depends on the results of our field work and on orders from the main office. We doodlebuggers have to move on the spur of the moment because of the secrecy of our work."

Mother frowned. "Spur of the moment?" Dropping her darning, she looked Daddy straight in the eye. "Moving around with three children would be no picnic, especially with a little boy as active as Skippy is!"

"I know, and I'd help you in every way possible."

Mother sighed. "If only . . . if only you could find a job that didn't involve traipsing around like a band of gypsies."

"The country is still suffering from the Depression, Hon. My job on the doodlebug party is a good one and it pays fairly well. I'm lucky to have it. You know how tough things are these days. And if you and the children travel with me I'll get a larger allowance for moving and housing expenses."

Mother sighed again. "But I was thinking . . . if maybe we waited a while . . . something might turn up."

"No signs of that," Daddy said. "Plenty of good civil engineers are out of work these days. I want my family with me. Besides, there's something I haven't told you."

Mother was clearly out of patience. "What's that for heaven's sake?"

"We're working near Tulare right now, but rumor has it that we may be moving farther north. If that happens, I won't be able to get home at all on the weekends. It will be too far to drive."

"I'm only thinking of the girls," Mother said.

"In that case," Daddy said, "let *them* decide."

"*What?*" Mother looked startled.

"Yes, why not? We'll discuss it with them and see how they react."

Mother jabbed the darning needle into the toe of a heavy wool boot sock. A frown lingered on her face. "Children don't decide these things! That's what parents are for!"

"The girls are sensible. Let's explain the situation to them and see how they feel about it."

"They won't want to leave Lynwood," Mother said with a tone of finality. "I'm sure of it."

Daddy persisted. "And if they *are* willing to leave? Would you go along with it?" Daddy seldom pushed Mother, but this was important to him.

Several seconds went by before Mother answered. "All right. We'll put it to the girls. Let them decide. But I know what their answer will be."

Sunny

My little brother, Skippy, a freckled, red-haired dynamo, had been put to bed. The four of us, my mother, father, sister, and I gathered around the heavy, round oak table in the dining room. Mother looked serious, but she did not look angry. That was a relief! Daddy, who never looked angry, looked serious as well. Mother said, "Girls, I want you to listen *very carefully*." Daddy remained quiet. Nancy and I had no idea that we were going to make a crucial family decision.

Mother's penetrating gaze fell first on Nancy, whose wide eyes gazed back from underneath her Dutch boy bangs, and then settled on me. "You girls keep saying how much you miss Daddy. You know he tries to get home as often as possible, but sometimes he's just too far away to make the trip. Daddy wants us to go with him, but I think it would be a hardship on you girls."

Mother leaned back in the oak chair and folded her arms. "We'd be moving from town to town, and you'd have to change schools frequently. Not only that, but the San Joaquin Valley is *very* hot in the summer."

Mother looked me right in the eye as she pressed her point. "You'd have to make new friends, Sunny. Both of you would. We couldn't take many things with us. It wouldn't be easy for you."

Visions of adventure caused my heart to thump. What was coming next? Mother continued, "Daddy and I have agreed to let you girls make the choice. Stay here in this house, without having to change schools and leave your friends, or go with Daddy. It's up to you." Mother folded her arms and smugly waited for the answer she knew she would get.

With Daddy gone so much, life wasn't the same. Unlike Mother, he treated Nancy and me more like companions than children. It wasn't just the drives along the coast, the picnics at the beach or the swimming lessons at Belmont Shore near our home that we missed. We missed helping Daddy pluck and dress our Rhode Island Red chickens, gather the eggs and spread the chicken feed. We were by his side when he built a bookcase, repaired the plumbing or made a kite for us out of newspapers and sticks held together with flour and water paste.

We missed Daddy at dinner, which was always a complete meal with meat, potatoes, two vegetables and salad served in the dining room when he was home.

Mother served a less lavish, but still adequate, supper at the kitchen table when he was gone. And, importantly, Daddy's presence formed a buffer between Nancy and me and Mother's sharp impatience. With Daddy away, Mother had more time to focus on our behavior and we had no one to appease her on our behalf. When Daddy was home a spilled glass of milk was an unfortunate accident, cleaned up quickly and soon forgotten. When he was gone it was a misdeed punished by a few hard swats on the rear.

I was proud of my tall, athletic father, suntanned and hard-muscled from his treks across the hot, dry, dusty land of the San Joaquin Valley with his surveyor's rod and transit. Always willing to help Nancy and me with our homework, to explain a geological formation or the significance of tree rings, my father was the embodiment of patience and tolerance.

Mother, on the other hand, was quick-tempered. She had a fast way of doing things and was impatient with laggards. While Mother's domestic accomplishments were many, unlike Daddy she shunned the outdoors. Hanging out the family wash and cultivating her zinnias was as close as Mother got to participating in an active outdoor life. Already beginning to plump out a little, Mother's once slender figure was becoming more like that of her stocky German father than that of her trim Scots mother. Everyone Mother met fell under the spell of her pretty face, dark naturally wavy hair and easy laugh. But her public persona could change into a dark mood at home, causing Nancy and me to fall into the habit of testing the direction of the wind like sailors on an uncertain sea.

"Well, Sunny?" Mother prompted.

I blurted out, "Go with Daddy!"

Mother looked startled. A strained silence fell over the table. Mother patted her hair and rearranged the bun at the nape of her neck. She removed a large hairpin from the bun and started tapping on the table with it.

Mother looked at Nancy, who was wide eyed but silent, before flashing me one of her severe looks. "Think what this means, Sunny. You would have to leave your school (tap, tap), your friends (tap, tap, tap) and this house (tap). No more overnight stays with Cora Sue (tap, tap)! You'd have to go from school to school, town to town (tap, tap, tap). No more swimming at Belmont Shore on Sundays (tap, tap)."

"I want to go with Daddy," I repeated firmly, though not as loudly as before. Out of the corner of my eye I saw Nancy's head move slightly in a "yes" nod. Mother glowered at Nancy, then at me. Her lips tightened and a flush of red crept over her face. I glanced at Daddy. He was examining his hands as if there might be some dirt under the fingernails. I think I saw him smile, just a little. Neither parent spoke. Then Mother jabbed the hairpin back into her hair, got up and went into the kitchen. There was a clatter of pots and pans.

Nancy and I looked at each other. We knew better than to approach Mother when she was in one of her moods, and we didn't dare ask Daddy any questions about the decision to leave Lynwood for fear Mother would hear and send us off to bed.

To help diffuse the tension Nancy and I found two decks of cards and laid them out on the dining room table for double solitaire. Daddy walked through the kitchen and went outside.

Mother came into the dining room carrying the iced tea pitcher and put it on the sideboard with a thud. Brushing by the table she snapped, "Is that all you two have to do? Play cards? You girls did a sloppy job on the pots and pans and I had to do them over again. *And* wash and dry the pitcher, too."

Nancy and I exchanged glances again as we each put a deuce on the aces that were out. Silence, we knew, was our best defense. A few minutes later Daddy came into the kitchen with some eggs from our chicken pens and put them in the ice box. "Our neighbor Frank does a good job taking care of the chickens while I'm gone," he said. Mother didn't answer.

Daddy came into the dining room. "Who's winning?" he asked Nancy and me.

"It's about even," I replied.

When Nancy and I went to our room we talked softly for a while about the events of the evening. "Mom's mad at us," Nancy whispered.

"I know." My spirits, which had soared at the possibility

of traveling with Daddy, were now deflated. I was afraid we might have to stay in Lynwood after all.

Long after Nancy fell asleep I was still asking myself, "What have I done?" I had made a decision which affected the whole family. Of course, Nancy had agreed with me, but I was the one who had been vocal about it. I lay awake feeling fearful, excited and uncomfortable.

Part of my desire to go with Daddy was the "Osa Johnson" factor. I admired Osa Johnson, who, with her husband, Martin, spent years in Africa photographing wildlife. I wanted to be like Osa, taking pictures of lions, elephants and giraffes and providing game for the trusty native bearers. I read every book that Osa wrote, over and over again, and could recite parts from memory. I wanted adventure, and the change in our lives held that promise.

When I walked to school through the cornfield that belonged to the Wagners' farm at the end of the street, I was Osa Johnson in the dense African jungle. The stick I carried was my gun to protect me in case a lion bounded across my path or a boa constrictor slithered among the cornstalks. But this was kid stuff. I wanted something *real*.

After Daddy took Nancy and me horseback riding a few times, I begged my parents for a pair of riding breeches like Osa's for my birthday, and some boots. They gave me the breeches, but no boots. The breeches laced on the sides just below the knees, and to create the illusion of boots I wore a pair of Daddy's old wool boot socks with my regular brown school shoes. This would have to do until I could get a pair of boots.

Nancy turned over and mumbled something in her sleep. I was afraid that my restlessness had disturbed her, so I held still for a while then returned to my thoughts. If I had a pair of boots, even inexpensive ones, I'd be outfitted just like Osa, almost. I was saving money from my allowance to buy boots, but Mother disapproved. "There are more important things than boots to buy with that money. Don't be ridiculous!"

I knew better than to argue with Mother. When Daddy disagreed with her, he did so in private. Our parents usually presented a united front. The discussion about leaving Lynwood was an exception. I worried that Mother would continue to be angry with me for wanting to travel with Daddy, and that she would take it out on me somehow. Nancy and I had been asked to make a decision, and we had made it. Would that decision hold? I wasn't sure. Adventure was what I wanted. Sunny "Osa Johnson" Lockard was ready to go on safari into the great San Joaquin Valley.

While I idolized Osa Johnson, Mother wanted me to pattern myself after my eighth grade teacher, Miss Monique Le Blanc. Miss Le Blanc was young and pretty. She had stylish clothes and a smart little coupé of her very own. I remember the day Mother rushed into my bedroom and dropped the rotogravure section of the Sunday paper on my lavender chenille bedspread. "Sunny, look! Here's your teacher, Miss Le Blanc! Here she is!"

I looked at the picture. It was Miss Le Blanc, all right, dressed in a white sailor outfit reclining on the deck of a sailboat and smiling her radiant smile. The caption read, "Miss Monique Le Blanc of Lynwood relaxes on her fiancé's sloop, the Merry Girl. Miss Le Blanc and Dr. John Merry announced their engagement last week at the Commodore Yacht Club in Long Beach."

"You see? You see?" Mother said. "How adorable she looks!" Mother cut out the picture and gave it to me. "Take it to Miss Le Blanc." On my way to school the next day I crumpled the picture into a tight little ball and threw it away in the cornfield.

Mother was always bringing up her idea of a teaching career for me—a two-year career, that is. "Teach elementary school for a couple of years and then get married. Like Miss Le Blanc."

Once when my maternal grandmother, Mama Dot, was

visiting us and Mother began planning my future again Mama Dot remarked, "I suppose teaching is all right if you don't stay in it too long, become an old maid and lose your looks." To prettily petite Mama Dot a woman's "looks" were all-important.

"Just a couple of years," Mother emphasized. "That's enough. And if it became necessary, you'd have a career to fall back on."

"Marry somebody with *money*," said Mama Dot, shaking a fresh cigarette out of her Camel pack. "Someone who can provide a nice home, trips to Europe and a maid. Then, if anything happened, you wouldn't *need* to fall back on teaching."

Posing on a sailboat in a white sailor suit wasn't my idea of adventure. I piped up with my own idea. "I want to be an *adventuress*!" I had read that word in a novel I found in Mama Dot's bookcase at The Ranch, our grandparents' home on the Mojave Desert. I thought I knew what the word meant.

Mother and Mama Dot laughed, then Mother said, "Don't use that word. It's not nice."

Mama Dot leaned back and relaxed behind the red glow of her cigarette. Then, dismissing smoke with a wave of her hand, she delivered her final statement on the matter. "Just remember, Sunny, that money makes life easier."

I rolled over, rearranged my pillow and tried to fall asleep. Mama Dot and Mother could say what they liked, but I would marry for love. Some day I'd find *my* Martin Johnson and live an exciting life like Osa's. Osa hadn't said "no" to adventure, and I certainly didn't intend to.

Nancy

Leave Lynwood? My "yes" vote at the family conference was barely a nod.

Lynwood, then a community of some 8,000 south of down-town Los Angeles, was home—the only home I remembered.

Our street, Virginia Avenue off Long Beach Boulevard, was half farm land and half California bungalows. Peanuts grew in a field across from our house, and Daddy kept chickens in pens behind our backyard. The air bore the fragrance of orange blossoms from nearby groves, the saltiness of sea air wafting inland from Long Beach and the smell of oil pumped night and day from the forest of derricks that spiked nearby Signal Hill.

Our trees were palms and pepper trees and eucalyptus, our flowering plants lantana, hibiscus and jasmine.

Unlike my older sister, Sunny, already scholarly and eager to sample the world, and my little brother, Skippy, so curious as a baby that Mother put his crib by the light switch so he could examine his corner of the universe at three a.m., I was a homebody. My mind wasn't on how fortunate Daddy was to have a job—any job—during the Great Depression. I was fully occupied with everyday life.

My ten-year-old feet had already sprouted roots in Lynwood. I knew every zinnia, cosmos and geranium that grew around the foundation of our rented house. Every crack in the sidewalk in front of our house had been jumped, drawn over with chalk squares for hopscotch or avoided as I played jacks, scooping up the metal pieces while the bounced ball was still in the air.

The path I took to school ran through a cornfield planted by the Wagners, a farm family at the dead end of our street. I had finally earned the right to walk through the field without being bullied by Willy Wagner, my age but tough, his chest, arms and bare feet tan where they emerged from his overalls.

Every day as I walked home from school I would pull on stems of the long grass that grew among the corn until I found a piece hollow enough to make a good whistle by biting one end flat. Heart beating in anticipation of Willy's jumping out at me from behind a cornstalk as I neared his farm, I willed my whistled tune to protect me the way I'd read charms protected princesses in the *"My Book House"* fairy tales that sat in our living-room bookcase.

But Willy was never charmed. He would materialize in the middle of the path, standing still in the stalk-dappled light and grinning as I approached. When I came within range, he'd scoop up a handful of dirt clods and aim for the school dress Mother had made me, laughing as the clods exploded against the clean calico and dusted down my legs into my white socks. Then Willy would lunge for one of the puffed sleeves my mother had eased so carefully into my dress or grab at the little-girl bodice I hated but which showed off Mother's considerable smocking skills.

It was the day Willy ripped a sleeve half out of a new white dotted swiss dress that Mother intervened. As I opened our back screen door and stumbled into the kitchen, dirty and crying, Mother pushed a lump of pie dough aside and confronted me, arms akimbo.

"Another dress ruined," she scolded, examining my torn sleeve with hands still powdery with flour. "I may have just enough material left to piece together a new sleeve."

She pointed a flour-coated finger at my runny nose. "Nancy, you and Willy Wagner are the same age and size. I'm ashamed of you for letting him get the best of you. If you don't beat that boy up the next time he bothers you, you're going to get a hard spanking from me. Do you understand, young lady?"

Nodding and sniffling, I let Mother know I understood. At my age her hard spankings were rare, but I dreaded one more than any assault from Willy.

So the next afternoon Willy met his match—a flailing, kicking, teeth-gritting girl who thereafter passed unmolested through the cornfield to school.

A force less controllable than Willy Wagner, the March 1933 Long Beach earthquake, helped shape my affection for the Lynwood house. For days our stucco house shook and swayed and rattled, sometimes sending dishes out of the cupboards or plaster down from the ceiling but always settling back into the three-bedroom, one bath rectangle that was home.

When the 6.3 earthquake first hit, it was 5:54 p.m., and I was alone in the living room engrossed in the radio adventures of Little Orphan Annie.

The quaking found me drawing upon what I'd read in our collection of children's books for an answer. Just having started *"The Wizard of Oz,"* I decided a tornado had swept our house into the sky, and I thought that if I dared cross the pitching floor to the windows to look out, I would see the earth hundreds of feet below.

Mother had just driven into our garage from the grocery store. My sister Sunny was holding 18-month-old Skippy as she climbed out of the car, and the quake threw him out of her arms onto the concrete floor where he skinned his arms and legs and banged his forehead. Later we learned that the market's walls had given way with the first jolt, crushing cars where Mother had been parked just minutes before. Others were not so lucky. One hundred and twenty people were killed in the quake and damage amounted to more than $40 million.

Daddy was in the bathroom when the initial shock burst the medicine cabinet open, sending Bayer Aspirin, Milk of Magnesia and adhesive tape flying out past him into the bathtub.

With his civil engineer's approach to seismic activity, Daddy tried to calm Mother, Sunny, Skippy and me when we gathered in the rattling kitchen by giving us a technical description of what was happening. "We're on the Newport-Inglewood Fault, although the San Andreas is probably the best known in California," he explained between tremors. "Pressures must have built up below the ground, and now we're just experiencing shifts along the fault."

Mother, hugging an awed Skippy to her and eyeing the scrapes from his fall, was clearly experiencing tight-lipped fear along with an undisguised impatience with Daddy and his engineer's objectivity.

But I could tell by the relaxed way Daddy lounged against the kitchen sink and the spark in his hazel eyes that, underneath his concern for us, he was intensely interested in this geological phenomenon.

For days, many of the poorly constructed schools and other buildings in the Lynwood and Long Beach area crumbled to the ground in aftershocks. Huge cracks zigzagged down city streets and soup kitchens served free meals outdoors. Cautious about possible leaks in our natural gas lines, Mother and Daddy cooked our dinners in the backyard over an open fire, and we retreated to the family Oldsmobile parked on the street when the swaying and creaking inside the house got too intense.

Once when all five of us were in the car, a jolt caused the street lamp above us to shatter, sending broken glass hailing down on the metal. Daddy was more concerned, though, when he heard that gas tanks from a nearby "gas farm" had exploded. He had worked at a boiler plant in the Signal Hill oil fields and knew the danger.

But what I remember most was sitting in our living room and hearing the rumbles from the grinding earth followed by the rattling of window glass as the house began to sway. As soon as I saw the water in our fish bowl start to slosh, I would run to Daddy's overstuffed chair and brace against him for another shock.

But by now Daddy trusted the structure of the house, and, as always, I trusted him. He'd smile and say, "Here it comes, Nancy," just as calmly as he did when he and Sunny and I were wading out toward a forming ocean wave at Long Beach.

As the shock hit, I'd watch familiar furnishings dance away from their places. Our ornate little gas heater with ceramic elements would slide away from its gas-line tether, and the floor lamp by which Mother mended our clothes or Daddy read the *National Geographic* would sway on its wrought iron pedestal.

In the midst of it all, Daddy didn't hug me; he wasn't physically demonstrative. I can recall passing by the back of his chair at the dining room table and longing to hug him but being certain that the whole family would laugh at me if I did. Today when I see acquaintances hug each other in an easy show of affection, I wish I could go back to my childhood and give my father one of the hugs that we denied each other.

Still, there was a coziness to being protected in the center of danger, and I wasn't at all sure that such coziness existed anywhere outside of Lynwood.

It was not that life in Lynwood was free of childhood drama, it was just that it was familiar drama. Like an old shoe I knew where it pinched and where it molded to perfection.

Perfection came when Sunny said I could roller skate along the sidewalks with her and her friends. I'd slip my brown school oxfords onto my skate platforms and use my skate key to tighten the metal clamps that hooked onto the soles of my shoes. Then I'd tug on the leather ankle strap before I slipped the string with the key over my head, and I was off, trying to be daredevil like the older kids.

Sunny and the other kids would careen over the cracked, uneven concrete, jump over curbs and explore the next avenue, something I was forbidden to do. "Hey, wait up!" was my theme song because Sunny and her crowd usually skated off and left me to return home with skinned knees and a suspicion that I'd been ditched again.

There was the pride of being in a school play where my only lines, written especially for me, were, "Sing it again, Sister Sue." Each time I looked at Sue and said my part, the audience would laugh, so I felt there was a possibility of my becoming a child movie star. It was years before I realized I had been selected for the part because of my tendency to lisp and the comedy relief it offered.

Before I was old enough for kindergarten, I would run away to school through the cornfield because I envied Sunny her school projects and thought I was missing out. I would stand on tiptoe at the door of the kindergarten room and peer inside at the tables covered with colored craft paper and the rest-time mats stacked up against the wall under drawings made by the children.

One day, when Mother arrived at school for her runaway, she didn't grab me by the shoulder as usual and scold, "I thought I'd find you here, young lady." Instead she, the kindergarten teacher and I went into the wood-paneled principal's office where arrangements were made to allow me to attend kindergarten early. I was thrilled, but what I wasn't told was that I would not be allowed to leave kindergarten until I was the proper age for the first grade.

I loved school, pasting and coloring and shaking the tambourine with gusto at music time. I rested on my very own gunny sack filled with shredded bits of old newspapers. I was certain I had done well—at least as well as anyone else in my class—until one day the teacher sat us all down on the floor in a circle saying, "Those of you who have worked hard will soon be going into the first grade. That is, except you, Nancy." I sat still. Every boy and girl in the room turned and stared at me. Baffled, I couldn't stop tears from running down my cheeks. What had I done wrong? Why was I the only one not "graduating" into the first grade?

No one ever explained, and it wasn't until I overheard Mother and Daddy telling friends years later how I had run away to school that I realized I hadn't been the dumbest one in the kindergarten class after all.

Other memories are fragments—Daddy at the kitchen table tenderizing abalone he had dived for, Mother handing me a piece of buttered pumpernickel bread as I came in the back door from roller skating, holding Skippy on my lap to comb his red curls around my finger, running after the ice wagon to pick ice fragments covered with splinters out of the rear of the truck and offering the ice cream vendor flowers in exchange for a cone and wondering why it didn't work the second time.

I remembered learning to swim in the lagoon at Long Beach and thinking Daddy was holding me up in the water only to look back and see I'd been swimming on my own for yards, shivering on the sand until my teeth chattered and then feeling Daddy slip a dry Mickey Mouse sweatshirt over my head, taking a nap with my pet desert tortoise asleep on my chest, playing kick-the-can in the long midsummer twilight.

Had I actually voted to leave Lynwood?

CHAPTER 2

Snapshots

Sunny and Nancy

When we girls decided the family should leave Lynwood and follow Daddy, Mother must have remembered only too well those first six years of her marriage, moving first with one small child and then another. No wonder she was reluctant to face it again, this time with three of us.

During those first years, Mother and Daddy lived in the southern part of California: Santa Paula, Ventura, Fillmore, Santa Barbara, Los Angeles and Long Beach, settling in Lynwood for eight years after Daddy was hired by The Texas Company.

As each baby came along, Mother, ever alert to emerging personality traits, gave us labels which tended to be accepted and then reinforced by other members of the family.

"Sunny's so pretty," Mama Dot would say as she curled Sunny's springy hair around her fingers into the dangling mass of coils that later became child star Shirley Temple's trademark. "Nancy is cute," she would add charitably, glancing at Nancy's straight and fine hair that was best managed in a Dutch Boy bob named after the house paint ads.

When we began grade school and report cards were sent home, Mother and Daddy would sit at the kitchen table and look them over before signing them. Mother would read one teacher's remarks out proudly, "Sunny is a top student . . . a joy to have in class!"

Daddy, without censure, would read, "Nancy is doing acceptable work but needs to try harder."

As Mother and Daddy signed the cards, their daughters were assigned roles. Sunny was the scholar, and Nancy was average.

Eavesdropping when Mother had company, we could hear Mother describing us. "Nancy is so outspoken. When Mrs. Tingley was here Nancy asked her if she dyed her hair! Of course she does, but leave it to Nancy to ask outright. Then she asked her if she still had that little dog that looks like a drowned rat! Fortunately Sunny pulled Nancy out of the living room and told her she wasn't acting like a lady."

Mother would continue, "Sunny seldom spilled her milk, even as a baby. Nancy's milk still tumbles over at almost every meal! And Skippy, well, he's very active and pugnacious, but we have every reason to believe he may be a genius!"

Skippy was indeed precocious. When he was nine months old, however, the opposite appeared to be the case. Mother was worried. "Do you think his eyelids are too heavy for a baby?" she would ask Daddy. "Do you think he breathes through his mouth too much?"

Mother, frustrated in her desire to become a doctor, nevertheless kept an interested watch on medical developments, and she read a good deal about the fad of the day, abnormal psychology. At last she came to the deep-sigh conclusion that Skippy might be a mentally retarded child. For a woman who wanted each of her children to excel, this was a blow.

After telling Daddy to expect the worst, she had a child specialist come to the house to examine their spunky little son who was so physically attractive. During the thirties, doctors routinely made house calls, and when the specialist came out of the nursery, leaving Skippy playing in his crib, he looked at Mother and said, "Mrs. Lockard, I have only one thing to say. *You* should have had the examination."

But, as a youngster, Skippy's intelligence was mostly manifested in little show-off tricks such as his imitation of sultry movie star Mae West, whose daring gowns and on-screen innuendoes kept the movie censors on their toes. Skippy would put his chubby hands on his hips and peer out of half-lidded eyes to murmur, "Why doncha come up and see me some time," his version of the famous line from her 1933 movie, "*She Done Him Wrong.*"

It was Hollywood's age of lavish musicals and irresistible child stars, entertainment aimed at cheering up Depression-weary citizens. Even families like ours, far from starstruck, were giving their children music, dancing and elocution lessons and parading them in front of relatives to strut their talent.

Mother's two salesmen brothers, Clayton and Phil, taught Skippy to memorize captions from the risqué cartoons in the *Esquire* magazines they brought to our house. Skippy was able to open *Esquire*, flip by the "Petty Girl" pinup pictures to a cartoon of two showgirls chatting in front of their makeup mirrors and recite, "I said, 'No,' and he said, 'Why not?' He had me there."

Audience appreciation was guaranteed, and occasionally when he got the captions and cartoons confused, he was rewarded by even more titters on the part of the women and knee slapping on the part of the men.

Skippy's performances were played out in front of friends and family. One evening he brought out a new piggy bank to show his captive admirers, and each dropped a coin into it. From then on the piggy bank was part of Skippy's routine although fewer and fewer coins found their way into the slot as his jaded audiences claimed to be out of small change.

Just one snapshot, taken on our maternal grandparents' front lawn in Los Angeles, records the marriage of Dorothy Belle

Schuster, 22, and Bruce Hall Lockard, 24, in December, 1921. The ceremony at the informal family affair was performed by Daddy's father, the Reverend Earl Tubbs Lockard, a stern Scots Presbyterian who came to the West Coast from Pennsylvania in 1883 and established churches in California.

Mother often made fun of Daddy's humorless bearded father. "He says grace for so long before dinner that I've never eaten a hot meal in his house." She also ridiculed the framed sampler hung over the bed where she and Daddy slept on their first visits to the Reverend's Santa Barbara house after they were married. The cross-stitched piece of linen, bordered by purple morning glories, proclaimed, "He who rises late will work all day and scarce overtake his duties by nightfall."

Mother was certain this message was directed at her since her idea of heaven was to sleep in whenever she could arrange it. She imagined that Daddy's mother, Grace, a good minister's wife and a recognized California artist, had embroidered the message after Mother's first visit to the house as a new bride when she slept late enough to miss breakfast. But Grace Barnard Lockard was so quiet and self-effacing that we could never believe that Mother's suspicions were justified.

In the wedding photo, Daddy is dressed in a suit and wears a stiff white collar. Nearly six feet tall, his dark hair is neatly cut reflecting his recent duty as a naval officer. He is saved from being dashingly handsome by his shy smile and his "Lockard nose," which is on the long side of being perfect. The fourth of five Lockard children who grew up in coastal California, he sometimes made the trip from Santa Barbara to Los Angeles with his father, riding through the now commuter-jammed Cahuenga Pass in a horse-drawn buggy.

Mother is slender and feminine in her pale silk dress with its spray of embroidery on the bodice and sleeves trimmed with fluted lace. Her wavy brunette hair is pulled straight back from her forehead and worked into a pouf over each ear. The black and white photo doesn't show her violet eyes but sculptures her movie-star nose in all its not-too-pert, not-too-long, not-too-wide perfection. Later we had reason to be grateful for Mother's nose since it undoubtedly rescued us from inheriting a true "Lockard nose."

Perhaps more photos were not taken of the wedding because our maternal grandmother, Mama Dot, saw no reason to celebrate it.

Mother was dreaming of college and then medical school when she graduated from high school, but Mama Dot had other ideas. Marriage to a wealthy man was all she, who had been a southern belle, could envision for her attractive daughter; a ticket to an easy life bought quickly while Mother was at the peak of her youthful beauty. Mama Dot was not cruel, but to steer Mother toward this "easy" life, she did a very cruel thing to her daughter and Daddy after they first met at a dance for Navy men in Los Angeles.

Mother and Daddy fell in love and planned to marry when Daddy returned from his tour of duty aboard ship. Daddy wrote to Mother faithfully as soon as his ship sailed for Marseilles, but Mama Dot took the letters from the mailbox first and destroyed them, leaving Mother to think Daddy had forgotten her.

Mama Dot didn't dislike Daddy, but he was not wealthy, which, in her view, automatically disqualified him as a son-in-law. She pushed her disillusioned daughter into a marriage with an older well-to-do man—a marriage that lasted less than thirty days.

After listening to Mother's tearful account of her husband's bizarre behavior on their honeymoon, even Mama Dot agreed that an annulment was necessary. Still, she left Daddy to find his own way back to Mother after he was released from naval duty, and if she felt remorse about destroying his letters, she never spoke of it to Mother.

Finally, when she realized the young lovers were determined to marry, she told Mother, "Bruce will always find a way to support his family, but you'll never have much money." That turned out to be true, but money couldn't have bought the love and caring Daddy always gave his wife, his children and his reluctant mother-in-law.

The 1930s were Depression years. Between his pick-up jobs as roustabout, draftsman, timekeeper, boiler tender and lab tester, mostly in the Southern California oil fields, Daddy found construction jobs or helped out at his parents' Santa Barbara dairy. So many men were out of work that even his dangerous boiler tender job on Long Beach's Signal Hill made him the envy of the neighborhood.

Daddy was a perfectionist, but not a fussy one. He had a Zen way of doing things, giving his undivided attention to even the simplest of tasks.

On one family camping trip to Yosemite, we recall his taking our green Coleman stove out of the trunk of the car to get it ready for two weeks of cooking outdoors. We sat down by him as we loved to do and watched. He spread newspaper out on the picnic table, dismantled the entire stove, then patiently cleaned and oiled each part. He whistled softly as he reassembled the parts into a perfectly working stove, each burner lighting with a reassuring pop and settling into even blue flames.

During our flycasting lessons, we would inevitably tangle our fishing lines on our reels after our practice casts, and Daddy would sort out the mess with unhurried patience.

Mother didn't belong in the twenties and thirties although she tried hard enough to win the Good Housekeeping Seal of Approval as a wife and mother. When she married Daddy, whom she loved, she dived into marriage with the intelligent zeal she might have spent on becoming a physician. But Mama Dot's disapproval wasn't the only obstacle to Mother's realizing her dream. Women's magazines of the day told her how to bake perfect cakes, sew perfect curtains and be a perfect wife and mother. The short stories the magazines ran carried the message that if women aspired to more than home and hearth, they would cheat their families and destroy their femininity.

Often Mother's buried frustration peaked into a rage, and she would bang pots and pans around in the kitchen or slam her iron down on Daddy's shirts. Daddy's "What's troubling you, Hon?" would just elicit more iron banging as she hung a perfectly starched work shirt on a hanger and took another sprinkled and rolled item out of her ironing basket. There was no women's movement to tell her she was not alone in her desire to be more than "just a housewife."

CHAPTER 3

Middle Class Migrants

Nancy

Everything we took with us when our family drove away from our Lynwood house had to fit into our new 1935 black Oldsmobile sedan and the small canvas-covered trailer we pulled behind. Daddy had traded our 1933 Olds five-passenger coupé in for the newer model four-door sedan because of its reputation for a well-designed transmission, a necessity, he felt, when towing a trailer.

Mother and Daddy had spent weeks selling chickens from our backyard pens, packing furniture, dishes and books for storage and deciding what was absolutely essential for a family of five that might be moving as often as the San Joaquin Valley's migrant farm workers.

Before we left, Daddy gave me his battered tan leather suitcase. He put it on my bed, unbuckled the softened-from-use leather straps that reached around it and snapped open the brass lock, revealing frayed grosgrain lining and an inside pocket that expanded with puckered elastic.

I thought the suitcase was beautiful. It smelled of saddle leather, reminding me of our camping trips with horses and pack mules.

The glamour of far-away places also emanated from the bag. I had often watched Daddy pack it with the work clothes he took on his trips with the doodlebug party, always fitting in his copy of *"The Outline of History"* by H.G. Wells or the latest *National Geographic* magazine to read on evenings away from his family. Unbelievably, this veteran of adventure was now mine!

When Daddy sat on my chenille bedspread and crossed his legs, settling down for a talk, I knew what he would have to say was serious. "Nancy, this suitcase is yours now. You can take anything with you anywhere we go as long as it will fit in this case. That means your clothes, your books—everything."

I practiced opening and closing my suitcase as Daddy called to Mother, "Honey, do you know where Sunny is? I want to give her the other suitcase now."

In 1935 most children didn't have closets stuffed with clothes, shoes and games. I had a pair of sturdy lace-up oxfords, and when I outgrew them, Mother bought me a new pair. These brown leather shoes were selected carefully and always purchased at the most expensive shoe store in town, usually one with a trademark picture of Buster Brown and his dog Tige in the window.

"I won't economize where my children's feet are concerned," Mother would say, arms folded on her maternal bosom and lips on the ready for a retort in case anyone would dare to disagree with her. "They are going to have the best shoes made so their feet will develop normally."

My oxfords were considered adequate for school, play and rare dress-up occasions such as a movie or dinner at a relative's house. When my feet grew big enough that Mother could no longer fit her thumb between my big toe and the end of my shoes, she'd announce, "It's time for a new pair of shoes for you, young lady." Until then, my all-purpose oxfords were half-soled, and I'd sit in the shoe repair shop in my stocking feet waiting for the cobbler to cut new leather and glue it onto my shoes, trimming the edges and carefully beveling each piece toward the arch. I was proud of my half-soled shoes. The cobbler would polish them, making them smell even better than new ones.

I had four cotton dresses, a white blouse and a plaid skirt, all made by Mother. My wraps consisted of a hand-knit red cardigan and a navy blue wool coat that had been Sunny's the year before. White bobby socks, one flannel nightgown and five pairs of underpants completed my wardrobe. All this would fit in my wonderful suitcase with just room enough for "*The Wizard of Oz*," my daintily decorated green celluloid mirror, brush and comb vanity set and Kodak box camera.

Besides packing, I had a piece of unfinished business. Before we left Lynwood I wanted to get revenge on Willy Wagner for all the times he'd pulled my hair and torn my dresses before Mother made me fight back. My idea was not original. I planned to play the same trick on Willy that Mary Beth, our former next door neighbor, had played on me.

One year older than I, feisty Mary Beth was usually one up on me as far as pranks were concerned. When she told me to point to my head and abbreviate the word mountain, I shouted, "Emp—ty!" to the glee of Sunny and the other kids in the neighborhood. I lisped whenever I came to the letter "S," so Mary Beth directed plays on her front lawn in which my part required me to say, "Summer swans swim sweetly," or "Sing softly, Suzy."

One day Mary Beth told me that if I would loan her a nickel, she would pay me back a dime the next day. I ran into the house, got a nickel out of a matchbox in my top dresser drawer and handed it to her, feeling that Mary Beth was turning out to be a pretty nice girl after all.

The next morning when I ran across the driveway to collect my dime, Mary Beth's house was vacant. Cupping my hands to peer in through the uncurtained windows, all I saw was the sun slanting across bare hardwood floors. "Mary Beth has moved to Canada," Sunny informed me. "Didn't you know that?"

As we made our last preparations to leave Lynwood, I tried to play Mary Beth's trick on Willy Wagner. "I know you're moving away," Willy said, hitching up his overalls with one thumb. "Besides, I wouldn't be stupid enough to lend you a nickel, even if I had one."

So, in June of 1935, after school was out, our furniture went into storage. Daddy bought a small open trailer to hold our suitcases, bedding, dishes, pots and pans and Skippy's tricycle. Early in the morning he hitched the loaded trailer to our Oldsmobile. Now we were ready to head north out of Lynwood, over the Ridge Route and up highway 99 to our new home, Tulare.

As Daddy helped Mother into the front seat, she turned to Sunny, Skippy and me restlessly waiting in back. "You children mind your Ps and Qs. Here it is not even sunrise and I'm already exhausted. And Daddy will need to put all his attention to driving over the Ridge Route."

"Well, Hon," Daddy said, patting her knee before he shut the car door, "You married a civil engineer." Mother was quiet as Daddy walked around to the driver's side and slid in behind the steering wheel. It was too dark to see, but I was certain Mother blushed as Daddy turned to her and added, "And I'm sure glad you did."

Sunny

The night sky was just beginning to fade to gray as Daddy slowly pulled our car and trailer out of the driveway of our Virginia Avenue home and headed toward Long Beach Boulevard. Nancy and I sat on opposite sides of the back seat with Skippy in the middle. We spread a large quilt over the three of us to keep warm. Mother had told us to mind our "Ps and Qs," which proved an unnecessary warning to three children who had scarcely slept the night before.

Excited and apprehensive, I had lain awake for, it seemed, most of the night staring at the changing patterns of light on the bedroom ceiling. Nancy lay very still, a sure sign that she, too, was awake. Several times during the night I was aware of a soft yellow glow flooding the hall from Skippy's room, which meant that he had snapped on his overhead light to play with his toys. I guessed that he, too, felt the excitement of the new life which was starting for all of us.

When the snoring in Mother and Daddy's room ceased and Mother padded into our dark room and shook Nancy and me gently, I could not believe that the long sleepless night had ended and that it was time to start our big adventure.

"Come on, Sunny," Mother called from the kitchen, "your toast is ready." Nancy and I dressed, put our pajamas in our suitcases and placed them in the hall for Daddy to collect. I walked through our nearly empty house, the sound of my footsteps echoing along the rugless floors and bouncing off the pictureless walls and drapeless windows. I felt a strange sense of loss bolstered by determination of spirit.

Mother handed me a paper plate containing a mashed banana on toast with sugar and cinnamon. "Your milk is on the drainboard. Did you and Nancy fold your bedding? Keep out that Log Cabin quilt to throw over you in the back seat."

After two bites of banana and toast I decided I wasn't hungry. When Mother left the kitchen for a moment I stuffed the rest of my breakfast in the garbage—being careful to cover it up with other trash so Mother wouldn't notice—and poured my milk down the sink.

As we headed north, I made a pillow out of my sweater and nestled against the car window. Glancing at Nancy I saw that she had done the same. Skippy slumped against my arm. Succumbing to the rhythm and hum of the car's motor I drifted into a comfortable sleep.

Some time later the warmth of the rising sun and the new sound of frequently shifting gears awakened me. Skippy was still asleep and Nancy was beginning to stir. Seeing low, brown hills on both sides of the car I asked, "Where are we?"

"We just passed through the San Fernando Valley and we're in the foothills of the Santa Susana Mountains," Daddy answered. He added, "There's a bridge a few miles ahead, and when we get there I want you girls to look down into the canyon and tell me what you see. I'll slow up a bit."

"I don't want the girls looking around too much," said Mother. "They haven't been carsick yet and I want them to stay that way."

"I feel all right," Nancy said. I didn't feel all right. My stomach was gnawing and I had a headache.

When we reached the bridge Nancy, who was sitting on the right side of the car and had a better view of the canyon, said, "I see some big pieces of something down there, like cement chunks, *big* ones!"

I craned my neck and made a slight pretense of looking past Nancy and into the canyon, then settled back into my corner.

"That's right, Nancy," said Daddy. "Those are parts of a dam which broke when you were only three years old. The water that came down the canyon destroyed bridges, houses, and part of the highway."

"And people?" Nancy asked.

"Yes, people too, unfortunately."

Skippy sat up and rubbed his eyes. Mother turned around, then said to Daddy, "I think it's time we stopped."

"We'll pull off at Castaic," Daddy said. "It's about four miles ahead. We can all get out and stretch and I can check the car."

Mother asked, "How's the radiator? I don't hear it boiling."

"It's fine so far. We have to climb about 3,000 feet be- tween Castaic and the Tejon Pass, so I want to take it easy. We're pulling quite a load." Daddy was quiet for a moment, then, grinning, he said to Mother, "Maybe we'll have to do like the covered wagon pioneers did and dump some of our belongings along the trail to lighten the load."

"Tain't funny, McGee," Mother said, parodying the popu- lar radio show *"Fibber McGee and Molly."* "I don't even want to *think* about what we've had to leave behind. Our good beds, for example."

Daddy reassured her. "Frank will store them in his ga- rage for us. He felt the chickens we gave him were a fair exchange."

"I'll miss Frank and Nellie," Mother said. "They were good neighbors."

At Castaic Daddy checked the gas, oil and tires and put water in the radiator. We stretched our legs and Mother of- fered us apples, raisins and crackers. I chewed on a couple of crackers but was barely able to swallow them. When we got back into the car Daddy said, "Girls, we'll be going slower for a while because there's a lot of climbing to do. Between here and Gorman—to the right—you'll be able to see parts of the old Ridge Route that was constructed in 1919. It had a lot of hairpin turns and switchbacks. At that time it was con- sidered the most dangerous road in America."

"I'm glad we're not on that one," Nancy said.

Mother said, "This one's bad enough."

"I traveled the old Ridge Route once," said Daddy. "It was really something. More twists and turns than a corkscrew. The new section—the one we're on now—is about two years old."

"Isn't the old road called the Grapevine?" Mother offered.

"Yes, but there's also a town called Grapevine near Fort Tejon and there's a Grapevine Canyon. People seem to use the term 'Grapevine' rather loosely when they talk about the Ridge Route."

A long, steady grade brought us to Gorman, where we stopped. Daddy checked the car again and Mother passed the cool, plaid-covered canteen of water around.

Daddy said, "We can eat lunch at Fort Tejon."

"If anyone is still hungry," said Mother.

The ache in my stomach said I was hungry, but I didn't think I could eat.

A mile and a half climb brought us to Tejon Pass summit, where a sign said "Elevation 4,182 feet." From there we dropped down, first to Lebec and then to Fort Tejon. Daddy seemed relieved. "How about lunch, everybody? From here on it's downhill, then flat. We're making good time, so we can stay here for an hour or more. It's 35 miles from here to Bakersfield." Daddy turned the car into Fort Tejon and parked.

"How far to Tulare?" Nancy asked.

"About 60 miles from Bakersfield."

"A long way, Daddy."

"Yes, but the road is straight and flat. No hills to climb."

We found a picnic table. Mother spread out a lunch of salami, macaroni salad, pickles, cookies, oranges and bananas. None of it looked good to me. So Mother wouldn't think I was sick I munched on a cookie and ate part of a banana. She had a thermos of hot coffee for herself and Daddy and a thermos of cold milk for Skippy, Nancy and me. After lunch Skippy ran off to climb a pile of rocks not far from our table.

"I'm surprised that you girls have done so well on this trip," said Mother. "Nancy, you ate a good lunch, but Sunny, you hardly touched anything, and you've been very quiet. Is something wrong? Do you feel all right?"

I hastened to reassure her. "I'm O.K. Just tired of being in the car."

"We're all tired of being in the car," Mother answered, packing up the remains of the lunch.

It was true that I had said very little. I was concerned about what lay ahead and I felt the heavy responsibility of having been the major decision maker. The heady excitement I had initially felt about making such a big change was increasingly eroded by fear of the unknown. I decided that I had better say something or Mother would assume I was pouting or, worse still, that I was ill. It was best to avoid being questioned, and I certainly wouldn't want Mother to think I had misgivings about our new life.

I looked around at the old army outpost and the surrounding hills and mentally fumbled for something to say. "These mountains aren't as big as the Sierras, and they aren't as pretty. Not as many trees, either."

"The Techachapis are beautiful in their own way," Daddy said. "Fort Tejon was an army fort established in the 1850s. Also, the army had an experimental camel train which didn't work out because the camels' tender feet couldn't adjust to the rocky soil. 'Tejon' means badger in Spanish. At one time there were plenty of badgers in this area."

I was glad that Daddy had gone into one of his detailed explanations. I hoped it would take Mother's attention off of me.

"The wildflowers on the hills are so colorful," said Mother. "I love the brilliant orange of the poppies and especially the deep purple of the lupine. I hope we see more as we descend into the Valley."

"We should see some," Daddy said, "although I've heard they're at their best through May."

A trip with Daddy was always an event. There seemed to be no end to his knowledge of the history, geology, flora and fauna of California. As he pointed things out to us he was never overbearing or pedantic. However, when Nancy and I were older and going through the blasé phase which seems to afflict all teenagers, we referred to trips with our father as "guided tours."

As we dropped down into the San Joaquin Valley Mother said, "Oh, look! There are lots of wildflowers still! It looks like a patchwork quilt!"

"May we pick some wildflowers?" Nancy asked.

"No," Mother replied. "We have to get to Tulare and see if we can move into the house that your father rented for us."

"Anyhow, Nancy," said Daddy, "wildflowers wilt pretty fast. It's better to enjoy them where they are."

"Is Tulare very big?" I asked.

"About 7,000 population, I think," Daddy answered. Turning to Mother he said, "We'll stop in Bakersfield. We'll probably make Tulare by early evening. It's a straight shot from now on."

Nancy

Our "straight shot" to Tulare was interrupted by two experiences reflecting the hostility that settled residents of the San Joaquin Valley felt toward the migrants pouring into their valley looking for farm work. While our car was new and our trailer neatly packed, we still drew suspicious stares as we drove through Bakersfield, pulling to a stop at a shady city park to eat oranges and let Skippy run off some of his pent-up energy.

As our family gathered back at the car to continue toward Tulare, two work-hardened men in ranch straw hats and short-sleeved cotton shirts stood glaring at our California license plates.

"Had those plates on long?" the shorter man challenged Daddy, who was making room in the back seat for our food sack.

"Guess you'd say so," Daddy said pleasantly as he straightened up.

Probably because Daddy spoke without the southern or midwestern accent the men expected, they looked confused. Mother and Sunny were standing aside, two pillars of dignity ready to get huffy at the first sign of an insult. Mother's hands were settling on her hips, a sure sign that her indignation would soon be expressed verbally.

I took Skippy's hand, noticing that his brown and white Little Lord Fauntleroy suit Mother had made out of Indian Head cotton was smeared with dirt where he wiped his hands after drinking out of the park's fountain. I was Skippy's protector when I wasn't siding with Sunny as his tormentor.

The taller man took a step toward Daddy. "'Spect you're not looking for farm work in Bakersfield with that new rig and all. Good thing, 'cause there isn't any." Deliberately he spat on the curb just inches from the rear door of our Olds. "Every damn fool in Texas, Missouri, Arkansas and Oklahoma is either here or on Route 66 trying to get here in some beat-up jalopy. Not enough cotton or potatoes in all of Kern County to keep half of them busy."

"No," Daddy said evenly. "Not looking for work. Just looking to head out of here in a few minutes."

Mother snapped open her white envelope purse, drew out a bottle of Coty's Emeraude, "the fragrance of ecstasy," and dabbed a drop behind each ear. Handing Sunny the perfume to hold, she opened a compact and powdered her nose with Lady Ester for brunettes. "It's so much hotter here than in Lynwood," she said loftily. Thrusting her cosmetics back in her purse, she snapped it shut and secured it under her arm. "I don't know how people can stand it. Come on, children, let's get in the car." Turning her back on the men she added, "And don't step on that filth on the curb."

After conferring with each other, one of the men decided to smile. "Family heading toward the Sierras? Sequoia National Park maybe?"

"Guess you'd say we're headed in that direction," Daddy answered, leaning his head out of the car as he eased the Olds into first gear and pulled away from the curb toward the highway.

"Imagine Bruce," Mother said, fanning herself with her purse. "You, a civil engineer, looking for farm work. I'd like to have given those Bakersfield men a piece of my mind."

She circled her head toward the back seat to make sure we children heard her declaration. "And I would have too, if it hadn't meant giving away your father's line of work. Imagine!"

Since Daddy usually championed any kind of worker, no matter how lowly in Mother's eyes, I was surprised when he just drove along in silence.

The smell of the remaining oranges, mixed in with the dinner sandwiches and date bars in our food sack, reminded me of the air that often blew over Southern California's orange groves and perfumed our house on Virginia Avenue. I was homesick already, but my mood lifted when Sunny whispered in my ear that we should fool Skippy into thinking we'd come upon a series of red and white signs posted along the road advertising Burma Shave brushless shaving cream with a catchy jingle.

The three of us loved to spot the signs on car trips, and Skippy had a record to maintain of seeing them first. Although he couldn't read most of the words, he'd always call out, "Burma Shave!" at the first sign and was invariably rewarded by Mother and Daddy's exaggerated praise.

Sunny and I whispered and giggled back and forth, finally chanting out our invention: "Put your/campfire out/with water/if you don't know/you surely oughter/Burma Shave."

"I didn't see it! I didn't see it!" Skippy yelled, bouncing from back to side window in distress. "We were going too fast! I didn't see it!"

Sunny and I laughed and would have contined teasing Skippy for miles, but Mother, tired of the ruckus in the back seat, gave us a scorching look as she told Skippy, "There weren't any signs. The girls just pretended they saw them. Now be quiet, all of you. Maybe there will be some real Burma Shave jingles up ahead."

Skippy managed to kick each of his sisters before settling down with folded arms, puckered lips and a scowl to catch the first glimpse of any roadside signs ahead.

All of Daddy's passengers must have dozed, for when he pulled off the highway behind an old black Ford sedan heaped with cardboard boxes, pots, farm tools and mattresses, Mother's head jerked up, alarmed. "Bruce, is something wrong with our car?"

"Not our car," Daddy said. "Looks as if those folks ahead could use some help though."

Mother viewed the scene ahead with distaste. Two fair-haired girls about Sunny's and my age and a boy about Skippy's were sitting on the rear bumper of the car, straining the wires that held it to the car's frame. Absently kicking the dirt with their split shoes as we pulled up, all three simply stared when we stopped.

A tall thin man wearing a cap was looking under the hood of his car, and a gaunt young woman in a faded cotton dress leaned in what little shade the car provided, nursing her baby.

"Bruce," Mother pleaded, "don't you imagine someone else will stop to help these people? We need to get to that house in Tulare and unpack." She folded her arms and sat back against the car seat. "This is one time when I don't think we can afford to be Good Samaritans to everyone on the road who didn't set out properly prepared."

Daddy was already out of the car. "I won't be a minute, Dorothy, and I doubt if they'll get any offers of help unless another car like theirs comes along. Just wait here."

Mother called Daddy "Bruce" whenever she wanted to emphasize a point, and I knew Daddy called Mother "Dorothy" only when he was angry with her. Our parents didn't bicker or raise their voices—they just became increasingly formal when their opinions clashed.

While Daddy and the man inspected the stalled car, Mother stared. I knew she wouldn't have looked so hard if the woman hadn't turned her back to us as she continued to feed her infant.

"I have to go wee wee," Skippy announced, seeing an opportunity to get out of our car and approach the boy who was exchanging a kid-to-kid smile with him.

Mother sighed. "Oh, all right. Go way away from the road behind that first row of cotton. Watch for rattlesnakes and come right back to the car."

Grabbing Skippy's arm as he climbed out, Mother lowered her voice. "I don't want you playing with that boy, Skippy. Do you hear? His hair might be full of lice, and his mother looks wasted enough to have T.B. They're Okies for sure."

Sunny corrected Mother with teenage logic bordering on impudence. "Their license plate says 'Arkansas.' " Both Sunny and I knew Mother wouldn't have used the term "Okie" if Daddy had been in the car.

I wanted to get out too and was about to ask when Daddy stuck his head in the car window. "All they need is a new fan belt. We've got a spare that will fit okay. Won't take long for me and the gentleman to put it on." When Mother didn't comment, Daddy added, "Seem like nice folks—the Turners from Conway, Arkansas."

Daddy rolled up his sleeves and found the belt in his toolbox. "Was afraid their radiator might have been cracked. That would have been real trouble."

"It looks to me as if they have plenty of trouble as it is," Mother said testily. But her voice softened with genuine concern as she added, "Bruce, what will they do? They're clean, but they look hungry, all of them. That poor young woman with a baby. . . ."

"They didn't get any warmer reception in Bakersfield than we did," Daddy said. "When their car's running they plan to drive on to Wasco or Shafter hoping to pick potatoes. The fellow's a good mechanic, too. He drove that load across the desert at night to Barstow and then over the Tehachapi

Mountains, keeping it together with spit and baling wire, I suppose."

As soon as Daddy left with the fan belt, Mother turned around to Sunny. "Hand me that food bag. I'll be right back. You and Nancy can get out and talk to those girls if you want, but don't get close. And keep an eye on Skippy."

When we were on the road again, Mother fretted, "I wonder what those children will have to wear to school in the fall. Maybe there's a sewing machine tucked away on top of that car somewhere. I wish I could send the mother some material."

"If they find work grubbing potatoes the whole family will pitch in," Daddy said. "Regular school may not be in the cards for those kids."

Mother gave one of her martyred shrugs. "I guess that means that they'll be in school just off and on, making it hard for the teachers to give the college preparatory students like Sunny and Nancy the attention they deserve." Her compassion continued to wane as she focused on her own children. "I certainly don't like the idea of that!"

Because of our stop, it was too late to move into the house in Tulare when we arrived, so Daddy pulled into an auto court, parking next to the office. "Just stay in the car until I see if they'll let us have a cabin," he said. "I'm afraid I've got to convince the manager we're not a migrant family." Before getting out of the car he added, "Of course in a way we are. The only difference between us and that family from Arkansas is that I have a job to go to."

"Humph," Mother replied, letting us know that being taken for a down-and-out family from the Dust Bowl seeking farm work in California would still be an insult as far as she was concerned.

In fact, Mother made it clear that even staying in an auto court was an indignity that she wouldn't have had to face if Sunny and I had elected to stay in Lynwood. "It's probably filthy," she warned us as Daddy came back with a key and drove our car and trailer into the car shelter next to our cabin. Our home for the night was green and white and looked to me like a storybook cottage.

Sunny, Skippy and I started climbing over each other trying to get out of the back seat to explore our temporary home, but Mother turned around warning, "Don't anyone leave the car until I clean the place with Lysol and put paper bags over the door knobs. You don't know what kind of people have been staying here. And don't any of you walk around inside in your bare feet! There are probably athlete's foot germs living in the rug." Even more seriously Mother added, "And don't any of you sit down on the toilet seat!"

Mother was convinced that the only people who stayed in auto courts were fast men with shady ladies, traveling salesmen and gangsters, all of whom had dirty hands, bugs in unmentionable places and infected feet. As far as she was concerned, decent families stayed home, visited their friends on vacations or, if they could afford it, stayed in hotels such as The Biltmore in Los Angeles. But her prejudices couldn't dampen her children's excitement. Sunny and I viewed the auto court as a romantic spot where anything could happen. After all, tonight weren't we far from Lynwood and deep in the San Joaquin Valley?

Finally Mother stood in the doorway, framed by the bare light bulb hanging from the ceiling inside. She wiped her forehead and sighed, waving her Lysol-scented rag toward the car. "You can come in now," she said, "but don't sit on a bed until I put one of our own blankets down over the spread."

"Yes," Sunny echoed, stepping into the room first. "They might not have washed it since the last people stayed."

Mother gave Sunny a quick look, then decided that her sometimes smart-alecky daughter was not making fun of her. "That's right, Sunny. Well, it's been a trying day. Let's all have some crackers and cheese and then go to bed." Mother didn't mention that she'd given most of the contents of our dinner sack to the family by the road. It felt strange, though, to go to bed with a little gnawing of hunger in my stomach.

Skippy was almost asleep on the folding cot the manager had brought in. Sunny and I were in our nightgowns, sharing the twin bed by the window whose green pull-down shade didn't shut out the light from the auto court's "Vacancy" sign. The light from another sign saying "Modern" blinked on and off.

"I feel like Osa Johnson on safari in Africa," Sunny whispered to me. "It's still hot outside, and those trucks going down the highway could be elephants stampeding through a native village."

Ripe aromas from a dairy farm across the highway made Sunny's fantasy seem more real.

I lowered my voice and introduced a spooky waver, hoping to get a rise out of Skippy. "Maybe a tiger is waiting out there ready to jump through the hole in the window screen the minute we're asleep. Or maybe a bear will push the front door open."

"I'm scared," Skippy obliged, sitting up.

"There aren't any bears or tigers in Africa," Sunny hissed to me just before Daddy warned softly, "Now you girls settle down and go to sleep. And quit trying to frighten Skippy."

"Sunny brushed all her cracker crumbs over to my side of the bed," I complained, but Daddy just repeated, "Go to sleep, all of you."

Just before dawn Skippy sat up on his cot yelling, "Tigers! tigers! I hear tigers out there!"

All of us waked up to the sound of scores of animals snorting and snuffling just outside our door. "Tigers, tigers," Skippy repeated, pointing to the door which led to the wilds of Tulare.

Daddy got up, daringly walked across the rug in his bare feet and pulled the shade aside to peer out the window. He tried to keep his face serious as he turned back toward Sunny, Skippy and me, but even in the dim light I could see a little smile. "There's a truckload of hogs parked out there," he said, "and I don't see stripes on any of them, so you three better get back to sleep."

As he climbed back into bed with Mother, I could hear her chuckle, and the sound made me feel warm. Mother happy! What a welcome sound. She and Daddy weren't cross with each other any longer. As I snuggled back down to sleep, I knew the tiger story would become a family classic that Mother would tell over and over, adding her own embellishments. Well, the San Joaquin Valley wasn't going to be so bad after all.

Sunny

We moved into a furnished white frame house in Tulare on a tree-lined street not far from the center of town. The houses on each side of us and across the street looked much like ours. Nancy and I shared a bedroom and our parents took the larger bedroom in the front of the house. Skippy's bed was placed on the rear screened porch just off the kitchen, near the laundry trays. The bathroom had a claw-footed tub and a pull chain toilet. The floor in the combination living and dining room sloped slightly. A few flattened tin can lids were nailed to the floor and also to the floor of the covered front porch.

Daddy's toe pointed to one of the tin can lids. "That's a creative way to cover a hole," he said, chuckling.

Mother looked at the can lids in disgust. "I'll have to get some little rugs and cover as many of them as possible," she said.

I followed Mother into the small kitchen. To Mother, who spent so much time in it, the kitchen was the most important room in the house. I lifted the top of the old oak ice box and Mother and I sniffed. It smelled dank and moldy. Directly across from the ice box stood a black four burner gas range.

The chest-high oven had a large white ceramic plate on the door with "Wedgewood" stamped across it in bold blue letters. White ceramic taps turned on the gas burners. On the wall above the stove was a metal match dispenser containing a nearly full box of Blue Diamond matches. Mother opened the oven door, peered inside and closed it with a sharp click.

Mother walked over to the sink, turned on the hot water faucet, then the cold, and turned them off. "Look at that sink!" she exclaimed. "It'll take a lot of scrubbing with SOS to get those stains out!" A wooden drainboard sloped gently towards the stained white ceramic sink. Underneath the drainboard were dusty, open storage shelves.

On the wall opposite the sink was a built-in breakfront. Mother ran a critical finger through the dust on the long open shelf but tapped approvingly on the frosted glass doors of the dish cupboard above.

A clear glass pull knob fell on the floor as Mother bent over opening and closing a series of drawers. As I put the knob on the shelf for Daddy to fix Mother rose saying, "All this needs to be cleaned and lined with paper."

The kitchen woodwork had been recently painted in a high gloss cream-colored enamel. The wallpaper was a faded barnyard scene with chickens and ducks. "Well," Mother sighed, surveying the kitchen as a whole, "I guess it could be worse."

Mother's glance fell on the well-worn, hexagonal patterned linoleum, and her hands immediately went to her hips. Then she pointed to buckled spots in front of the kitchen sink, the stove and the ice box. "Right where I'll be standing most of the time!"

Skippy ran into the kitchen racing from one buckled spot to another, jumping up and down and watching the linoleum deflate and inflate. "Stop that, Skippy," Mother said. "You'll make it worse. Your father will have to fix those loose spots if I'm going to do any cooking in *this* kitchen."

All the windows in the house had yellowed pull-down shades on rollers and cotton lace curtains frayed at the edges. Mother looked at the curtains in the living room and sighed.

"These curtains are old," she said, "and dirty. They'll have to go." She fingered the edge of one of the curtains in disgust, then wiped her fingers on a towel she was carrying.

Daddy was bringing a large box into the house. "Well, Hon," he said, putting the box down, "it was the best I could do. Rentals are scarce here, especially furnished ones, and with the children . . ."

"I know," Mother interrupted. "New curtains will make a difference. Let's see . . ." Her voice took on a cheerful edge as she looked at each window, mentally measuring the yardage it would take. "Probably about . . ."

"Don't forget that we might not be here very long," Daddy reminded, "and new curtains would mean that much more to pack. Also, would they fit the windows of our next house?"

"I can *make* them fit," Mother emphasized. "But, better than that, maybe I can get the landlord to buy the material if I make the curtains." Warming to her idea Mother turned to me. "Sunny, go out to the back porch and bring me that stick. I think it's about a yard long."

I brought the stick and gave it to her. Extending her right arm stiff and straight to the right of her body, she measured the stick from the tip of her nose and along her arm to her middle finger. "Just about a yard," she said. I had seen women measure yardage like that many times, even in dry goods stores, and I always wondered if women with long arms got more fabric.

Daddy went outside to bring in more boxes. "Hmmm," Mother said as she did some quick measurements with the stick. "Some unbleached muslin, I think . . . I'll look for a sale . . . maybe just the living room and kitchen . . ."

Daddy came in with a box and a suitcase. "Don't forget, Hon, you don't have your machine."

Mother plopped into a chair, looking upset. "I forgot. How soon can we get it here?"

Mother's Singer treadle sewing machine had been left behind with a neighbor because there was no room for it in the trailer. Daddy had promised to bring it to Tulare as soon as possible.

"If no one on the doodlebug party is going down that way soon, I'll go get it some weekend. We'll get it here somehow," Daddy promised.

"Maybe I can rent one," Mother said. She looked unhappy. "Maybe the landlord . . ." She got up abruptly without finishing her sentence. "This whole place needs a good cleaning," she snapped. "Come on, girls, we have to get busy."

We turned over lumpy mattresses and covered them with clean mattress pads before the beds were made. We swept the floors, dusted the furniture, cleaned the mirrors and windows, wiped shelves and lined them with paper, disinfected the bathroom, scrubbed the kitchen and waxed the worn, buckled linoleum.

Nancy and I worked along with Mother and did our best to keep up with her, but it was like chasing a whirlwind. We weren't fast enough or thorough enough for her taste. She prodded us with "Come on, girls," and "You call *that* clean?" While we were cleaning Daddy unloaded the car and trailer and kept Skippy out of our way. When we were finished Mother declared, to no one in particular, "We'll get those curtains . . . you'll see!"

And it did happen. The sewing machine was delivered two weeks later by an employee from the Los Angeles office who was going to the Sierras on a fishing trip. The landlord furnished the muslin through his sister-in-law who owned a dry goods store, and the new curtains went up at the end of week number three. Mother's clever measuring and cutting gave her enough fabric to do the whole house. Mr. Bromberg, the landlord, was very pleased.

When Nancy and I inspected the front and back yards we were disappointed. We tried to jab sticks into the ground, but it was dry and hard everywhere. Where was the green grass that we had had in Lynwood? Where were the zinnias, cosmos, calla lillies, snapdragons, sweet peas, castor bean trees and lantana bushes? The only tree was a scraggly elm at the curb, one in a line of equally scraggly elms on each side of the street. The only plants were dried up Bermuda grass and some tall brown weeds. There was no indication that any kind of a flower garden had ever been in the parched yard.

"Maybe we could plant something," I said.

Nancy, ever ready with a smart quip, said, "Well, Osa, You got your wish! You're in Africa now! It looks just like pictures in the *National Geographic*!"

"Shows how much *you* know, dummy," I replied. "Africa has trees and grass and lots of green stuff!"

"You been there?" Nancy shot at me.

"Ut-shay up-yay," I replied, annoyed.

Mother let us buy a few little plants and we put them in the holes that Daddy dug for us in the unyielding ground. While Nancy and I argued over whose turn it was to water our little garden, the plants died.

In the rear of the Tulare house there was a clothesline attached to the garage. The Valley climate had turned most of the garage paint to little curls. The garage leaned slightly to the south, taking the clothesline with it.

Tulare was hot: daily temperatures varied from the upper 80s to the upper 90s, and many days were in the 100s. Our house had a "desert" or "swamp" cooler, a large metal box with a fan which blew air through an excelsior pad kept wet with running water. Our cooler was mounted in one of the dining room windows and blew directly on the dining table. We turned it off during dinner so that the food would stay warm. The cooler lowered the temperature in the dining and living rooms somewhat, but the other rooms remained out of reach of this scant relief.

In the mornings after breakfast Mother would close up the house and draw the shades in an attempt to keep some of the slightly cooler night air inside. Soon, however, the heat of the day seeped in.

In the evenings after dinner we often sat on the front porch while Skippy rode his trike on the sidewalk. Later, when we went inside to listen to"*Amos and Andy*" or "*George Burns and Gracie Allen*" on the radio or to go to bed, the house would still be hot. In Tulare, and in other towns we lived in in the San Joaquin Valley, the summer nights were often so uncomfortable that Nancy and I put a wet sheet over ourselves so we could sleep.

Still, Mother cooked a hot meal every night. Daddy did not like cold food, except on a picnic. Our dinners consisted of meat, potatoes and gravy, at least one vegetable, bread or rolls, fruit, Jell-O or one of Mother's angel food cakes for dessert. Nancy and I set the table, made a big pitcher of iced tea with lemon and poured a glass of milk for Skippy. After dinner we did the dishes, arguing over whose turn it was to wash, pinching each other and kicking each other in the shins. "Cut it out, girls!" Mother would call from the living room. Nancy or I would whisper, "Give me the scissors and what shape?" and giggle. We were careful that Mother did not hear us. We knew that it would mean a reprimand. "Impudence" was never excusable in our home.

Skippy was a pest as far as I was concerned. I referred to him as "little brother without the 'r'." He had flame-red hair and freckles, and his energy and curiosity often led him into mischief. Mother and Daddy would sometimes laughingly say to people that Skippy got into so much trouble that, to insure his good behavior, they ought to spank him before they took him places.

One day soon after we moved into our Tulare house I was helping Mother fix dinner when Nancy ran into the kitchen yelling, "Mom! Mom! I have to go to the bathroom and Skippy won't let me in!"

"What's he doing in there?" Mother asked.

"He's been in there a long time," Nancy replied.

Mother dropped the carrot she was scraping, wiped her hands and left the kitchen, followed by Nancy. Curious to find out what Skippy was up to, I tagged along.

Mother tried the knob on the bathroom door. It was locked. Then she banged on the door with her fist. "Skippy, unlock this door *immediately!*"

There was a sharp click as the bolt was released, then Skippy opened the door a few inches. Mother pushed the door open and grabbed Skippy's arm. "What are you . . . I told you never to lock the door!"

There was water all over the bathroom floor. The long toilet pull chain was lying in the corner like a coiled serpent. The old-fashioned high toilet tank was slightly askew.

Mother shook Skippy. "Young man, what were you doing?" Not waiting for an answer, she gave Skippy a couple of whacks on his rear and said, "Go out on the porch and sit on your bed! I'll deal with you later. Nancy, go get your father and tell him to bring his tools and the stepladder. Sunny, get the mop and the bucket."

Skippy ran for the porch and Nancy ran to get Daddy, who had gone out to the car to bring in a lug of apricots destined to become Mother's delicious apricot jam.

Dinner was delayed an hour while Daddy repaired the toilet and I mopped the floor. Skippy, in disgrace, was sent to bed right after dinner and denied his favorite dessert, chocolate pudding with whipped cream and a cherry on top.

Over a cup of coffee Daddy said, "Maybe I'll move the

toilet chain higher so he can't reach it."

"Leave it where it is," said Mother. "He has to learn. I paddled him hard. I don't think he'll do it again."

Nancy spoke up in defense of Skippy. "He was playing Tarzan," she explained, "swinging through the trees in the jungle on a vine. I heard him giving the Tarzan yell."

Daddy snickered. Mother said, "*What?* And I suppose he'll blame the whole thing on his imaginary playmate, Skippy-Jack."

"That's right, Mom," Nancy said. "He told me that Skippy-Jack did it."

"Skippy's a brat," I said.

"Now, Sunny," said Mother, "he's your brother, after all."

Tulare was typical of the small rural towns in the San Joaquin Valley. It had a department store, "Mom and Pop" shops, a grocery store or two, a feed and farm equipment outlet, a movie theater and a drugstore with a soda fountain.

Nancy and I enjoyed going into the fan-cooled drugstore, sitting on the tall, worn red leather soda fountain stools with our elbows on the slick black and white marble counter top and ordering ice cream sodas or chocolate malts. Sometimes Mother let us order tuna sandwiches, a very special treat. These were heavy with mayonnaise slathered on white bread and served with a huge dill pickle and crisp potato chips. We thought they were the best sandwiches ever made.

The feed store was a big barn of a place with a dark, creaky uneven wood floor burnished to a high polish by the boots of thousands of farmers. Once inside customers inhaled a pleasant combination of scents from sawdust, hay, chicken feed, gunny sacks, paints, varnishes and new farm tractor tires. Nancy and I would walk among the huge piles of bulging feed sacks and marvel at the barrels of nails, spools of barbed wire, saddles, horse blankets, harnesses, rakes, hoes, brooms and every kind of hardware imaginable.

Saturday night was Bank Night at the local theater. You wrote your name on the back of your ticket stub and dropped it into a box as you entered the theater. The show was stopped between the double features, the manager came up on the stage and asked a child from the audience to draw a name for a prize of $50. No one in our family ever won, but it was fun, anyway.

On hot summer days in Tulare Nancy and I read our library books, investigated the neighborhood, went shopping with Mother and played in the backyard if the day wasn't a scorcher. Daddy often took us swimming in the city pool on Saturday. On Sundays we went for a ride in the family car before the sun reached a full blaze, and Mother bought fruit and vegetables from the Japanese farmers. School seemed too far off to worry about.

Nancy and I didn't have any playmates that summer in Tulare. There weren't any other families on the doodlebug party at that time. The men were either single, newly married or had left their families behind. One evening when all of us were sitting on the front porch waiting for the house to cool off, we had a surprise visit from the boy next door. He sat on the porch steps with his back to Nancy and me.

"Hello!" said Mother. "What's your name?"

"Billy," was the reply. "Billy Martin." Billy wore a pair of faded blue overalls and no shirt. His short, light blond hair stood straight up like the stubble in a newly harvested wheat field. Nancy and I had noticed Billy coming and going from the house next door, but we had never talked with him.

"What grade are you in, Billy?" asked Daddy.

"Eighth. That is, I'm going into the eighth."

"Well," Mother said. "Nancy, here, is in the sixth grade and Sunny is in the ninth."

Billy didn't look at either Nancy or me. He turned to

Daddy and said, "I read history all the time."

"Really?" Daddy replied. "Is history your favorite subject?"

"Sure," Billy answered. "Only they don't teach enough in school, so I go to the library and get history books."

"That's wonderful," said Daddy. "What are you reading now?"

"About the Civil War. And I just finished a book on the American Revolution."

"Very interesting," said Daddy.

Nancy and I had nothing to say. We were prolific readers, but not in the area of history. History was *boring*.

"Got to go now," said Billy. "Got lots of reading to do."

Mother said, "Come over again, anytime."

Billy did come over again, in fact, he drifted over many times, usually in the evening to join us on the porch. He paid little attention to Nancy and me. He talked briefly—always to our parents—about the Peloponnesian War, the Crusades, the fall of Rome, the Russian Revolution. To Nancy and me it seemed that he went on and on, ad nauseam. Daddy encouraged him, saying, "Well, tell us about what you're reading."

Mother thought that Billy was an odd boy, but Daddy often reminded her, "A lot of successful people seemed out of step when they were kids." Daddy, who had a profound respect for learning, thought Billy was a wonder.

One night Billy told my parents a little about the history of Tulare County. "A lot of Portuguese people settled here. They were from the Azores. They worked mainly in the dairy industry."

Daddy perked up. "Is that so? I've been to the Azores. I served on a naval vessel, the U.S.S. Sierra, during World War I. We went to Marseilles to bring back troops and we stopped in the Azores."

"You did? Gee, I hope I get to do something like that."

"Yes, it was quite an experience. Billy, we've seen quite a few vineyards. What else is grown here?"

"Cotton, sugar beets, grain, fruits and citrus. Lemons, limes, grapefruit and tangerines."

Mother said, "I'm surprised that the crops don't burn up in all this heat."

"It's the winter frost that the growers have to watch out for," Billy replied. "And did you know that eastern Tulare County has more than 110 mountain peaks?"

"Billy," said Daddy, "I predict that you'll be a historian when you grow up. Actually, you already are."

Billy Martin lived on one side of us, Mr. Cavendish on the other. Mother felt sorry for Mr. Cavendish.

"Such an elegant name for a poor little man in a rundown old house," she remarked one day after bringing in the mail and finding a letter for Mr. Cavendish which had been delivered to us by mistake. She handed me the letter. "Here, Sunny, take this over to Mr. Cavendish and put it in his mailbox. No, I'll do it," she decided, snatching the letter out of my hand. She held the letter to the light and turned it around a few times. "Hmmm," she said. "It might be a check."

Mother took the letter over to Mr. Cavendish as soon as she was certain he was home. Peeking through a front window I could see her chatting in a lively manner with him on his front screened porch. Mother could be very charming when it suited her, and people seemed to enjoy her animated, friendly conversation.

That evening at dinner Mother said, "Poor Mr. Cavendish. He's not a widower after all. He lived in that house with his sister and she died a couple of years ago. His sister did all the cooking and took care of the garden. Now he eats out of cans and the garden is all dried up. She had a little money, though, and he gets something from her estate every month. Maybe that's what was in the envelope today."

Daddy looked at Mother. "Well, you seem to know a lot about our neighbor. How did you find out all this?"

Mother told him about the letter and her chat with Mr.

Cavendish. "Such a nice little old man," she said, "and *so* polite. He calls me ma'am. I think I'll send him a piece of cake after dinner."

Mother, who always came to life over a piece of gossip, had been in a good mood ever since the letter incident. When she returned from her chat with Mr. Cavendish she had baked one of her specialties, a chocolate angel food cake.

"Sunny," Mother said when she was cutting the cake that evening, "you can take Mr. Cavendish a piece of cake."

"Let Nancy do it," I suggested.

"No, you're the oldest." Mother handed me a plate with a generous hunk of chocolate angel food on it. "And don't go inside," she cautioned.

I went next door with the cake, and just as I was about to knock on the door of the screened porch I noticed that Mr. Cavendish was sitting on the porch in a chair by his radio and that he was asleep. The radio was playing softly and Mr. Cavendish was breathing in little snorts. I opened the screen door slowly and it groaned just like the door on the "*Inner Sanctum*" radio mystery program, but Mr. Cavendish did not stir. Taking two steps across the squeaky wood floor of the old porch I decided to leave the cake on the table by the radio. Mr. Cavendish kept on snoring. I tiptoed out—which didn't do much good, since the floor creaked badly—and started home. Suddenly I realized I had smelled a very peculiar odor on Mr. Cavendish's porch, an odor like Fels Naptha laundry soap and grass and lemon mixed together. Phew! I wondered what it was.

Several days later Mother said, "I think we ought to invite Mr. Cavendish over for dinner. Poor man, he never has a good home-cooked meal. And he *loved* the cake, he told me so. He was very appreciative."

So Mother wrote a note inviting Mr. Cavendish to dinner and I put it in his mailbox. On the appointed night he arrived dressed in a shabby, shiny, ill-fitting black suit, a white shirt with a creased and frayed collar and a striped tie with stains. The minute he entered our house I smelled the peculiar odor again.

Daddy said, "Take off your coat, Mr. Cavendish, and feel free to loosen that tie! It's too hot tonight to be formal!"

Reluctantly Mr. Cavendish removed his suit coat revealing a tattered, unironed shirt. Apparently the coat was intended as a cover-up for the shirt, and also as an attempt to give a "tone" to the occasion.

I went to the kitchen to help Mother. "Mr. Cavendish stinks!" I told her. "It's the same smell I noticed when I took him the cake."

"Never mind," Mother replied. "Help me get this food on the table."

We had fried chicken, biscuits, mashed potatoes and gravy, peas, a pineapple and cottage cheese salad and for dessert strawberry shortcake with real whipped cream. All of this Mother had prepared in a kitchen only a few degrees cooler than Death Valley in summer.

Mr. Cavendish operated a very busy fork, a little like an active steam shovel. In between bites—big ones—he would mutter, "You're a marvelous cook, ma'am." Mother giggled and said, "It's all in a day's work. I just threw it together." It was clearly a big boost for her, though, to have someone compliment her cooking. We were spoiled. We took her good cooking for granted.

Mr. Cavendish wasn't much of a conversationalist. Daddy tried several leads, none of which came to anything. Mother, hoping to glean more gossipy tidbits, had even less luck. This made me wonder how she ever got so much out of him when she delivered the letter. Mr. Cavendish seemed to be unwilling to put his fork down long enough to answer the queries. After dessert and coffee Mother packed up some leftovers and sent them home with him. When he was safely out of earshot I asked Daddy, "What was that awful smell?"

"Oil of citronella," Daddy replied, giving his nose a twitch. Then he laughed a little. "He told me he combs his hair with it to keep the mosquitos away."

I remembered that Mr. Cavendish's hair was slicked back and looked oily. "It sure stinks," I said.

"Well," Mother said, "it doesn't smell *that* bad, and he's a very nice man. He calls me ma'am. It's 'good mornin', ma'am,' 'good afternoon, ma'am,' and 'good evenin', ma'am.' He's very polite."

Although many pieces of angel food cake, sponge cake, apple pie and banana cream pie were sent his way, Mr. Cavendish was never invited to our house for dinner again. When I delivered the plates of cake or pie to him I held a handkerchief over my nose and mumbled something about getting a summer cold.

CHAPTER 4

Boots and Glamour

Sunny

This was the summer that I met Aunt Irene. I was so dazzled by Aunt Irene that she nearly replaced Osa Johnson as my heroine. I still admired Osa, but Aunt Irene appealed to me in a different way. She didn't photograph lions in Africa but she brought sophistication and style into my life.

It began with a letter which came to Mama Dot while she was visiting us in Tulare.

One afternoon during Mama Dot's visit Mother brought in the mail and handed an envelope to her. "Here's something forwarded to you from Adelanto. It has a Seattle postmark and a Seattle return address, but no name." Mother was dying of curiosity.

Mama Dot looked puzzled. "Seattle?" She opened the envelope and read the letter. Then she said, calmly, "Well. From Phil. He waited long enough to write."

"Phil?" Mother was surprised. "In Seattle? What is he doing?"

Phil was Mother's brother, Mama Dot's youngest child. Mother was the oldest, then came Clay, followed by Grant De Philip, whom we called Phil until, later, he asked all of us to call him Grant. I had known "Nunkie Phil" when I was a small child, but I scarcely remembered him. He left home in his early twenties and seldom wrote to his parents.

Mama Dot folded the letter, put it back in the envelope and lighted a cigarette.

"What does he say?" Mother asked anxiously.

Mama Dot shifted in her chair and blew smoke toward the ceiling. "He's married. He's on his honeymoon and they'll be stopping by The Ranch." She busied herself with her cigarette more than usual, I thought.

"*Married?*" Mother gasped. The mail slid off her lap and hit the floor.

"Her name's Irene," said Mama Dot matter of factly. "And it seems that Phil has a good job in Seattle." She got up and walked toward the kitchen. "I believe I'll have another cup of coffee."

Mother followed Mama Dot into the kitchen. "Maybe they'll come by here!" she said, excitedly. "Perhaps even today!"

"Maybe." Mama Dot struck a match and lighted a fire under the aluminum percolator. She let it perk just long enough to warm the coffee, then poured herself a fresh cup. "Coffee, Dorothy?"

"No, thanks. If they're stopping by The Ranch, they'll get our address. After all these years! It's a long drive back to Seattle . . . they'll have to stay *somewhere*." Mother, of course, was planning to put up her brother and his bride should they come by. At night Mama Dot slept on the nubby orange and gray plaid sofa, well-used by a succession of renters. This was the only extra "bed" in the house. "The girls could sleep on army cots."

"The newlyweds might *prefer* a hotel," Mama Dot said flatly. "*If* they come by."

"Just the same, I'll have Bruce bring the cots in from the garage," Mother replied. Phil and Irene can have the girls' room."

Mother put the house on a state of alert. "I'll cook a big roast for dinner. The cold leftovers will slice nicely for sandwiches or a Dutch lunch. Sunny, I have jobs for you and Nancy."

"Really, Dorothy . . ." Mama Dot protested.

Mother got out the wet mop, the dust mop, the broom and cloths for cleaning and dusting. When Mama Dot saw that Mother was determined to scrub, clean, dust and polish the same things which had been scrubbed, cleaned, dusted and polished only a few days before she, never one to waste much time and energy on unrewarding household chores, said, "I'll take care of Skippy." She walked Skippy to the park where she let him play on the swings, slides and teeter totter for three hours, just long enough to miss the mop and broom barrage.

Nancy and I always enjoyed Mama Dot's visits. She didn't have the traits commonly associated with grandmothers, and that is what I liked about her. She wasn't loving, comforting and indulgent. She had an air of independence, of superiority, of quality. She was an iconoclast, and I loved to hear her take potshots at religion or politics while flicking ashes from her ever-present cigarette. I was too young to understand all of her remarks, but her attitudes were clear.

When President Franklin Delano Roosevelt's name was mentioned Mama Dot would toss her head, look at the ceiling and utter a sharp "Humph!" in distaste. She fancied herself a member of the elite upper class in spite of the fact that she had little money. Roosevelt's concern for the unemployed and Eleanor Roosevelt's empathy for African-Americans (then called "Negroes") drew many a "Humph!" from Mama Dot.

I adored Mama Dot, but I found her prejudices embarrassing. When she began her favorite story about Willy Mae Johnson I mentally shrank myself to the size of a gnat and tried to blend in with the specks on the wallpaper. Even though Daddy got along with Mama Dot quite well, the Willy

Mae story so repulsed him that he would leave the room the minute it started. Mother, on the other hand, smiled politely, but without comment, at the end of the story. This is Mama Dot's account:

"As a girl in Louisiana, my family had this wonderful Nigra cook, Wilma Mae Johnson. When we moved to Texas, she came right along with us. Well, I married Louis and moved to Los Angeles, and the years went by. Imagine my surprise when one day there was Willy Mae at my front door!"

Mama Dot, usually so reserved, would warm to her story. "Willy Mae was completely gray and missing a front tooth, but I'd have known her smile anywhere. I was so glad to see her that I burst into tears. But . . ."

Then Mama Dot would sit up straight and turn smugly to each person in the room. "I didn't open the door all the way. I didn't forget for one minute that I'd been brought up a southern lady. I said, 'Willy Mae, now you just go around to the back door.' "

Mama Dot would nod to her listeners, certain of their approval. "Then I ran through the house and flung open the kitchen door for her. That old Nigra and I hugged each other for dear life. We talked and cried over a whole pot of coffee in my kitchen before Willy Mae had to leave."

I knew that it was useless to disagree or argue with Mama Dot. Instead, I ignored the part of her I didn't like or understand. I think Daddy did the same.

The next morning, as Mama Dot and Mother were chatting over a second cup of coffee in the living room and Nancy and I were clearing the breakfast dishes from the table, a car pulled up very slowly and stopped in front of our house.

Mother jumped up. "Could it be Phil?"

All four of us rushed to the front window. A good-looking, well-dressed man got out of the stylish coupé and walked around to the passenger side.

"It's Phil!" Mother gasped. Mama Dot said nothing.

Uncle Phil opened the car door and helped Aunt Irene out of the car. They exchanged a light kiss.

Mama Dot stared. "*What* is she wearing, for heaven's sake?"

Indeed, this was a good question. Aunt Irene was dressed in a very smart riding outfit, and she even carried a riding crop. From her highly polished boots to her paisley ascot and jockey cap she looked like pictures of society women I had seen in the Sunday newspaper supplement. But, I wondered, if they have been horseback riding why wasn't Uncle Phil dressed in a riding outfit also? As they approached our front door I could see what a handsome couple they were: he with his navy blue sports coat, gray slacks, red and blue ascot and dark wavy hair and she in her snappy riding outfit with wisps of light blonde hair below her cap.

Mother went to the door and greeted them, but Mama Dot waited in the living room. When Uncle Phil saw Mama Dot he kissed her and introduced Irene, but Mama Dot did not respond with any warmth. She sat in a chair, lighted a fresh cigarette and waited for others to talk. Mother filled in the gaps, asking about their honeymoon trip, Phil's job, how long they had been married, how they met, where Irene was from, the usual. Phil was head of personnel for a Seattle firm. Irene, originally from San Francisco, worked in his office, and that's how they met. When they married, she had quit her job. It was expected in those days.

Aunt Irene removed her cap and put it on the floor with the riding crop. Her blonde hair, cut very short in a tousled little boy look, was much shorter than most women were wearing their hair in those days, but it suited her. She had lovely big expressive eyes. She was slender and very attractive, not beautiful, but striking. Aunt Irene had the kind of "good bones" which keep a woman looking magnificent into her 60s and 70s. I watched her in fascination as she talked. I still hadn't heard why she was wearing riding clothes and Uncle Phil wasn't.

Mama Dot finally spoke to Irene. "Have you been horse-back riding?" Her tone was lofty.

"Oh, this," Irene laughed, pulling on the sides of her riding breeches with both hands. "I was so nervous about meeting all of you, and I couldn't decide what to wear, so Grant told me to wear this because he likes it on me!"

Mama Dot turned to Uncle Phil. "So, it's 'Grant' now, is it?"

Uncle Phil laughed. "Yes, people call me Grant. More dignified, you know. The riding habit was my idea. Doesn't she look terrific?" He put his arm around Irene and gave her a squeeze.

Mama Dot ground out her cigarette and said nothing. Mother said, "Sunny has a pair of riding breeches. Why don't you show them to Aunt Irene, Sunny?"

Irene jumped up and, putting her right hand over her heart, exclaimed with delight, "Oh, Grant, Grant, I'm an *aunt*! An *aunt*! Come on, Sunny, let's see your breeches!" She grabbed my hand and pulled me out of the living room. It was several years later that I found out Aunt Irene was an orphan, and that she was thrilled to have a family, even a family by marriage.

Reluctantly I led her into my bedroom, but I didn't want to show her my riding breeches, so obviously inferior to hers. Besides, I had no boots, nor did I have a pretty white silk blouse like hers or a cap, or an ascot or a crop. Once proud of my riding breeches, I now saw them as cheap and drab.

"First I have to use your bathroom," said Aunt Irene, disappearing around the corner into the hall. Did this wonderful aunt have bodily needs like other people, I wondered?

I took the breeches out of a drawer and put them on the bed. How ugly they looked!

Aunt Irene came into the bedroom. "Do you have a comb I could use? I left mine in the car." Oh, what a privilege! I handed her my comb, checking first to be certain there were no hairs caught in the teeth. Watching her comb her hair I was mesmerized by the flash of diamonds on the third finger of her left hand. "Do you have some lipstick?" she asked. "Powder?"

"No," I replied. "Mother won't let me . . ."

"Oh, well," Aunt Irene said. "No matter. I'll tell you what! I'll send you some lipstick in a very light shade that your mother won't object to."

"Oh, would you?" I gushed.

"Of course. Now, let me see those breeches."

I handed her my riding breeches. She held them up and turned them around. "These are very nice. Put them on."

"But . . . I don't have any boots!" I blurted out.

"You can try mine on." She wiggled out of her boots and gave them to me. "I think we're about the same size."

I put on my breeches and Aunt Irene's boots. The boots fitted me perfectly and made my breeches look ever so much better. "I wish Mother would buy me some boots," I said.

"She won't? Well, I'm going to send you these when I get home. I'm buying a new pair anyhow, black ones, to go with my new outfit."

Boots! I was actually going to get boots *and* a lipstick! I could hardly believe it!

I returned the boots to Aunt Irene and thanked her. She looked me over from head to toe and said, "You know, I think you could wear some of my clothes. You're thinner than I am, but if your mother can alter a few things, you could wear them. Would you like that?"

"Oh, yes, Aunt Irene!" I was transported into another world, a world of elegant possibilities. "Mother is very good at sewing. She makes most of the clothes that Nancy and I and Skippy wear."

"Then it won't be a problem," said Irene. She gave me a hug. "You and I are going to get along well."

I hugged her back. She smelled so good, of some exotic perfume I did not know existed. I was intoxicated with heavenly scent, fine leather, soft silk, rich gabardine and glittering diamonds.

There was a knock on the bedroom door. "Are you girls about through in there?" asked Uncle Phil. "Let's go for a little drive before lunch. Nancy wants to sit in the rumble seat."

Uncle Phil and Aunt Irene took Nancy and me for a ride in their 1934 Dodge coupé. Nancy and I stepped on the running board and climbed into the rumble seat, putting our feet on top of suitcases and boxes. Uncle Phil drove around the neighborhood, then up and down the main streets of the town and finally a few miles out of town along the highway. I waved to people even though I didn't know anyone. I was positively bursting with pride. I hoped that some of the kids I waved to would recognize me when I entered school in the fall, and that they would remember the coupé with the side-mounted tires, luggage rack, and white sidewall tires.

We came back into town and turned onto our street. Through the rear window of the coupé Nancy and I could see Uncle Phil and Aunt Irene talking, waving their arms and laughing. Uncle Phil pulled up in front of the corner grocery store and got out of the car. "How about ice cream for dessert?" he called to Nancy and me. "I'll have the clerk pack the carton as full as possible." Aunt Irene turned around, waved to us and smiled.

Mother tried to talk Uncle Phil and Aunt Irene into staying all night. "Bruce will be disappointed if he misses you," she said. "If you'll stay I'll make your favorite banana cream pie for tonight's dessert, Phil."

"What a temptation, Dorothy!" Uncle Phil replied. "But it's a long trip and we really should be on our way. I have to be in the office on Monday."

Aunt Irene gave me a goodbye hug. "You'll be hearing from me," she promised. Three weeks later the boots and lipstick arrived.

Several years later Uncle Phil and Aunt Irene took Nancy and me for another memorable ride, in another car. They had bought a "custom-outfitted" salmon-colored Ford convertible at a bargain price from a dealer who claimed that the couple who ordered the car had changed their minds when it was too late to cancel the order. Our family was spending a weekend at The Ranch. Uncle Phil and Aunt Irene had moved to Hollywood by that time. They drove up to The Ranch to spend the weekend and show off their new car. Late that night under a full moon, they took Nancy and me for a long ride along lonely desert roads, with the top down, the radio blaring ballroom dance music and the heater on full blast, all of us singing and laughing and cutting up. It was fun; *they* were fun. I loved being with them, and I loved hearing their stories about adventures in Hollywood.

Uncle Phil and Aunt Irene were an elegant looking couple. She, with her slender, blonde good looks—stunningly attractive, people said—had style and pizzazz. Her nearest look-alike in the world of Hollywood was Carole Lombard. Uncle Phil was suave, dark, movie-star handsome, with the looks and polished manners of a Clark Gable. Together they attempted to emulate the sophisticated life of Nick and Nora Charles in "*The Thin Man*" motion picture series, and to some extent succeeded, for a time. However, unlike Nick and Nora, neither Uncle Phil nor Aunt Irene was heir to a fortune in dollars and cents.

Always smartly dressed, with impeccable manners and devastating charm, Uncle Phil and Aunt Irene commanded attention wherever they went. People would stop and stare, certain that they must be Hollywood stars or somebody equally important. They were often approached for autographs which they scrawled carelessly but graciously, leaving the autograph hunter in total bafflement. They enjoyed going to nightclubs in Hollywood like Ciro's, the Coconut Grove or the Trocadero, where movie stars went in those days. They were always ushered to the very best table without hesitation. Reporters took their photographs and afterwards tried to figure out who they were, occasionally asking for autographs in order to solve the mystery, which, of course, was never solved.

I wonder how many flash photos of my aunt and uncle went into the wastebaskets of newspaper offices because these beautiful people couldn't be identified. "They must be *somebody*," was a reporter's comment that Uncle Phil overheard one night as he and Aunt Irene were leaving Ciro's. This delighted them both, and was repeated to us often in family gatherings. They enjoyed this deception: it was genuine fun for them. They saw no harm in it, nor did we.

I saw a lot of Uncle Phil and Aunt Irene during my teenage years and I loved being with them. They visited our family frequently and we saw them often at The Ranch. Sometimes in the summer I went home with them and spent a week at their house in Hollywood. They lived in a Spanish-style bungalow court with red tile roofs. The window boxes were bright with geraniums and broad-leafed banana trees shaded the front lawns. Irene would take me shopping in Hollywood and sometimes we would see a movie star at lunch in the Brown Derby, driving by in a car, shopping at Farmer's Market or just walking down the street.

In the thirties Hollywood was a small subtropical village set at the foot of hills decorated with an architectural hodgepodge of homes ranging from Spanish-style villas to fairyland castles. Oranges, grapefruit and lemons hung from front yard trees while bougainvillea vines festooned patios with cascades of purple and coral blossoms.

From the crest of the Hollywood Hills you could see a blue streak of the Pacific Ocean and, while winding downhill, pass the gated estates of genuinely-in-residence movie stars. Off Hollywood Boulevard, amidst lines of tall palm trees, snack stands took the shape of giant hot dogs, and real estate offices were marked by wooden spears that could only have been thrown by the mighty King Kong.

Drugstores offered an astounding variety of cosmetics to movie hopefuls while billboards along the Sunset Strip advertised cigarettes that promised movie-star sophistication for 15 cents a pack.

It was a Hollywood one could see best in a snappy convertible. Of course, if you were Joan Crawford, Clark Gable, Robert Taylor or Claudette Colbert following the searchlight emblazoned sky to a preview, the privacy of your chauffeur-driven limousine was advisable.

Shopping with Aunt Irene was an even bigger treat than looking for movie stars. She had unusual ideas about clothes. She dared to wear color combinations which were, at the time, considered to be unwearable together, such as blue and green, brown and black, red and pink, and red and green, the latter being reserved by everyone else for Christmas decorations. When Aunt Irene put these color combinations together, she was daringly *chic*. When I received clothes from her I changed them around quite a bit to make them more acceptable for the small towns I lived in. I didn't have Aunt Irene's ability to carry off the unusual. Although I loved her things, I knew I couldn't get away with them the way she did.

Once, when Aunt Irene heard that I was going to the senior prom, she sent me one of her evening gowns by way of Greyhound bus. I was very excited, thinking I'd be the belle of the ball in one of Aunt Irene's stylish gowns. When I opened the box what I saw was pure magic: a shimmering sleeveless shift of silver lamé. When I put it on what I saw in the mirror was a disappointment. Mother looked at me and shook her head. "It's not for you," she said.

Mother was right. I was very skinny, tall for my age and nearly flat-chested. Aunt Irene was slender, but she had curves in the right places. I lacked curves. The gown would have looked better hanging on a coat rack than on me. I had long, bony arms and my hip bones stuck out. Unhappily I returned the beautiful silver gown to Aunt Irene by the next Greyhound bus, then Mother and I went shopping. Mother usually made my clothes, but the prom was only two days away and there wasn't time enough, even for Mother's flying needle.

"We need something bouffant to fill you out," Mother said. The only prom dress left in town in my size was a baby blue net number with a big full skirt lined in blue satin. It had puffed sleeves dotted with pink satin bows. Even Mother agreed that taking the bows off the sleeves would improve the dress.

I went to the beauty parlor and had my hair swept up in a big reverse roll on each side and sprayed with lacquer so that the rolls wouldn't fall. Then the beautician sprinkled gold dust on my hair. My date took me to his house to show me off to his mother. "Doesn't she look wonderful?" he bragged. I didn't feel wonderful. The tacky blue net was no substitute for Aunt Irene's beautiful silver lamé dress.

I didn't get to attend that prom after all. When we arrived at the gym the Dean of Girls, Miss Barker, was waiting there looking grim and checking names on a clipboard.

"Sunny Lockard?" she inquired. She knew perfectly well who I was. I was in her chemistry class and I hated it.

"Yes?" I replied. What was wrong? Had I failed the last test?

"You were on the school bus trip to Fort Tejon on Thursday?"

"Yes." She knew that as well. What had I done?

"Well, I'm sorry, but you're quarantined. May Baxter was on that trip also, and she's come down with polio. Everyone who was on that bus is in quarantine, so you have to go home now."

May Baxter! Nancy was on that trip as well. We sat with May and her friend Amy the whole time and even shared sandwiches with them!

My date, a boy I had never been out with before and who had just asked me to go steady, rushed me home and left as fast as he could get away. Mother looked shocked when I walked into the house only forty-five minutes after leaving it. After hearing my story she said, "I wonder if we can return the dress?"

Nancy, of course, was in quarantine also. She became ill, and the doctor suspected polio. However, she recovered with no ill effects, our quarantine expired, and life went on.

The boots were Aunt Irene's first gift to me, and I wrote her a warm thank-you note. This established a correspondence with her which lasted for years. Whenever I had a new outfit, either purchased in a store or made for me by Mother, I wrote a letter to Aunt Irene and enclosed a detailed drawing of my new dress or suit. I sketched my new clothing very carefully, using art pencils to render the colors as accurately as possible. I even snipped a bit of material from one of the seams or the inside of a hem if I could do so without damage to the fabric and I included this in the letter. Aunt Irene always responded enthusiastically and added her ideas for accessories.

Mother made me a blue and white striped dirndl with a white dotted swiss blouse. "Buy a wide bright red patent leather belt," wrote Aunt Irene. "It will complete your outfit perfectly." And it did. About a dark green plaid dress with a narrow yellow band worked into the plaid she wrote, "Wear a shiny gold belt and replace the green buttons with gold ones that match the belt." For a navy blue dress and matching bolero Aunt Irene advised, "A brilliant orange scarf and matching lipstick would be a knockout!" *Orange?* Did anyone wear orange if it wasn't Halloween? The flashy orange scarf and matching Tangee lipstick that I bought changed my navy outfit from ordinary to smart.

I didn't send Aunt Irene a sketch of the blue satin and net formal with the puffed sleeves and pink bows that Mother sewed back on before she returned the dress to the store. Even then I had enough sense of Aunt Irene's style to know she wouldn't have approved.

From Aunt Irene I learned the meaning of *flair*.

Nancy

When Sunny opened her package from Aunt Irene and drew out a pair of brown riding boots, I was mute with envy.

"Oh, look! look!" Sunny gasped as she tore away the white tissue. I saw the boots were already creased around the ankles, letting the world know the wearer had broken them in by spending hours in the saddle.

The fact that Aunt Irene had probably gained all her riding experience on rented horses didn't diminish the glamour that emanated from the boots as the perfume of saddle soap and fresh polish wafted up from the tissue Sunny tossed aside.

My envy was not just that the boots were given to Sunny and not to me. I was used to the fact that coats and jackets were purchased for Sunny and handed down to me after she had outgrown them. I was accustomed to keeping an anxious eye on my favorites among her clothes, hoping they wouldn't have tears or stains by the time they were moved over to my side of the closet. And, I knew as I watched Sunny work her feet into Aunt Irene's boots, that eventually the boots would be mine. Aunt Irene's feet and Sunny's were already the same size, and Sunny's were still growing.

What I felt, and could not articulate, was that the boots fit more with my personality than Sunny's. It would have been more fair if Aunt Irene had given the boots to *me*. Teenage Sunny was concerned with "girl things" like bracelets and perfume. Even her idol, Osa Johnson, was reputed to carry a full makeup kit on safari. I felt sure Sunny only wanted the boots to appear fashionable—to emulate the horsey coeds from wealthy eastern families. She had spent a lot of time visiting Mama Dot at The Ranch, and Mama Dot wanted her granddaughters to acquire upper-class manners and attitudes. "Expect orchids and you'll get orchids," Mama Dot would advise us as she adjusted her single strand of pearls and blew smoke rings from her Camel cigarette.

Moreover, Sunny was going to be a schoolteacher if Mother had anything to say about it. I, on the other hand, planned to be a cowboy. Not a silly *cowgirl* with a guitar, big white Stetson hat and fringed leather skirt but a real working cowhand, riding a pinto pony out on the desert and sleeping by a campfire at night, my head on my saddle. Western movies were popular in the thirties, and I had drunk in Hollywood's version of the old West at Saturday matinées.

If no one in the family was aware of my plans for the future, it was because the fantasy life I acted out was mostly ignored. My favorite song was the popular cowboy tune of the 30s, "*Home on the Range*," but since I couldn't carry a tune, my singing was not encouraged. I spent hours in the backyard with a length of cotton rope trying to make perfect circles in the air with my lasso. When I was at The Ranch I walked far out among the Joshua trees and sagebrush, mentally saddling "Old Paint" for the last roundup.

I was different from Sunny, but Aunt Irene obviously didn't see that difference—didn't see that the boots should have been given to me.

Watching Sunny strut around the living room in the boots, I begged, "Let me try them on."

But Sunny slipped the boots off and began wrapping them back up in the tissue.

"Fat chance," she said, tucking them away in their box. "They aren't *children's* boots, you know. You'd clop around in them and run them over on the sides." Her voice took on a loftier tone as she reminded me, "Besides, you'd look silly. You don't even have riding breeches."

CHAPTER 5

Valley and Mountains

Nancy

On a clear day looking east, California's snow-covered Sierra Nevada mountains can be seen from the San Joaquin Valley towns lying between John Muir's "Range of Light" and the rugged but less spectacular Coast Ranges to the west.

Daddy loved the Sierras, and because of his civil engineer's way of describing terrain, Sunny and I knew they were some 500 miles long, 70 miles wide and boasted a peak, Mt. Whitney, nearly 15,000 feet high.

What I knew more intimately, though, from our family's trips into these mountains, was that I could be relied upon to get carsick no matter how carefully Daddy drove out of the Valley into the Sierra foothills.

Anxious questions from Mother to the back seat such as "Nancy, are you feeling all right?" or "Do you need us to pull over?" were voiced in part out of a concern for me but primarily because no one wanted to ride in a car that smelled of my regurgitated breakfast or lunch. Our family had strong olfactory memories of that experience because my stomach always rebelled at the curves and switchbacks that brought us up through the manzanita scrub then Douglas spruce, sugar pine and silver fir to destinations such as Sequoia or Yosemite.

87-GALL

Among Mother's emergency supplies were two glass jars that might as well have been labeled, "Nancy." One jar contained a washcloth floating in water with baking soda. This was for disguising odors. The other contained a washcloth floating in soapy water. This was for wiping up mouth, arms, knees, shins and any other parts of my body that might become decorated with semi-digested bits of my last meal.

One trip to Giant Forest Village comes to mind. I sat in the back seat of the car between Skippy and Sunny—since it wasn't my turn to sit by a window—and peered up front through the windshield, keeping my gaze to the center of the road as Daddy recommended. I tried not to listen to the sloshing emanating from the two jars on the floor in the back seat and periodically pleaded with Sunny, "Roll your window down!"

I emphasized my request with an elbow jab into Sunny's ribs as she answered, loud enough, she hoped, to get Mother on her side, "I don't want my hair to get messed up."

Daddy, perhaps remembering how long it took to clean out the back seat after one of his children had thrown up, answered, "Roll your window back down, Sunny," in a voice that meant business.

Sunny cranked her window down slowly then begin inching it back up by degrees so small that I knew it would be another stomach-lurching ten miles before I could complain again. She gave me a smug glance, and I answered with my I'm-going-to-get-even stare. Skippy wrinkled his nose at us with a now-I've-got-something-on-both-of-you look, and another family car trip to the Sierras was underway.

Mother carried a change of clothes for me in a paper sack which she placed handily by her feet in the front seat. It never occurred to anyone that I should ride in the front seat, which, in those days, was not split to house the gear shift but extended the width of the car with ample room for three people. Riding in front, though, was a privilege often accorded to

Skippy—not because he was the son and heir but because his anatomy allowed Daddy to partially solve yet another problem of traveling with children: requests for frequent "I-have-to-go" stops.

Skippy, active and restless, found car trips boring and discovered he had the power to stop the car and enjoy a few minutes of running around the side of the road by announcing, "I have to go wee wee!" In between these "Skippy" stops he declared, "I'm thirsty!" thereby ensuring that, before long, he could not only get Daddy to stop again but could prove, as he postured between our car and the road's shoulder, that the stop was really necessary.

Both Daddy and Mother were on to Skippy's tricks, but Mother had read that it was unhealthy for a child to wait too long to urinate, so she insisted Daddy stop each time Skippy said he had the urge.

Typically, Daddy solved the problem in a practical way. He ran a length of garden hose from alongside the gearshift through the floor of the car, and, thereafter when Skippy felt the call of nature, he would be allowed to climb into the front seat of the car and answer, leaving moist little echoes along the highways of California.

But, until we moved to Tulare, we could only enjoy the Sierras on Daddy's annual two-week vacation. Now, with these magnificent mountains a mere 50 miles away, we could explore them on weekends or even drive up to a foothill lake for a summer-evening barbecue.

The ever-present Sierra Nevadas stood over us to the east as if to say, "How bad can the heat, tule fog, dust and bugs of San Joaquin Valley be if we're here?" Our trips to the Sierras were among the sweetest of Sunny's and my memories.

A grown Skippy put our feelings into words after he took a break from his job as professor at the University of Washington and camped on Washington's Olympic Peninsula with his wife and their young son, Eric, and daughter, Kim. "I was hunched by our tent in the drizzling rain," he told Sunny and me, "trying to keep the children amused and the campfire going. I started wondering how Daddy managed to infuse our camping trips with so much magic. Maybe in retrospect all we remember is the good times, but they really were special, weren't they?"

Camping isn't everyone's cup of hot chocolate, but it was clear that Daddy, along with John Muir, was most at home among ". . . the noonday radiance on the trees . . . the flush of the alpenglow, and a thousand dashing waterfalls . . ."

Mother, on the other hand, would have enjoyed a vacation at a hotel where meals were served, beds made and dance music played in the evenings. Since the family budget wouldn't allow for such luxuries, she didn't campaign for her dream vacations. Too, she believed in giving her children "experiences" and wouldn't have left us behind at vacation time.

So Daddy whistled as he packed the car with our huge cotton tent, army cots and blankets. Mother's face took on an air of resignation as she got together our cast-iron frying pan, tin plates and cups, blue speckled coffee pot and food.

The food box always contained dry macaroni, canned tomatoes and Spanish onions, essential ingredients, along with fresh ground meat purchased as we neared our destination, for our first night's meal of Daddy's famous "Indian Macaroni."

Daddy told us the story of how he got the recipe many times, but we children always begged him to tell us again.

"I was out near Kettleman Hills late one afternoon surveying a possible rig site when I came across this old Indian sheepherder," Daddy recounted. "There wasn't a house in sight, just oil rigs and sagebrush covered-hills as far as you could see. I didn't have any food with me, and it had been a long time since lunch. I was getting hungry."

Daddy paused, and we listened intently. "I got to talking to this wonderful old gentleman as he was frying meat and macaroni and chopped onions in a big skillet. When the macaroni was good and brown, he poured a can of tomatoes in, stirred it and put the lid on. Boy, did it smell delicious as it simmered over that campfire."

We knew what came next, but we waited. "Well," Daddy continued, "he asked me to join him for dinner. But first the old Indian got up, walked over to a patch of sagebrush and picked a few leaves. 'Going to add my secret ingredient,' he told me. 'Keep it under your hat. Wouldn't want it to get around.' We sat on some rocks and finished nearly every bite that was in that black skillet. It was delicious." Daddy looked at us seriously. "The recipe is a secret, though. That Indian asked me not to give it to anyone."

"What was secret about it?" we asked, pretending not to know.

Daddy leaned closer and spoke softly, "Just before he took the macaroni off the fire, the sheepherder took those sage leaves and rubbed them together in his hands over the skillet. I could smell the aroma that sage gave out as it fell into the sizzling sauce."

We swore we'd never tell, although all our lives we've told everyone who would listen.

Daddy's Indian Macaroni saved Mother from cooking many a camp dinner and is still a favorite with Sunny and me, although Sunny now makes her version without the meat, and I add garlic to mine and sprinkle cheese over the top just before serving. The real secret, though, is browning the macaroni.

Sunny

Daddy always took his annual vacation the last two weeks of August, ending on Labor Day, and we went to either the beach or the mountains. We usually camped, but once in a while we rented a rustic beach cottage or a mountain cabin. These were concessions to Mother because she did not like camping. In describing her role on the family vacation Mother often complained, "I do the same things I do at home but under primitive conditions."

Mother would have preferred a vacation in the city. She would have thrived on bustling department stores, crowded streets, and restaurants with waiters who called her "madam." We didn't have the money for that kind of a vacation. Even if we had been able to afford it, it would not have suited Daddy. He was an outdoor person in every sense of the word. He disliked cities and crowds. In fact, he disliked everything about a city that Mother liked.

What Mother saw as refinement, like obsequious waiters, for example, Daddy saw as pretense. To my father a city was a disagreeable place where one had to go on business occasionally or through which one had to pass to get to an agreeable place. For Mother, a city was a longed-for destination.

Daddy was sensitive enough to Mother's dislike of camping to relieve her of much of the burden of housekeeping in camp. He set up the camp, kept it tidy—with help from Nancy and me—and did quite a bit of the cooking. He fixed flapjacks or bacon and eggs for breakfast. For dinner he often made his specialty, Indian Macaroni. If the day's fishing had turned out well, he would fry trout or, on the coast, ocean perch for dinner.

Since Mother didn't go hiking or fishing with us, there was little for her to do on these trips except worry about one of us getting stung by a bee, bitten by a rattlesnake, pawed by a bear, or attacked by a batch of poison oak when we squatted to relieve ourselves in the bushes. Mother stayed in camp reading the *Woman's Home Companion, Good Housekeeping* or a lending library selection. She also occupied herself with knitting, playing solitaire and writing long letters to friends and relatives complaining about the dust, flies, yellow jackets, rain, cold nights, sagging camp bed and lack of sanitary facilities. Here is a portion of a letter which Mother wrote to me in late August, 1941. I was away at college, and this year the family vacation was at North Lake in the eastern Sierras.

> *Dear Sunny,*
>
> *I am writing this from North Lake but I won't be able to mail it until we leave as there is no place here to mail a letter. There is nothing here, and I mean nothing! We are the only people here. We are camped by a lake in a very rocky area—rocks everywhere and hardly any trees. Your father had a hard time finding a spot without too many rocks which was level enough for the tent. There isn't a picnic table like you find in many camping spots, so we make do with an army cot, if you can imagine sitting around that for our meals! It is cold here, especially at night, but Nancy and Skippy don't seem to mind, and of course you know your father, he is happy in a remote, isolated place—which this certainly is—and he doesn't mind the cold or other discomforts.*
>
> *We have eaten all the fresh food we brought, and are now eating out of cans. We have trout every day and it is getting tiresome. There is no way to take a bath excepting to heat some water in a bucket and sponge inside the tent, but that's not the worst of it! For our "toilet" your father dug a hole and put a large tree limb over it to sit on. After we do our business we cover it (the "business") with dirt! Be thankful you are not here. This is the most primitive "vacation" experience I've ever had! Fortunately I brought along plenty to read, my knitting and a pile of mending.*

This is the first page of the letter. The rest has been lost, along with the envelope. The letter is not dated, but I remember the time because I had just entered the University of California at Berkeley as a junior. I was settled in a boarding house near the campus and feeling absolutely devastated because I couldn't be on the family vacation.

In 1935, while we were living in Tulare, Daddy decided that the family vacation that summer would be at Huntington Lake, about 120 miles northeast of Tulare in the Sierra National Forest. Mother never participated in choosing the sites for these trips. I suppose that, in her opinion, one camp was much like another, with more or less the same inconveniences, so it did not really matter to her where we went. In any case, for her our vacations boiled down to two weeks of discomfort and boredom, wherever we were.

The night before we were due to leave for the lake Nancy and I helped Mother pack canned goods, pots and pans, kitchen utensils, dish towels, bath towels, soap, iodine, bandages and other necessary items for the trip. Finally she sent us into our room to pack our clothes.

"Now, remember," Mother said, "you girls get only one suitcase between you. We don't have room for two, so all your things have to go in one. You can use Nancy's leather case."

Nancy and I sorted through our clothes and made two separate piles on our double bed. Shorts, shirts, socks, underwear, sweater, sweatshirt, bathing suit, pajamas, bandanna. We would wear our boys' jeans and our old brown oxfords in the car on the way. Our old school shoes—which still fit because Mother was always careful to buy them big enough to last at least half a year—would do for the trip. Waiting in our closet were new shoes to be worn to our new school in September.

I put my riding breeches and the boots Aunt Irene had sent me on top of my pile. Nancy stared at my stack of clothing and put her hands on her hips just like Mother did when she was annoyed. "What do you think you're going to do with *those*, Sunny-funny?"

"They're on my pile, aren't they?" I answered. "So they go into the suitcase, Nanny-goat."

"Not in *my* suitcase!" Nancy stamped her foot. "There won't be room for anything else!"

"What do you mean, *your* suitcase? It's half mine for this

trip!" I gave her a shove. She ran into the kitchen to tell Mother, then marched back to the bedroom with Mother close behind.

"Sunny," Mother said, in her no-argument tone, "you can't take the boots. Leave them here."

"But, Mom . . ."

"I said to leave them here! You can't hike in those. They'll hurt your feet. Besides, we don't have money for horseback riding this year." With that she picked up the boots and handed them to me.

Fighting away tears, I put my boots away in the closet. Then I picked up the breeches to put them away too. "You can take *those*," Mother said, pointing to the breeches. I put the breeches back in the drawer.

Wear them without the boots? No. Mother didn't understand. She wasn't *stylish* like Aunt Irene.

"Well," Mother said, "suit yourself. Don't forget sweaters and sweatshirts, girls."

"In our piles," said Nancy.

Mother went back to the kitchen. I stuck my tongue out at Nancy. "What a tattle-tale you are, Nancy-pantsy!"

"One of these days," Nancy said, in her best haughty tone, "*your* feet will be too big for those boots and *my* feet will grow and the boots will be just right for *me*! So there!"

"I'll wear them *out* first!" I promised.

We were all up early the next morning. Daddy didn't start packing the car until everything had been assembled and put on a large tarp which he had spread out on the ground next to the car. Then he cautioned, "Is everything here? Because once I start packing nothing can be added, not even a toothpick."

Daddy was a whiz at packing our sedan for a camping trip. First he put a few layers of army blankets on the rear seat where Nancy and I would sit. A couple of suitcases went on one side of the seat, leaving the middle and the other side for Nancy and me. The floor of the car in back was carefully filled with canned goods, cooking utensils and other items until it reached the level of the seat, then it was covered with blankets. This made it impossible for Nancy and me to put our feet on the floor and we had to ride with our legs stretched out straight.

Mother discouraged us from lying down or curling up on our sides, especially as Nancy tended to get carsick. Skippy often rode in front with Mother so that he could use the hose in the floorboard to relieve himself. Mother and Daddy were fond of telling friends and relatives about Skippy's hose, but I found this so embarrassing that I left the room whenever this subject came up in front of company.

Our car did not have a top carrier, but Daddy was a genius at packing the top. First he put an old blanket or a canvas tarp on to protect the car finish. Then he arranged army cots, the Coleman stove and lantern, the tent, boxes and suitcases on top of the tarp, bringing up the sides of the tarp to cover everything. Another tarp went on top, then he tied the whole bundle down with ropes lashed to the car bumpers.

Daddy finished securing the top bundle after Mother, Skippy, Nancy and I got into the car. He had a way of tightening up the straps which went through the side windows after he got into the car. Once in, the straps prevented us from rolling the windows all the way up or opening the car doors. The straps had to be loosened to allow us to get out of the car. The trunk of the car was fully packed as well.

We carried a large canvas water bag on the front of the car in case the engine overheated and the radiator needed water. The last thing that Daddy tied on to the top pack was a long-handled shovel. In those days everyone who camped was required to carry one. In case of a forest fire male campers in the area could be commandeered to fight the fire. The shovel that Daddy carried on our trips was used to make a temporary latrine, dig a drainage ditch around our tent in case of a thunderstorm, pitch dirt on a campfire or kill a rattlesnake.

We were finally ready to go. The last things Mother packed were bacon, sausage and leftover pot roast. These she put in a bucket with a piece of dry ice from the corner grocery. She placed the bucket on the floor of the car near her feet and covered it with towels to keep it insulated. "Keep your hands off the dry ice," Mother warned Skippy. "It will burn, and take the skin right off."

As Daddy backed the car into the alley, Mother gave us our final orders: "Now girls, look straight ahead when we get to the winding mountain road and you won't get sick. I've told Daddy to take it easy on the curves. Behave yourselves, and no fighting! And trade places once in a while, so you can take turns sitting by the window."

My excitement increased when we turned off the main road and began to slowly wind our way up through the sloping foothills of the western face of the Sierra range. After we had gained only a few hundred feet of elevation the air seemed fresher and cooler and the Valley floor began to fade into the distance.

Daddy pointed out things along the way. "Look, girls, I think that's a red-tailed hawk up there," he said, pointing to a big bird gliding on the air currents high above. Nancy and I scrambled over each other to catch a glimpse from one of the windows. As we climbed a little higher Daddy said, "See that big pile of dark rocks to the right? That's the top of an old lava flow from a volcano. Nancy's eyes grew big as she uttered a long drawn-out "Ooooh!"

Later we drove over a bridge which spanned a meandering creek. "Those trees along the river," said Daddy, "are called quaking aspen. Aspen is a species of poplar." I watched the leaves quiver in the breeze, as if some unseen hand was gently shaking each tree. When the leaves caught the sun just right they became silvery for a second, then turned green again. I imagined the leaves made a magic tinkling sound that I could hear if I walked along the river.

Daddy said, "Oh, oh. A rattlesnake in the road." Nancy and I whipped around and looked out the rear window but didn't see anything. Skippy jumped up and yelled, "Snake! I wanna see!"

Mother told Skippy to sit down and be quiet. Turning to Daddy she said, "I think it's best if the girls look straight ahead from now on."

Nancy and I settled down and watched the road. We were out of the grasslands and oaks now and among a few pines and firs. A rabbit ran across the road and we saw a few deer high up on a hillside. "I wanna see a bear!" Skippy yelled.

Nancy grabbed her towel and covered her mouth. "Stop," she mumbled.

"Daddy!" I yelled. "Nancy wants to stop!"

"I told you," said Mother.

Daddy slowed the car down and parked on a wide part of the shoulder. Then he unfastened the front overhead strap which was securing the load. "Climb over the seat," Daddy urged, "Come on, I'll help you." Nancy climbed over, and I followed. I decided that I was feeling woozy, and it wouldn't hurt to get out. Then Skippy wanted out. Daddy walked Skippy up and down by the car, holding him by the hand.

Mother stayed in the car. She handed me the canteen through the open window. "Give everyone a drink, and stay away from the road and the edge of the cliff!"

After a few minutes we were on our way again. Tall pines, firs and cedars were now abundant. Eventually we came around a curve and I saw the blue expanse of a lake. "There it is!" I shouted.

"That's Shaver Lake," Daddy said. "Huntington is beyond that."

Nancy, recovered from her carsickness, perked up. "I'm gonna catch a big fish!"

Daddy laughed. "I hope so. I hope we catch a lot of fish."

Daddy had arranged to rent a tent-cabin at the lake. It

was built on a large wooden platform and covered with heavy canvas. On the platform outside the tent-cabin was a large picnic table, some shelves, and a cupboard with doors.

Daddy had packed a small tent for Nancy and me, which he erected next to the platform. He set up army cots in our tent and put one in the tent-cabin for Skippy. Mother took one look at the bed she and Daddy would share, a double-sized metal camp affair with a waffle work of wire which served as springs, and said, "Ugh!"

"We can pad it up pretty well," Daddy offered.

"Not much we can do about the sag," Mother grumbled.

Within an hour we had settled into our camp, a beautiful spot on the edge of the lake. The elevation was 7,000 feet and it was very chilly at night. I loved the cold nights and the snugness of my warm blankets. Tulare's hot nights were forgotten.

Daddy caught rainbow trout in the lake, and Nancy and I also caught several. Towards the end of the first week Daddy heard that there was very good fishing in some of the upper lakes. He decided to hike to Lower Twin Lake and he asked Nancy and me to go along. We were excellent hikers and always eager to go with him. The hike was about five miles each way, easy for two active kids and a healthy man in his late thirties.

The day of the planned hike, at breakfast, Nancy let out a giant sneeze, and her nose began to bleed. Mother was concerned. Nancy had frequent nosebleeds, which were often hard to stop. Mother applied a cold washcloth to Nancy's forehead and another one to the back of her neck. Soon the bleeding stopped. "She'll be all right," Mother said, "but she's not going anywhere today. Maybe it's the altitude, or she may be coming down with something." Nancy's eyes filled with tears of disappointment.

"Well," Daddy mused, "I suppose we could go another day." He thought for a minute, then said to Nancy, "Suppose we plan something special, just for you? You stay in camp and rest today, and we'll see what tomorrow brings." I could tell that Daddy didn't want to put off the hike, that he was thinking of all the fish waiting for us. "We'll bring you a nice fish for dinner," Daddy continued. "You can have the biggest one!"

Tears rolled down Nancy's cheeks. Her mouth trembled, but she managed a weak smile. "O.K., Daddy."

I felt sorry for Nancy, but I didn't want to miss going with Daddy. I was very careful not to cough or sneeze or in any way appear to be "coming down with something."

Daddy and I were off before lunch. My small rucksack held two salami sandwiches and two oranges. Daddy carried our fishing poles and a creel containing the salmon eggs we used for bait, hooks, split shot and leaders. We drove to the trailhead and parked. When we started on the trail I was so elated that I skipped, hopped and jumped.

"Conserve your energy, Sunny," said Daddy. "There may be some stiff climbing ahead, and anyhow you're raising dust, which is not good hiking etiquette."

I reined in my enthusiasm. It was a beautiful day. Except for a few wispy clouds the sky was clear and bright blue. The warmth of the sun felt good, but in the shade it was still cool enough for a sweater. We hiked on, past open sunny meadows, through pine forests and along rivulets and springs trickling over granite rocks. Every turn in the trail exposed us to breathtaking vistas of towering mountain peaks, deep valleys and distant waterfalls.

After about an hour and a half Daddy called a halt in an open space along the trail. "Let's stop here and eat our oranges," he suggested. We weren't hiking very fast. Daddy's hiking method was hike ten minutes, rest some. In this way the scenery could be enjoyed thoroughly as we went along. Daddy didn't believe in endurance hiking.

We sat on some almost flat granite rocks and ate our oranges. A gray squirrel scampered across the trail, on its busy way. We scattered our orange seeds among the sparse, low scrub brush by the trail, but the orange peels went into my rucksack to dispose of back in camp. Daddy had reminded me, "What you pack in must be packed out."

Against the background of vast wilderness silence I concentrated on the mountain sounds I loved: the rustle of the wind in the trees, the faint noise of water running over rocks, and the occasional raucous call of a stellar's jay. I inhaled the pine aroma carried on updrafts from the forests below.

Daddy stood up and looked up the trail ahead of us. "Someone's coming," he said.

"A . . . bear?" I ventured, uneasily.

"Yep, a bear that whistles."

I listened intently then heard it: the light rhythmic crunch of granite pebbles on the trail and low whistling. I looked up the trail and saw a tall figure just appearing over the crest of the next rise. The hiker appeared and disappeared, growing bigger and bigger, the whistling becoming more audible. Soon he was approaching us, hiking fast.

Daddy greeted the hiker. "Hello, there! How's the fishing?"

"Great!" the man answered. "Got some nice rainbows." He unfastened the strap of his creel and opened the lid to show Daddy the fish. He lifted the top fish up to show the ones underneath, all neatly packed in reddish-green leaves.

I looked at the fish too, and unconsciously put my hand lightly on the edge of the creel. Daddy grabbed my hand, saying, "Don't touch."

"That's all right," said the man.

"I hate to tell you this," Daddy said, "but you've packed your fish in poison oak."

"Poison oak!" the man exclaimed. He peered inside the creel. "Damn!" Looking at me he said, "Oh, I'm sorry! Worse luck. *Darn!*"

The man went on down the trail, shaking his head from side to side, and not whistling. Daddy said, "I'll bet he repacks those fish before he shows them to his buddies!"

So far the trail had been fairly wide and easy, but now it became narrower and steeper. My old school shoes slipped on the pebbles and slid back on the steeper slopes, but I kept my balance. We trudged along a set of switchbacks and came out among some giant granite boulders. Then we saw our destination, Lower Twin Lake.

"It sure is blue!" I exclaimed, taking a deep breath. Both Daddy and I were quiet for a moment, taking in the beauty around us.

"Sure is," Daddy replied. "Let's eat our lunch by the lake."

We walked down to the lake and sat on a couple of rocks and ate our sandwiches. From our vantage point we could see the whole lake. We were the only human beings there. It was still, peaceful. I wanted to say, "I love this beautiful place." I felt that Daddy was thinking the same thing, so I didn't say it. Our family wasn't given to open expression of feelings, anyhow. That's just the way we were.

I was happy to be with Daddy, doing something we both loved to do. I was sorry that Nancy had been left behind, but being with Daddy alone was a very special treat. I was very proud of him and I thought he was the most wonderful father a girl could have.

"Not the best time of day to fish," said Daddy. "So they say."

"Why not? Who are 'they'?" I asked

"I suppose it's just an old fishermen's tale. I don't know how true it is. They say the fish bite in the mornings and evenings, not in the middle of the day."

"Do you believe it?" I asked.

"Sometimes. Well, let's find out."

Daddy rigged up his fishing pole and helped me with mine. We found a nice deep pool that looked promising. I perched on a large rock overlooking the pool and dropped my line in the water. The rock was warm and felt good on my bare legs.

"You want to stay here for a while?" Daddy asked. "I'm going to fish around the lake. Try my luck here and there. I'll always be where you can see me. By the way, don't forget to check your bait once in a while."

"I won't forget."

For a while I watched Daddy fishing in one place and then another across the lake. The warm rock, the soothing breeze, the sunshine bath and my full stomach made me drowsy. I made my sweater into a pillow and stretched out as best I could on the rock, clutching the fishing pole in an iron grip. I knew if I lost a fishing pole my life wouldn't be worth two cents. It would be better if I drowned along with the pole.

I didn't intend to fall asleep, but I did just that. The next thing I knew Daddy was shaking me gently by the shoulder. "Hey, lazybones, any bites?"

"Guess not," I replied, grateful that I was still clutching my pole. I reeled in my line. The bait was missing.

Daddy said, "Either something stole your bait or you didn't put it on well."

I felt a tinge of guilt. "Catch anything?" I asked.

"A couple," Daddy replied, "and some bites. Maybe those old fishermen knew something."

"I think I'll fish around the lake," I said, and I started off with my pole.

"Stay where I can see you," Daddy called.

I walked slowly around the opposite side of the lake, crawling over boulders and dropping my line in the water in places that looked like the kind of pools in which trout hide and feed. I must have done this for about an hour, without even a nibble. Finally I came across a pool that looked so inviting that I decided to swim instead of fish. I peeled down to my underwear, secured my fishing pole among some rocks and jumped in.

The water was icy but refreshing. I thought I was as close to heaven as one could get on this earth. I splashed around, swam under water, and floated on my back for a while, watching several dark flocks of birds pass overhead. When I got out of the water I shivered in the sun for a few minutes waiting for my underwear to dry. Then I got dressed and went back to where I had left Daddy.

"I thought I told you to stay where I could see you," Daddy admonished.

"I went swimming," I explained.

"Now the fish *know* we're here," said Daddy in an amused tone.

"Does it make a difference?" I asked, seriously. I remembered that fishermen didn't like any noise or disturbance near where they were fishing. "Can the fish hear noise, see people?"

"Maybe," Daddy replied. "Let's wait for a while and try again. Maybe our luck will change. Maybe fish have short memories."

Daddy had packed the two fish he caught in some wet grass from a little spring near the lake and put the fish in his creel in the shade. We sat silently for a while, thinking our own thoughts. Then Daddy asked me, "Do you mind going to a new school?"

"No," I replied. "I don't mind. It's all the same." I really did feel that way. I wasn't saying it just to please Daddy. Being with Daddy was more important to me than staying in the same school, but I couldn't say that out loud.

"Moving around will be hard on your mother, but I know you girls will help." With that Daddy turned away. He glanced at the sun, which was now well past the meridian and heading towards the western horizon. "Well! About time to sneak up on those fish!"

We walked down the trail towards the end of the lake. Keeping about a hundred feet apart, we dropped our lines in the deep pools along the edge. I was careful not to let my shadow fall on the water where I was fishing, as Daddy had taught me.

Right away I caught a big rainbow trout and then another. I looked at Daddy and saw him reel in a good-sized fish. Our luck had changed! At the next pool I had nibbles only, so I moved on. I saw Daddy pulling in one fish after the other. We kept moving along the lake, and I caught three more trout. One was too small, so I carefully removed the hook and threw it back in. After that it was nibbles only, but I was pleased with the four I had caught.

I glanced at the sun. It seemed to me that it was getting late. Daddy was still fishing, so I put fresh bait on my hook and dropped my line in the water. Not even a nibble this time. Then I saw Daddy retracing his steps and coming my way, a big smile on his face.

"How many?" I called. "I caught four good ones!"

"Good!" said Daddy, approaching me. "I'm over the limit, so I'll give you some of mine."

Daddy's fish were beautiful, big plump ones. He packed them in more wet grass, then, using the waxed paper left over from our sandwiches, he made two packets of fish, putting one in his creel and the other one in our lunch bag for me to carry. "Your rucksack will never smell the same," he joked.

"I don't care!" I replied, happily.

Daddy took our fishing poles apart and put the remaining bait, leaders, shot and hooks in my rucksack.

We started down the trail. It seemed a bit late to me, but I had confidence in Daddy. He could tell time by the position of the sun. He knew so many things. It never occurred to me that he could be wrong about anything. We hiked on.

The trail was mostly downhill, so we could go a little faster than coming uphill. After a while we came to a small spring trickling out of the side of an embankment. I remembered the spring because I had scooped up water in my hands for a drink on the way up. In those days we did not need to carry water on the trail in the high country. We drank out of lakes, rivers and springs and suffered no ill effects.

Daddy and I both cupped our hands, dipped up water from the spring and drank. We soaked my bandanna in the cool water and squeezed it over the fish.

We went on. "I think this is where we ate our oranges," Daddy said, pointing to some rocks in an open place on the trail. Then we heard voices, and a few yards farther down saw a man and two boys camped in a large flat area near the trail. The man and older boy, about my age, were struggling with a tent. The younger boy, maybe about eleven, was trying to build a fire.

The man called out to Daddy, "How's the fishing?"

"Can't complain," Daddy replied. He walked over to the man and showed him the fish. They exchanged a few words, then Daddy said, "How about some help with that tent? I have one just like it."

Daddy put the creel on the ground and steadied the tent pole. I watched the younger boy, who was attempting to build a fire with a couple of damp sticks and no kindling, and could contain myself no longer. "You'll never get a fire started that way," I said. "Here, let me do it."

I put my rucksack aside and gathered a pile of dry pine needles, then I put twigs on top of these. Next I put on some small dry branches which I found on the ground nearby. Finally I tucked two pinecones underneath the branches. "Now try it," I said.

The boy lighted the fire and it burned well, as I knew it would. "Where did you learn that?" he asked.

"From my father," I answered. "He taught me lots of things."

"Like what?"

"Like how to fish, hike, swim and shoot. My dad can do almost anything."

"I didn't know girls cared about stuff like that. Swimming, maybe."

"My dad can tie a diamond hitch on a mule," I bragged. "Hardly *anyone* knows how to do that."

"What's a diamond hitch, anyway?"

"It's a special way to tie a pack on a mule, as anyone who's been on a pack trip would know."

I moved away from the fire and sat on a log. The tent was up, and Daddy and the man were talking. I could hear "Lynwood," "Signal Hill," "Long Beach," "fishing trip." They seemed to have a lot to say to each other. The boys were sitting by the fire, poking it with sticks. "Leave it alone," I called out. "Let it burn down a little and then put on a bigger piece." The older boy stared at me, but they stopped poking the fire. I knew I sounded bossy, but I felt superior to these two kids who didn't even know how to build a fire.

I looked at the sky. It was getting dark, and we still had a way to go. I felt uneasy. It was getting cooler. I pulled my sweater tightly around me and buttoned it up the front. My arms were itchy and my face was hot. I wanted Daddy to finish talking so we could go.

Daddy reached in his creel, took out three trout and gave them to the man. "For your dinner," he said. The man thanked him. Then Daddy came over to me, patted me on the shoulder and said, "We'd better hit the trail."

And hit the trail we did. It was almost dark now and getting hard to see. We hiked at a fast pace, almost a run. I stumbled over some rocks and fell a couple of times, but picked myself up and went on. I had a tight grip on my rucksack so I wouldn't lose any fish if I took a tumble.

After what seemed to me like miles of running and stumbling along the trail we came out to the road and found the car. We started for our camp at Huntington Lake.

"That boy didn't know how to start a fire," I remarked. Daddy smiled. "They're greenhorns."

We pulled into the parking spot for our campsite and Daddy turned off the motor. Then, looking towards our camp he said, "What the . . . ?"

A forest service pickup was parked next to our tent-cabin. Mother was standing on the edge of the platform talking to two forest rangers. We gathered up our fish and walked over to the tent-cabin. Mother looked at us, but said nothing. Her mouth was turned down at the corners and there were dark circles under her eyes. I knew that look. My stomach did a flip.

Both of the rangers turned to Daddy, and one of them spoke. "Mr. Lockard? Your wife was afraid something might have happened to you. We were discussing a possible search."

I could see the embarrassment, guilt and anger mixed in Daddy's face. He talked with the rangers while Mother grabbed my arm and pulled me away. "Young lady," she said, "you have a terrible sunburn! And look at those knees! What happened?"

"I fell down . . . on the trail." I had had a wonderful day with Daddy, and here was Mother ready to spoil it for both of us.

"Come with me. You're going right to bed! Put that rucksack on the table. It stinks! Your father will take care of the fish."

I had learned not to answer Mother back, not to be accused of sassiness and have a privilege revoked. No matter what Mother said, I was determined not to let her ruin this day.

Mother washed the dirt from my knees. I winced as she applied iodine to the scrapes. Then she dabbed vinegar on my sunburn with a wad of cotton. "We'll repeat this every hour," she said. My knees, legs, arms and face were on fire, but I knew that complaints would be useless.

I heard Daddy and the rangers talking in low voices, and once in a while laughing. We were late getting back, of course, but we hadn't been in any danger. Mother had no way of knowing that. To her the mysterious mountain world beyond our camp was treacherous terrain where raging rivers, slippery rocks and rough trails lurked, ready to trap the unwary.

Nancy put her head into the tent, took a sniff and said "Phew!" She held her nose and went right out again. A few minutes later I heard the ranger pickup drive off.

Mother came in with a peanut butter and jelly sandwich for me, a cup of hot chocolate and a banana. These were some of my favorite foods, but I couldn't eat. My stomach just wasn't up to it. I got dabbed with vinegar two more times, then fell asleep. When I awakened the next morning, Nancy was getting dressed. "You stink!" she said. Then she added, "Daddy and I are going to the store at Shaver Lake and you can't go!"

"I don't care," I answered, and I didn't. My sunburn hurt and my legs were stiff, but my stomach was back to normal.

I called out to Daddy, "May I have one of our trout for breakfast?"

"They're already sizzling in the frying pan," he answered.

Nancy

The boots Aunt Irene had given Sunny stayed in Sunny's side of the closet until the year Daddy decided our camping trip would be to Kings Canyon National Park in the Sierras.

As we were packing for the trip, Sunny took the boots from our closet and began pulling out the newspaper she kept stuffed in them. As she held the right boot up to blow off the dust, I realized that my turn for the boots might have come at last. I was about to bet her that she could no longer get them on when she left the room and called to Daddy, "Is it O.K. if I borrow your brown shoe polish? I want to shine my boots."

Daddy came back into the bedroom with Sunny, the can of polish in his hand. He picked up the left boot and lined it up alongside Sunny's left foot. I could feel my heart racing. The boot was definitely shorter than her school shoe.

"Maybe Nancy should take the boots this year," Daddy said. "I think by now they're more her size."

Quickly Sunny unlaced her school shoes, sat down on the bed and struggled to pull a boot on. She tugged and tugged. Trying to hide a grimace of pain as her toes finally scrunched up into the end, she assured Daddy, "They fit fine. I can still wear them." Her offhand tone was supposed to let Daddy know that his help on this subject was no longer needed.

But Daddy sat on the end of the bed and crossed his legs as if he meant to relax awhile. He gave Sunny his "let's-wait-and-see" look before turning to me with the tiniest of conspiratorial glances. I just sucked in my breath. I knew enough to be quiet.

"Why don't you put on both boots then walk around a little?" he suggested to Sunny.

She slid off the bed and took several steps, trying to smile as if her toes weren't crumpled like the newspaper she had taken out of the boots. I knew she was thinking that on horseback in Kings Canyon it wouldn't matter if the boots were too tight. She just wouldn't walk in them.

But Daddy had a little trick in mind. He pulled it on Sunny with an innocent-sounding request. "Oh, Sunny, I was packing the car when you asked for the polish. I'm afraid the neighbor's dog might jump in the trunk and get into our groceries. Would you go out and close it for me?"

As Sunny hobbled down the hall and out the kitchen door toward the garage, her curly brown hair bouncing in determination, Mother stood in the hall doorway, hands on her hips. "For heavens sake, Bruce, tell Sunny to give those boots to Nancy. She will ruin her feet if she doesn't fall down and fracture her skull first. I never saw anything like it. You'd think those darn boots were Cinderella's slipper."

"Those darn boots" went into my suitcase, but I polished

them first, which gave all my camp clothes, including my new boys' Levi's that girls had started wearing after school, a glorious odor of well-loved leather.

We set up our tent beside the Roaring River—which leads into the South Fork of the Kings River—in Kings Canyon. Mother had been apprehensive as we circled the campground looking for a suitable site. "I saw some CCC boys working on the road as we drove in," Mother warned Daddy. "Remember, both the girls are teenagers now, and those boys don't come from the best of families. I don't want any of them hanging around our camp on their time off."

"I don't think it will be a problem," Daddy said, a note of curtness in his voice as he pulled into a campsite with level ground, a view of the river and just the right amount of dappled shade from three giant sequoias.

Daddy thoroughly approved of President Roosevelt's Civilian Conservation Corps which FDR established in 1933 to put unemployed youths, mainly single men from 18 to 25, to work. The young men worked on trails, firebreaks and roads in the national parks and sent much of their meager pay home to their often needy families.

That evening as our family sat around the group campfire with the other campers, a brown-skinned CCC worker brought out his guitar and, in the firelight, began coaxing "*Noche Azul*" from its well-worn strings. As he sang of the starry blue sky in soft Spanish, I felt the magic of the night, the fire and the stars sprinkled among the lacy tree tops in a disturbing new way. Mother's warning to Daddy about the possible lure of the CCC was well founded!

When the last notes of "*Noche Azul*" faded into the low-burning fire, Daddy asked, "Conoce usted la canción '*Malagueña?*' " When the young man smiled in our direction and stroked out the chorus in a spirited flamenco tempo, I knew that, at this enchanted moment, I had begun to leave my childhood behind. Like *"Malagueña's"* composer, I couldn't "escape from my heart."

To prove how grown-up I was, I wore my boots every day, but on the day Daddy rented three horses and a mule from the pack station so he, Sunny and I and even Skippy could go riding, my boots got me into a lot of trouble.

As the four of us walked down the dusty trail to the pack station to pick out our mounts, the cowboy walk I was affecting in my Levi's and boots was barely masking the apprehension I always felt around horses. Horses were so big! And, they had minds of their own—horse minds that never paid much attention to my tenderfoot orders. I could yell, "Whoa!" or pull back on the reins or kick my heels into their flanks but my horses continued to trot or eat grass or circle back toward their corral.

Sunny, Skippy and I had been riding before but had never had lessons. Skippy's experience was limited to pony rides at carnivals, and Sunny and I had taken trail rides with Daddy on vacations. Daddy had schooled us in horse lore, though, and we knew never to stand in back of a horse or try to mount with our right foot or let our attention wander. Daddy showed us where a farm horse had bitten a piece out of the back of his neck when he was a boy.

Above all, we were warned never to let a horse know if we were afraid. "Horses can smell fear," Daddy warned, "and they won't respect you if they get a whiff of your fright. They'll know they're in control instead of you. You can't let that happen."

I was mystified. I had no idea how to keep "scared" odors from wafting up from my body to a horse's quivering silver-dollar-sized nostrils. I always suspected that my horse lost respect for me the minute I put my left foot in the stirrup and grabbed the saddle horn to pull the rest of my body up onto the western saddle. Sunny had told me that riding while holding the saddle horn was bad form so I let loose as soon as I was up. Maybe the horse knew it too. It was worse than bad form; it was gauche.

To the female side of our family, Mother, Mama Dot, Aunt Irene, Aunt Jewell and Sunny, the sin of all sins was to be tacky or gauche. Sunny was the self-appointed critic of my behavior, much of which was both tacky *and* gauche, and this morning she was free with her advice on how to ride with style.

"You hold the reins in your *left* hand, leaving your right hand free," she said. This made sense to me. After all, you might need to lasso a calf with your right arm or tip your hat to a friend as you rode by. Next came her most important admonition. "Never, never hold on to the saddle horn. It's very bad form. Good riders *never* do it. Only toddlers on pony rides do it."

I had *done it* on every ride until now, as Sunny well knew. She gave me a stern look as the smell of hay, horse sweat, saddle leather and pine needles surrounded us. In passing the boots on to me, she expected me to uphold the image they conveyed.

"Remember, no saddle horn," she reminded me as Daddy and Slim, the wiry packer who was taking a last draw off his hand-rolled cigarette, saddled her horse.

Skippy, his red curls catching the morning sun, was already astride an old mule named Sea Biscuit, who had decided to close his eyes and rest until the trail ride began. Skippy was trying to look indignant not to have been put on a lively horse, but I could see the glimmer of excitement that overrode his effort.

"Don't worry, Skippy," Sunny called. "We'll put one horse behind Sea Biscuit and one ahead of him and then he'll go." Skippy stuck out his tongue.

For a moment I wished I too were safely on a docile Sea Biscuit. Then Slim handed the reins of Sunny's horse, Miranda, up to her and turned to me. "Well, Missy, what strikes your fancy?"

Miranda shook out her mane and rattled the bit in her mouth. Sunny sat tall in the saddle holding the reins correctly in her left hand. Her right hand was free, obviously avoiding the saddle horn. She gave every impression of being a young lady quite accustomed to an early morning ride.

"Well," I said to Slim, kicking a crushed pinecone to one side, "I don't want *too* big a horse."

Slim squinted as he looked me over. He looked like a real cowboy, but he was too creased with grime and shriveled up to be glamorous. Maybe I didn't want to be a cowhand after all.

Then Slim decided, "Got just the little mare for you. Name's Peewee."

As he led Peewee out I could see she was the smallest and most compact of all the horses in the packer's corral. The fact that Slim kept holding her reins and steadying her with a "Whoa, girl, whoa," as I mounted didn't give me enough of a warning about this little horse. And, since Peewee and I trotted out of the corral behind Daddy's big steady horse, Babe, Peewee kept her real agenda—that of getting rid of me and galloping off to the nearest meadow—to herself for a good prancing and snorting mile.

As the four of us rode up to our tent to tell Mother we'd be back late that afternoon, a group of young CCC men who were maintaining the campgrounds took surreptitious looks at Sunny. When one of them waved his bandanna at her, Peewee decided to make a break for it.

She spun around and took off down the dirt road at a full gallop. Too busy at first to be terrified, I tried all the commands I knew. Peewee sped on. I hugged her with my knees, eyeing the saddle horn and wondering how long I could stay on Peewee's back without grasping the horn in a gauche way. I wondered if Sunny were watching.

Peewee and I sped through the entire campground circle,

and, as we passed our tent, Daddy yelled, "Nancy, quit show-ing off!" The CCC workers, glad for a little excitement, stopped work and stared.

My answer didn't reach Daddy, for by the time I yelled, "I'm not! She won't stop!" he couldn't hear me.

By now my fear of being gauche had been overruled by my fear of falling off. I grabbed the saddle horn with both hands. Then, remembering the riders in the Saturday matinée westerns, I took my hands off the saddle horn, pulled on the reins and headed Peewee up a steep embankment. Surely this would stop her. But Peewee simply leapt up the knoll, pranced over rocks and through a stand of pines and leapt down onto the road once more, resuming her runaway pace. I could hear Daddy still yelling for me to quit showing off.

My last effort was to head Peewee toward a pine tree with a sturdy branch reaching out over the road. In the west-erns, I'd seen riders grab branches like this and swing into trees. I'd have to give it a try. I didn't know that stunt riders did these tricks, not actors. My brain was frantically going down the list of possible solutions to my situation, and this suicidal one came up.

Just like in the movies, help galloped up alongside of me barely in time to avert disaster. Daddy grabbed Peewee's reins and slowed both Peewee and Babe to a trot and then a walk. I didn't have to explain that I wasn't showing off. Daddy could see it in my face. "Come on," he said when we stopped. "You get on Babe and I'll take Peewee. She looks like quite a handful."

Daddy held feisty Peewee's head and examined the bit in her mouth. "Oh, oh," he said. "A Mexican curb bit—a mean one. No wonder Peewee's unhappy. Slim never should have given you this horse."

We joined Sunny and Skippy, and the four of us rode up a steep trail, the horses pawing at the rocks on switchbacks and Skippy's Sea Biscuit plodding reliably along. Little Peewee calmed down under Daddy's weight and experience, and Daddy tried to be careful of her tender mouth. Besides, the telltale odor of fear wasn't emanating from *his* body.

Slim, however, had to answer to Daddy when we came down the trail and rode the animals back to the pack station. "Hell," Slim apologized, "I thought she could ride. Saw them boots and all. Never would have given her Peewee otherwise."

CHAPTER 6

The New Kids

Nancy

The move to Tulare was my initiation into a child's nomadic life on a doodlebug party. At first the adventure took on the cheerful "make-do" spirit of a camping trip with Daddy home every night to put his calm engineer's perspective on any traumas the day might have brought.

Mother was not one to dump trivial household concerns on Daddy the moment he walked in the door, though. Quite the opposite, she could wield a paintbrush as well as a hammer and screwdriver and usually dealt with landlords, shopkeepers, doctors and teachers with the charm of a diplomat.

She could turn leftover food into tasty casseroles and odd pieces of material into quilts or braided rugs. A lush sweet potato vine usually graced our coffee table, and she taught Sunny, Skippy and me how to make beanbags out of calico scraps and treasure chests from empty Quaker Oats boxes.

Old dress patterns ended up on the back of the toilet, and we would find ourselves turning around from "the throne" to reach for a piece of tissue that said, "skirt, front" or "cut two pieces." We were taught not to be wasteful but to tear these large pieces in half or settle for others marked "collar," "belt" or "facing." Our everyday drinking glasses had previously held grape or strawberry jelly, and our dishtowels had been flour sacks. We were not poor, just part of the frugal middle class sobered by the Great Depression.

Both Mother and Daddy had a spirit of proud independence, and while we children were carefully protected in most ways, we were told to stand on our own two feet, an expectation that often caught me off guard. I never knew when Mother would take up my cause with all the protectiveness of a mother grizzly or would shove me out on my own as she had with Willy Wagner.

My family reputation for scrappiness, I feared, was overrated. I was shy and down deep wished that Mother would fight my battles for me. And, once Mother had settled an issue, appealing to Daddy was never very successful. He was loyal to her even when he didn't completely agree, and his first question to me, Sunny or Skippy was, "What did your mother say about this?"

So when school was about to start and I heard Mother tell one of the other wives on the doodlebug party that she was just going to drop her two daughters off in front of their respective schools and let them register themselves, I was terrified.

Was this the same Mother who befriended every teacher in my Lynwood school? Who talked them into letting me go to kindergarten early? The Mother who baked the lavishly iced and decorated three-layer cakes that always sold first at the PTA bake sales? The Mother who spent so much time at school that she was considered part of the administration? Now was I to go to a strange school in a strange town and search for the principal's office while all the other girls and boys headed for familiar classrooms?

I said nothing about Mother's overheard remark but hunkered down into a silent dread of the first day of school. As a distraction, a clinging to the last days of summer, I borrowed the shovel Daddy kept in the car in case we got stuck in sand on our trips to the Mojave Desert and started digging a hole in the backyard for my 17 tadpoles that were swimming in the laundry trays on the back porch.

The dark wiggly creatures had begun to grow little arms and legs, and their transparent leaf-shaped tails were shrinking. Soon they would be frogs, and, as I dug, I envisioned a clear pond in the backyard where they would swim and croak at night in gratitude.

Billy, the history buff from next door who ignored Sunny and me when he visited our family on the front porch, crawled through a hole in the wire fence separating our backyards and grabbed the shovel. "Let me do that. I'm a lot stronger than you are."

I hung onto the shovel, my experience with Willy Wagner standing me in good stead. "I want to do it. It's my yard and my shovel." I glared at him. Billy pushed me, and when I fell into the half-dug hole, he landed on top of me.

As I lay pinned in the dirt, I felt his arms reach around me and heard him whisper "mein frau" in my ear before he jumped up, crawled through the fence and disappeared into his house.

From my German-speaking grandfather I knew what "mein frau" meant, and an "icky" feeling filled me as I thrust the shovel into the hole, tossing more dry dirt into a pile. I knew there was something sexual about what had just happened, but I didn't know how to deal with it.

When the hole seemed big enough, I filled it with water from the hose, caught the tadpoles, put them into a Mason jar and carried them out to my pond. To my horror, after I poured them into the water, the "pond" stayed muddy instead of settling into clear water, and I couldn't see a tadpole anywhere.

The next day when I went out to inspect, I saw that the "pond" had dried up, and muddy lumps that could only be dead tadpoles covered the bottom. I felt like a murderer, but no one in the family commented on my blunder. I think Mother was just glad to have my tadpoles out of her laundry trays.

When Mother let me off in front of my new school, I was aware that my school dress, a "straight-from-the-shoulder" pattern babyish even for Lynwood, was much too childish for Tulare. How I hated that hand smocking Mother was so proud of!

Spotting a string on the sidewalk, after Mother drove away, I tied it around my waist for a belt. I stepped into a school corridor wondering what to do next. When a teacher stopped and asked, "Do you need help?" all I could say was, "I'm new." I didn't realize that I was just one of many new students that year. In 1935 about 7,000 people made their home in Tulare, and the town was growing fast. Most of the newcomers were from the Dust Bowl.

I was taken to a special room to take the I.Q. and other tests required for all new students. Heart beating, I worked all of the problems I could, grateful that Daddy had taught me the distance from the earth to the sun and who discovered the North Pole. Palms sweating, I flipped through the test answering all the questions I could, then I went back to the beginning and made guesses on the ones I'd skipped.

When I returned to my assigned classroom, I realized something peculiar about the other students in my room. Most were tall and strong looking, almost like high school students! They sure grew them big in Tulare!

I knew Mother would be waiting for me in the car, so when the bell went off after school and I stood up to leave, I untied the string from my waist and slipped it into the toe of my oxfords. I'd need the string again tomorrow if I wasn't to look like a Lynwood baby. Now that I was 10 I wanted to dress like the other kids. As I walked out, I saw my starched dress was wrinkled from the string. I felt like a silly Japanese fan!

"What's wrong with your dress and why are you limping?" were Mother's first words as I opened the car door and slid into the front seat. "I hope you didn't pick up athlete's foot off the rug in that awful auto court!"

"My sock is just wadded up, I guess," I mumbled, ignoring Mother's reference to my dress as I patted down the crinkles. Capitalizing on Mother's usual interest in school tests I said, "I spent all afternoon taking a test in the back of the room. They didn't tell me what grade I got, though."

Mother beamed as she drove toward Sunny's school. "They won't tell you, but I'm sure you did very well. We've always had plenty of books at home, and I taught you how to read before you went to kindergarten." A good driver, she negotiated a turn with confidence. "And then, your father is strong in science."

Turning toward me she added, "Tonight we'll work on any parts of the test you didn't understand. You can remember the questions, can't you?" I nodded. The Tulare tests had been just like the Lynwood ones.

"The kids in Tulare are sure big," I said, changing the subject. "Some boys in my class are almost as tall as Daddy and strong, too."

Mother thrust her left arm out of the car window and down to signal her abrupt pullover to the curb under a chinaberry tree. She glared at me, incredulous. "Do you mean to tell me they put you in a class with *migrant workers*, Nancy?"

"Well, I don't know," I answered. Now I was on Mother's hot seat. "I told them we just moved here and probably wouldn't stay too long." The first day of school had been bad enough. What had I done wrong? Why couldn't we just go ahead and pick up Sunny? I longed for my sister's moral support. "What I said is true, isn't it, Mother?"

Mother put the car into first gear, burning a little rubber as she headed for Sunny's school. She looked straight ahead as she continued to shift. "What you said was true, Nancy, but you certainly gave them the wrong idea. Those big kids stay out of school half the time to pick cotton and grapes and who knows what. Then they move on as soon as crops ripen in other parts of the Valley."

She was the mother grizzly now. "We'll see about this! I'm not having my child thrown in that class. How could you ever learn anything?" With a sharp turn she pulled over to where Sunny was waiting. "Migrant workers! We'll see about this!"

The next day I was in the same corridor in the same dress but without my string belt, being dragged to the principal's office by my indignant protector. Mother wore her best blue rayon crepe dress into which she had pinned white underarm shields in anticipation of a hot day and a possible steamy confrontation. She wore a blue and white straw hat with a veil to emphasize that *she* was not a migrant worker and neither was her child.

In the principal's office, Mother spoke in her most charming voice and used as many big words, such as *differentiate*, as she could logically fit into the discussion. Then she came to the point. "You don't mean to tell me that you think Nancy belongs in *that* class, do you?" She tipped her head to one side, violet eyes flashing. "It was recommended that Nancy skip a grade in Lynwood. I'm sure when you see the results of her I.Q. test you'll know why."

I stood behind Mother, wishing I were invisible. I didn't feel particularly smart. Maybe, as Mother bragged, Sunny was a brain and Skippy a genius, but I felt I couldn't possibly live up to her exaggerated claims for *my* intelligence. Hadn't my kindergarten class sailed into the first grade leaving me behind?

Still, the next day I found myself in a class of local children more my size. That's where I met my first boyfriend, Johnny Able.

Johnny and I might never have talked outside our classroom if Mother hadn't decided I should walk home from school. In the 1930s children were safe on small town streets unless, of course, their parents were rich and famous like the Lindberghs. Besides, hadn't Mother taught me how to deal with bullies like Willy Wagner?

The second week of school Johnny caught up with me as I shifted my books onto my hip and walked toward my house. As he fell into step beside me, saying only, "Hi," I just said, "Hi," back, a pleasurable feeling shooting a blush up into my face.

I was such an easy blusher that when Sunny and Skippy got bored, they'd say things to me that would turn my face pink and then laugh at my distress. I hoped Johnny hadn't noticed. Even if he had, I hoped he wouldn't let on. Johnny had a polite way about him. He was just my size, without the hard muscles and deep voices some of the boys at school had already. His hair was brown and straight, and he had skin I knew would tan instead of sunburn like mine. His brown eyes, which would look less enormous when his face began its masculine angling out, were extravagantly lashed. Johnny had the face of a poet. He was sweet and he wanted to walk me home. I sighed.

When Johnny turned toward me and offered, "I'll carry your books," I handed them over although I knew I was just as strong as he was. As he swung both of our books onto his hip, I noticed he was wearing ironed cotton slacks and a clean long-sleeved shirt. I wondered, as we walked under the chinaberry tree where Mother had stopped in a fury a week ago, if Johnny dressed for school this morning with this walk in mind. I decided to wear my plaid skirt tomorrow in case he caught up with me again.

After that, Johnny walked me home every day. Sometimes he would shift our books over to his knee as he picked up a good whittling stick. He had been given a pocket knife for his birthday and carved little pieces of wood whenever he got a chance. Carrying that knife in his pocket was the only school rule he broke.

One Tuesday afternoon it began to sprinkle as we walked toward my house, and we stopped under the chinaberry tree. "Do you want to stay here until the rain lets up?" Johnny asked, tucking our books under his shirt to protect them from the drops that found their way through the tree and slid off its lower leaves.

"I like to walk in the rain," I answered, to let him know how adventuresome I was. As drops collected on my hair I went on recklessly, "My sister Sunny won't go out in the rain. She's always worrying about getting her curly hair too frizzy. She's such a pill."

Johnny looked at me, brown eyes half reproving and half sad. "You shouldn't run your sister down, Nancy. She's family. You should stick up for your family no matter what."

I knew he was right. Why had I blabbed about Sunny? I loved her, and she stuck up for me more times than not. She hadn't even told the family about Johnny. In fact, she had advised me to say goodbye to him a block from home every day just in case. "No point in giving Mother something to gripe about," Sunny said.

I knew I couldn't erase my catty remark. I felt tears blurring my eyes and hoped they would get lost among the raindrops on my face. Johnny wiped the cuff of his shirtsleeve across my cheek. "Let's hurry." he said. "I think the rain has let up. You'd better go home."

As I walked up our front porch, shaking off as much water as I could before opening the front door, I was surprised to hear Daddy's voice in the kitchen. He wasn't usually home this time of day. Still, I went straight into my bedroom, wondering if Johnny's "You'd better go home" meant he didn't like me any more. After what I said about Sunny, he probably thought *I* was a pill. But when I saw my brown leather suitcase open on my bed, I had another more pressing question. Were we going on a trip?

Daddy came into the bedroom. He was still in his work

boots, and there was the usual green 4H pencil and engineer's scale in the pocket of his khaki shirt. "Better get all your things together, Nancy," he said. "This weekend we're moving."

I stared at Daddy and the suitcase. "But I've only been in school here four weeks!"

"We're moving to an interesting town," he said. "I think you'll like it. "When Sunny gets home I'll tell you both more about it, but I can't name the town until we leave."

As Daddy looked into my face I knew I was expected to be a good sport. I didn't want to let him down, so I tried to arrange my face into an eager expression. I must have looked silly, my eyes wide and my mouth turned up while tears slid down my face.

Daddy ruffled my hair and pulled a clean white handkerchief out of his back pocket. "Here, young lady," he said, "blow. I think I hear Sunny now."

As Johnny caught up with me the next day I blurted out to him, "We're moving this weekend, but it's a secret." Neither of us had anything else to say. I had told Johnny about the doodlebug party, but the role it would play in my life was only now becoming a reality. Leaving Tulare and Johnny was going to be hard.

That Friday when Johnny fell into step beside me, he handed me a small rectangular piece of redwood, sanded smooth. The letters "JA" and "NL" stood out in relief. Between our initials was a perfect heart.

Johnny must have carved in secret for hours. I kept his beautiful gift for more than 40 years.

Sunny

When I told Daddy, on our fishing trip to Lower Twin Lake, that I didn't mind going to a new school, I really meant it. I didn't feel the least bit apprehensive about starting the ninth grade in Tulare. I assumed, if I thought about it at all, that school in Tulare would be much the same as school in Lynwood.

My model for school was based on Lynwood, where I had many friends in my class, where all the teachers, and even the principal, knew me and spoke to me, and where Mother was known and appreciated for her contributions to the PTA bake and rummage sales. When Mother dropped me off in front of the junior high in Tulare on the first day, I walked into the building confidently, a bounce in my step. After all, wasn't I Sunny Lockard, teacher's pet, even principal's pet, in Lynwood? How different could it be? Besides, I was a *ninth grader*, big stuff in a three-year junior high.

I found the admissions office, walked up to the counter and waited. The room, with its dark oak paneling and yellowed window shades drawn against the relentless morning sun, was dim and stuffy. The blades of a large electric fan, mounted high on the wall, turned at a slow, creaking pace against the dense, stale air.

Behind the counter two women, one tall and thin with darting bird-like movements and the other short and stout in her rose-splashed dress, were frantically shuffling through piles of papers on a large table. Bird-woman said, "It must be here somewhere. Everything got blown around when the fan was on high."

The heavy woman dabbed at her forehead with a white handkerchief. "Whew! It's going to be a hot one today." Then, still wiping the beads of perspiration from her brow, she came over to me and smiled. "Do you have your schedule, young lady?"

"No," I replied. "I'm new here."

"Didn't you register last week? Last week was registration."

"No. We were on vacation."

She gave me a form to fill out. When I finished I stood at the counter again and waited. Finally, Bird-woman took my form, saying, "I'll look for your transcript."

After what seemed like a long wait I heard my name. "We don't have a transcript for you," Bird-woman said. "Did your parents ask the school in Lynwood to send us a transcript?"

"I guess so," I answered.

"Well, we don't have it. And you made a mistake on the form. If you're twelve years old, you can't be going into the *ninth* grade."

"I'll be thirteen next month, and I *am* going into the ninth grade."

Bird-woman sighed. "We'll need proof. Tell your mother to write to Lynwood for a transcript. When you come to school tomorrow, bring a note from your mother about your grade level, and bring your last report card, if you have it. All I can do today is put you in temporary classes."

"I want *ninth-grade classes*," I said, hoping I didn't sound too bossy.

"Well . . . just a minute." A balding, red-faced man had just entered the room from a door behind the counter. His tie hung askew from his loosened collar and little patches of perspiration showed through his starched white dress shirt. Bird-woman showed him the form I had filled out, and spoke to him in a low voice. He turned, looked at me, then came over to the counter, carrying the form. His smile looked forced.

"Sunny Lockard?" the man asked, looking intently at the form. "I'm Mr. Dolan, the principal."

"How do you do?" I said, politely. Mother had taught us *manners*.

"You're twelve?"

"Yes. Thirteen next month."

"Did you skip any grades?"

"Yes. Second grade."

"I see. Do you have a telephone at home?"

"No."

"Your father is an engineer?"

"Yes."

"Where does he work?"

I hesitated on this one, remembering how many times Mother or Daddy had cautioned us not to reveal the details of Daddy's work, because prospecting for oil was secret. After a moment I said, "He works for The Texas Company."

Mr. Dolan sniffed. "We don't have a business around here by that name. You mean he works at the gas station out on the highway?"

"No." At that precise moment something happened which was a relief to me, and probably to Mr. Dolan as well. Birdwoman dashed to the counter. "We found her transcript!" She handed it to Mr. Dolan and ran off to attend to someone else.

"Well!" Mr. Dolan exclaimed. "I see you *are* in the ninth grade! I also see we'll be putting you in academic classes. Well, well. Mrs. Barnes," he called to the heavy woman in the rose-patterned dress, "see that Sunny gets the right classes, will you? She's a *college prep* student." This time Mr. Dolan's smile looked sincere.

My ninth grade program turned out to be English, Spanish, World History, Algebra, Physical Education and Home Economics. "Do I *have* to take Home Ec?" I sighed.

"*All* the ninth grade girls take Home Economics," Roselady replied, patting her face and neck with a fresh handkerchief.

At dinner that evening I complained about having to take Home Ec. "Won't hurt you a bit," said Mother.

Daddy was proud of my academic subjects. He said he'd be able to help me with my algebra homework, if I needed it. He was pleased that I was taking Spanish. Daddy grew up in Santa Barbara and learned Spanish from the Mexican American kids he went to school with. He loved the language.

I talked about my experience in the school office that day, but I didn't call the women in the school office "Bird-woman" and "Rose-lady." Mother would consider that disrespectful. Daddy laughed when I mentioned that Mr. Dolan had asked me if my father worked in the service station out on the highway, but Mother said, "*What?*" After I mentioned the misplaced transcript she said, "Good thing they found it, or they'd be hearing from me!"

Mother told about Nancy's being placed in the class for migrant workers, and said that she was going to take her to school the next day to see that Nancy was placed in the proper class. "And while I'm at it," she continued, "I'm going over to your school, Sunny, and meet this Mr. Dolan. Your father working in a *service station*! Indeed!"

"Now, Honey," Daddy said. "Any job is a good job these days. And remember, our work is supposed to be . . ."

"I know," Mother interrupted. "He won't get anything out of *me*, don't worry! But they need to know who they're dealing with! Now, who wants cake and ice cream?"

My classes went well, all but Home Ec. Our first project was to make a slip, at that time an essential undergarment in every girl's or woman's wardrobe. Mother bought me the required yardage in a cheap, bilious pink cotton fabric. She wasn't going to waste good material on someone with my lack of interest in the needle arts! I took the material to school, but the teacher told me to take it home and shrink it before I could cut the pattern. Mother said, "I thought you were going to do that at school as part of the lesson!"

It took me two weeks to finish the slip, and I abhorred every minute of it. The best slips were kept at school for the Home Ec teacher to show off at Parents' Night. The poorly done slips were sent home with their owners. My slip, with its wavy seams, puckered corners and uneven hem, was sent home with me.

Mother took one look at the slip and said, "Maybe you'll do better on the next project."

I honestly did not feel like a failure with my first Home Ec project because I considered Home Ec to be a worthless subject, a total waste of my time and effort. A bad grade on an algebra test, now *that* would be a real failure!

The next Home Ec project was embroidery. Why anyone would want to spend so much time taking colored thread and patiently stitching little leaves and posies was beyond my comprehension. What was the point, when all you have when you're finished is a stupid "guest" towel which is too small to wipe your hands on or a pillow slip that will leave indentations on your face if you roll over on it? Of course, I didn't apply any questions like these to algebra.

My embroidery project was sent home. When Mother examined it, she made no comment. Mother's needlework, precise and beautiful, went largely unappreciated by Nancy and me. She was always knitting sweaters or socks, sewing clothes for us, making quilts, tablecloths, napkins, curtains, or layettes for the babies of friends or relatives. Mother knew how to embroider, cross stitch and appliqué, and she could also do fancy stitches like smocking. Needlework was what Mother did in her spare time, and I paid little attention to it. I had no interest whatsoever in learning these skills.

At the end of the fourth week of school in Tulare I realized I was lonely. I was the "new" kid. I hadn't grown up with any of the other pupils, so it wasn't easy to make friends. I was shy and younger than my classmates. With the exception of Home Ec I liked my classes but I knew that to my teachers I was just another kid in the classroom. In Lynwood, the principal, Miss Taylor, often stopped me in the hall to ask about my classes or just to say hello. Here, Mr. Dolan passed me by without a sign of recognition. I had gone from being special to being a nobody. What traveling around with Daddy really meant was just beginning to sink in, but, no matter what, I wouldn't complain. School in Lynwood might be better, but seeing Daddy only once in a while wasn't.

It was the fifth week of school in Tulare, and it was Tuesday. The Home Ec teacher had just announced our next project: learning how to wash dishes! What was there to learn, I wondered? At home, Nancy and I washed dishes every night! *That* was a school subject?

I walked home from school through alleys and vacant lots, kicking rocks and tin cans out of my way, picking up small stones and throwing them. Dishes! That time could be better spent on algebra.

Nancy was home already, and she ran to the front door to meet me. "Guess what, Sunny! We're moving!"

I didn't believe Nancy. Then I heard Daddy's voice in the kitchen, talking with Mother. Mother was mixing batter in a big bowl. Daddy was leaning against the stove, arms folded across his chest. He was wearing his work khakis and boots. "Daddy, are we moving?" I asked.

"Yes," Daddy replied. "On Saturday. You and Nancy will have to help your mother get packed, since I'll be working out of town until Friday."

"Where are we going?" I asked.

"Yes, where?" Nancy chimed in.

"I can't say just yet," Daddy replied. "Just go to school as usual for the rest of the week."

Mother turned to me. "I'll go to your school and Nancy's on Friday and make arrangements for your transfers. You're not to say anything to your teachers or the other kids."

Even though I knew it had to come sometime, Daddy's announcement startled me. A new school. The same problems all over again. A numbness crept over me.

Daddy reached out and patted me on the back. "Both

129

you girls will like the town. It's about seven times bigger than Tulare, and you know what? It's a port! We can see some big ships there. And we can take a trip to San Francisco Bay and see the big bridges under construction." Daddy turned to Mother. "I'd better get my suitcase. Roy will be by any minute."

Moving north! I had a good idea what town Daddy was talking about, but tomorrow I'd consult the California atlas at the school library.

"We're off!" Daddy waved as he went out. "See you Friday!"

By late Friday afternoon Nancy, Mother and I had almost everything packed. Nancy and I went to school every day that week and did our assignments as if we were going to be there for the rest of the school year. I kept my mouth shut about moving to Stockton. Secretly I gloated over missing out on the dishwashing instruction in Home Ec, which was scheduled to start on Monday. This week we were learning how to set the table, more useless business in my opinion. I mentioned to Mother how glad I was to miss the dishwashing instruction. "Nobody knows everything," she said. "There's always something to learn."

Daddy arrived home on Friday in time for dinner. Instead of her usual big evening meal, Mother fixed creamed tuna on toast and a salad. We had store ice cream with packaged cookies for dessert. "I've been busy," Mother apologized, "and most of the kitchen stuff is packed. Just cereal and milk for breakfast," she added.

After dinner I took the leftover cookies to Mr. Cavendish with apologies that the cookies weren't homemade. I told him we were leaving in the morning. He looked surprised and disappointed. "Tell your mother thanks," he said. "I'll see you off in the morning."

While Daddy was packing the trailer that evening Billy Martin wandered over. He stood by the trailer for a long time, hands thrust into his overall pockets, talking to Daddy. I watched them through the kitchen window while Nancy and I washed the dishes.

Early the next morning the landlord, Mr. Bromberg, arrived to inspect the house. "I must say, Mrs. Lockard," he said, "you're leaving the place in apple pie order. Better than it was, by golly. And those curtains are mighty fine." Mother beamed.

Mr. Cavendish knocked on the front screen door. "Your mother in?" When Mother appeared he said, "Just want to thank you, Mrs. Lockard, for all those good desserts. You folks were good neighbors." Mother beamed again, muttering "no trouble at all."

After a final check of the house for anything we might have left behind, we all got into the car. Daddy had managed to find a space for Mother's sewing machine by arranging for Roy to transport Skippy's tricycle in one of the company cars.

As soon as Daddy started the car Billy Martin came into his backyard and waved to us. Mr. Bromberg waved from "our" backyard and Mr. Cavendish gave us a salute. We did have friends in Tulare after all.

As we slowly moved down the alley towards the street Daddy grinned. "Next stop Stockton!"

CHAPTER 7

Almost a Big City

Sunny

Daddy said it was 170 miles from Tulare to Stockton, "give or take." Because of our loaded trailer the going was slow, and I had plenty of time to ruminate.

My enthusiasm for "going on safari" was not completely dead, but it was expiring. I wondered what Stockton would bring. Would we be there only a few weeks, barely get acquainted and then have to go somewhere else? Would I have to take Home Ec? Would I get my favorite classes, Spanish and Algebra? What would the kids, the teachers, the school be like? For the first time since joining Daddy on the doodlebug party I felt apprehensive. I was beginning to see that the pattern of life I had known in Lynwood did not apply elsewhere.

I watched the fence posts, the vineyards with migrant workers and the towns go by without really seeing them. When Nancy pointed to a flock of sheep and went "Baa," I paid no attention. Daddy and Mother were talking, but I didn't listen. Skippy sat in the back seat between Nancy and me. He and Nancy were hitting and poking each other. When Skippy hit me, I didn't respond. Soon he stopped and concentrated on Nancy.

I thought about Lynwood, about our backyard with the big swing and exercise bar next to the full-sized playhouse

Daddy had built for Nancy and me. The playhouse had a brick porch, a Dutch door and windows with real glass. I wondered if little girls were playing in it now or if boys were using it as a "no-girls-allowed" clubhouse.

My mind wandered among the events of our eight years in Lynwood. Mother sent me to school through the fifth grade in a navy blue pleated skirt with a middy blouse. I hated it. She twisted and brushed my wiry hair around her index finger until my head was a mass of bouncy curls. I hated that, too.

I remembered Daddy taking Nancy and me to Belmont Shore for swimming lessons. He put his foot on our backs and gently pushed us under the water to show us that we'd float right back up again. Nancy and I loved everything about the ocean. As soon as we could swim well enough, Daddy taught us to body surf the tame waves and then the bigger ones.

There were so many memories. They washed over me like the ocean waves I loved. Frank Sutton from across the street often dropped by with a wet sack of abalone—my favorite seafood—which he traded us for chickens and eggs. Nancy and I affectionately called him "Big Frank." Everything about Frank was big, from his generous nature and broad smile to his huge khaki shirts which must have taken his wife, Nellie, a long time to iron. I thought of Jolene, Nellie's niece, who came to stay with Frank and Nellie "for a while." Nellie brought Jolene, who was three years older than I, to our house the day after she arrived from Illinois. When they left, Mother said that Nancy and I weren't to go to the Suttons anymore because Jolene "wasn't well." After that we caught glimpses of Jolene rocking on the Suttons' front porch or getting into the car with Frank and Nellie. Jolene seemed to be getting fatter and fatter. One day Jolene wasn't there anymore, and Mother said we could visit the Suttons again.

One Christmas Mother gave Nancy and me each a Patsy doll, a popular doll with rosy cheeks, petulant mouth and bobbed hair. With the dolls were little steamer trunks full of carefully hand-stitched doll clothes which Mother had labored over at night after we had gone to bed. I rejected the dolls because I preferred books. Nancy was disappointed because what she really wanted was an electric train.

I remembered the frightening impact of the Long Beach earthquake of 1933 and the gathering thunder of the after-shocks which roared towards us like out-of-control locomotives. I even recalled the sweet smell of freshly ironed sheets and clean, soft pajamas when I was ill, and the good taste of milk toast to soothe my troubled stomach.

I was nostalgic for the familiarity, safety and security of the Lynwood days, yet I knew that, like the car in which I was riding, there was no going back. I had made a choice, and I would live with it without complaint, no matter what. And, maybe—just maybe—there was "adventure" still to come.

Nancy seemed unruffled about changing schools and towns. She was a straightforward, prickly and sassy kid, never moody or downcast and always ready with a smart remark or clever observation. Once, after I had done something for which I knew I'd be spanked and had burst into tears, Nancy, hands on hips, said, "Why are you crying? You're not spanked yet!" That was typical of her. Cute and perky with big blue eyes and a blond Dutch bob, Nancy was the very essence of practicality. She saved her allowance money, while I spent mine. When I borrowed money from her, I had to pay it back with interest, a concept she thought was her own invention.

I fretted about things; Nancy didn't. Even though I was almost three years older, Nancy kept up with me in most of our activities. In between fights—in which she gave me as good as she got—we were very companionable. I secretly envied Nancy's feistiness, something I thought I totally lacked. Once I overheard Mother say, "You have to pat Sunny on the back to keep her going." It hurt me, but I knew it was true. On the way to Stockton I needed that pat on the back, that reassurance that everything was going to be all right. Nancy unknowingly provided it a little later.

Daddy pulled into a Texaco service station to get gas and we all went to the restrooms, pronounced by Mother to be "cleaner than most." Mother produced a pair of scissors from her purse and two sheets of newspaper from a sack by her feet. She cut a big hole in each sheet and gave one to me and one to Nancy. "Put these on the toilet seat," she instructed, "and in the wastebasket when you're through. Don't touch anything with your hands or bottom!" She didn't have to add, "Wash your hands thoroughly with soap and water!" We *knew* about that.

Back in the car, Skippy moved to the front with Mother and fell asleep. Nancy was gazing out of the car window. Turning to me she said, "Well, Osa, we're leaving Africa. Time for something else."

That chance remark of Nancy's was full of meaning for me. *Leaving Africa. Time for something else.* Yes. It *was* time. Tulare was behind me. Lynwood was far behind me. I would work hard to make Stockton a good place. Daddy had spoken of the big bridges being built in San Francisco Bay, and he said that Stockton, although inland, was a port. I wanted to see San Francisco Bay and the big ships. Yes, something was ending and something was beginning. I turned to Nancy and said, "You can cut out that 'Osa' and that 'Africa' business!"

We stopped near Merced for lunch. Daddy pulled off on a country road and parked on a wide shoulder under a row of eucalyptus trees. Their mottled shade and pungent smell provided a pleasant picnic spot. After eating our deviled egg sandwiches we stayed there for a while to let Skippy run and play. "Anyhow," Daddy said, "the radiator needs to cool off a little."

Not too long after we started off again Nancy and I fell asleep. After what seemed like only a short time we were awakened by Daddy. "Wake up, girls! We're on the outskirts of Stockton."

"Look for a real estate office," Mother said. She pointed through the window. "Over there! Stop!"

Daddy pulled off the road in front of Valley Real Estate. "They're still open," Mother said. "I won't be long."

Mother went into the real estate office and came out a few minutes later with a map. "A nice man marked all the best neighborhoods for me, and the schools. That will save me a lot of trouble." She let out a girlish giggle. "I told him we were interested in buying a house."

Our final stop was an auto court where Daddy rented a cabin with a small kitchen. There were two double beds, and Daddy set up a cot for Skippy. Again Mother wouldn't let us go inside until she had gone over everything with disinfectant. "The bedding doesn't look clean," she said. "We'll use our own."

The next day, Sunday, we drove around Stockton to look at some of the neighborhoods marked on the real estate map. As we passed a large school Mother, looking at the map, said, "That's where you'll go to high school, Sunny. It starts with the ninth grade, so you'll be a freshman."

A freshman? On the bottom of the pile this time? "Mom!" I begged. "Can we stop? Can I look around?"

"I suppose so," Mother replied.

Daddy swung the car around and parked in front of the school. "Come on, Sunny," he said, "let's have a look."

"Take Skippy with you and let him run," Mother said. "He's driving me crazy."

Daddy and I explored the school grounds while Skippy dashed here and there near us. Nancy, who didn't seem interested in my school or concerned about hers, stayed in the car with Mother. We circled all the buildings. I peered in windows at empty classrooms full of lonely desks and clean blackboards, and through the glass of double doors down long shadowy deserted hallways. It was a big school, bigger than the schools in either Lynwood or Tulare, and it looked overwhelming.

Sensing my uneasiness Daddy remarked, "It looks like a nice school, don't you think?"

"It's big," I admitted. "But I think I'll like it."

Nancy

The task of finding a furnished house to rent in the metropolis of Stockton fell to Mother. Daddy had to report to the field office the Monday after our weekend move.

"You'll find something, Honey," Daddy assured Mother as the party's geologist drove up outside our auto court cabin to give him a ride. "*Every* landlord in Stockton can't be reluctant to rent to a family with three children. Most people are basically reasonable, I believe."

Mother believed differently. She sighed as she turned her cheek for Daddy to kiss goodbye. Her children were tumbling around in rumpled beds in their pajamas, breakfast dishes were unwashed in the tiny kitchenette, and all she knew about Stockton was what she had seen as we drove into town, our tightly packed trailer swaying behind us.

The brisk air that blew in the front door as Daddy stepped outside told us we were in Northern California now, less than 90 miles east of fog-cooled San Francisco. As I peered out the auto court window watching the company car drive away, I saw an avenue tunneled with green. Not one of the trees was a chinaberry! I remembered the last time I saw Johnny Able. The redwood plaque he carved for me was hidden inside a sock in my suitcase. Standing at the window, I tried to wallow in the sweet puppy-love sadness I'd felt leaving my first boyfriend. But I couldn't. Stockton was too exciting.

Mother's real estate office map was spread out on the kitchenette table. I had spilled a plop of strawberry jam on it and was relieved when Daddy, who had a surveyor's respect for maps, only commented, "Maybe that's where your mother should look first, Nancy."

"Humph," was all Mother said as she wiped up the jam, leaving a damp pink spot somewhere on the suburbs of Stockton.

"We'll all look together today," Mother said later as her three scrubbed children climbed into the car, Sunny in front to read the map and Skippy and me in the back seat. "Tomorrow I'll drop you girls off at school. You can register yourselves."

Register ourselves again! I was filled with dread. Mother continued, "And you, Skippy, had better behave. Whenever someone shows us a house, you are to be a perfect little gentleman. Do you understand?" Skippy assumed his "little brat" expression and aimed a make-believe slingshot out the car window. Mother sighed. Her house-hunting expedition had begun.

If Mother hadn't been determined, charming and resourceful, our doodlebug days might have ended right there in Stockton. Rentals were scarce, and none of the owners of the ones available wanted to take a chance on a family with three children. Mother drove up and down streets looking for "For Rent" signs. When she found one, she trudged up the steps and knocked on the door. She bought the Stockton paper and circled "For Rent" ads. She talked to grocers and filling station attendants. At one address she even had us huddle out of sight on the floor of the car while she pleaded with the landlord to rent to us. No luck.

Finally, when Mother stopped at a drugstore to buy some Balm Bengay for the "neuralgia" attack the househunting was bringing on, the pharmacist told her a widower in the neighborhood had said he was too sad to stay in his home now that his wife was dead. He was thinking of putting the place up for rent.

After conferring with the druggist in whispers over the cause of the wife's death and determining that it wasn't contagious, Mother drove by the house. We could tell by her silence she wasn't too impressed. Neighborhood markets and several four-story apartment buildings stood among the rundown Victorian homes. The widower's house, situated next to a faded pink apartment house, needed paint, and the front steps were sagging. Tired hydrangea bushes competed with weeds in the front yard.

Mother circled the neighborhood slowly in the car and saw that Stockton's mental institution was just two blocks away. Inmates were strolling around the fenced garden and several waved to us. Murdock's Studio of the Dance, where Sunny and I would later be enrolled, was across the boulevard. Both my school and Sunny's were within walking distance.

Mother took the house. The widower may not have dreamed of renting to a family of five, but he was no match for a woman, *a wife, a mother,* who knew where he was most vulnerable. She commiserated with his recent loss. She flattered him on his good sense in planning to move into a boarding house. She held out vague promises of a Sunday dinner that could include a lonely widower. The druggist, an acquaintance of a full ten minutes, was her reference.

Two days later she was taking "tacky" pictures off the widower's walls, turning his "tacky" sofa pillows around to hide mohair waterfall scenes and scrubbing every exposed surface with Lysol, Bon Ami (to which mother gave a French pronunciation) or Fels Naphtha. As she cleaned she issued a familiar warning, "Don't walk on the living room rug in your bare feet! It's probably full of athlete's foot germs!"

Sunny

The next day, Tuesday, we enrolled in our schools. This time I entered the school office with a sealed envelope from my school in Tulare and a note from Mother. I was enrolled in Spanish, English, World History, Algebra, Physical Education and Study Hall. Best of all, I didn't have to take Home Ec!

I *loved* my Spanish and Algebra classes, so much so that I could hardly wait to get to them. My algebra teacher was an easy-going, grandfatherly man whom I adored. The class was small, and we sat at long tables to do our work. I doted on the personal attention that this soft-spoken, attentive teacher was able to give me.

In my Spanish class we built a Mexican village on a table top, complete with trees, a lake, houses, people, a church, a plaza, sand and cactus. I was very fond of my teacher, Señorita Magdalena Ochoa, and I loved to hear the beautiful Spanish sounds rolling off her tongue.

On Fridays each student took a turn reading a newspaper article aloud in World History class. As dreaded Friday approached, I would search the newspaper for the shortest current event I could find, sacrificing content for brevity. I passed up lengthy articles on Mussolini's invasion of Ethiopia and Hitler's occupation of the Rhineland in favor of short accounts of the good deeds of the local boy scout troup or the doings of the Ladies' Orchid Society.

When the teacher called my name, I would rise weakly from my seat hoping that my knees, which were knocking together like castanets, would hold me up for the long trip to the front of the class. With sweaty palms and quavering voice, I delivered my current event. Current event Friday was wasted on me. I didn't learn a thing that hour. I was too nervous to hear anyone else's current event, and my own was meaningless words mechanically produced sound-by-sound.

An incident in Study Hall remains vivid to this day. My desk was in the back of the room, and in the front seat of my row was a boy with a head of bushy, unruly hair who must have done something the teacher did not like. The teacher, a large woman who wore a white scarf tied around her head to cover up her curlers, jumped up from her desk, grabbed the boy's hair with her left hand and started slapping his face with her right hand. She must have slapped him at least twenty times. The class watched in horrified silence. In shock and scarcely daring to breathe, I was overwhelmed with a sense that something terribly unjust was happening. The incident nearly made me sick, but in those days I did not question a teacher's actions.

Close to Stockton High was a mental institution, so close, in fact, that the school's baseball diamond adjoined the grounds. When my physical education class played baseball, some of the men from the mental hospital would wander over, sit on the benches and watch us play.

"Are they from the insane asylum?" I asked my P.E. teacher, Miss Gipson.

"They're from the mental hospital," she replied. "They're harmless."

A few days later Miss Gipson called me into her office before we went out to the field. "Your mother was in to see me," she said. "I assured her that those men from the institution are harmless. All they do is watch. Nothing to be concerned about." I felt my face turn crimson. Why did Mother have to come down to school and embarrass me? Why had I said anything about it at home?

Nancy

The I.Q. and other tests given to me in Stockton were familiar. The two-story school intimidated me, but I was no longer afraid of the test that I had taken in Lynwood and then Tulare.

Discovery of the North Pole? Easy. Distance to the sun? I knew it by heart. How many cubes in the picture? Sunny, who had special talents in spatial orientation, had taught me how to figure it out. The relationship of numbers? Daddy had drilled me on that with an engineer's thoroughness I found boring. Reading comprehension? I had listened to Mother and Daddy read to Sunny every night when I was a toddler still wearing Doctor Denton's gray one-piece sleepwear. And, the essay on one of the tests wasn't nearly as mysterious as "*Treasure Island*" and "*Heidi*" had been.

When I finished the last page and pushed the tests aside, the counselor flipped through the pages. "Are you sure you're through?" she asked sternly. "You have more time."

I just shook my head. I looked out the second floor window at the tree tops and saw that the leaves were turning red and yellow. I longed for my old familiar one-story Lynwood school set among palm trees—or even my Tulare class. To me, Stockton might as well have been San Francisco or New York. I felt like one of my Tulare tadpoles trying to swim in the muddy pond I had dug.

By the time Mother picked me up in the car (a first-day-at-school luxury since we lived just six blocks away), I was exhausted. The counselor had brought me longer and harder tests which took me the rest of the day to finish. Finally, she wrote a note to Mother and sealed it in an envelope so I couldn't read it. "Tell your mother we need to talk to her," she said, giving me a look I couldn't decipher. A big city teacher look.

I opened the back door to the car instead of the front and collapsed on the floor. I was tired and scared. I probably didn't measure up to Stockton's standards. Would I be put back a grade? What would Mother and Daddy think of me?

Mother turned around, alarmed. "Are you sick, Nancy?"

I just reached up over the seat and handed her the envelope. Then I sank down again and closed my eyes until we got home.

The next day Mother put on her going-to-see-the principal dress which was too summery for autumn in Stockton but still conveyed the message that she was a woman to be reckoned with. As the two of us took our now familiar walk down school corridors to the principal's office, I noticed that the Stockton girls were dressed in skirts and sweaters. No flowered cotton straight-from-the-shoulder dresses here. Smocking was out of the question. I wondered if I had anything in my wardrobe that would fit in. If I were demoted, I wanted to be as inconspicuous as possible.

I wasn't allowed in the conference, but, when Mother came out, she beamed. "You're to skip the rest of the fifth grade," she announced, giving a smug nod to the principal. "Tomorrow you'll go straight to the sixth-grade classroom. I'll show you where it is on our way out."

"Does that mean I did O.K. on the tests?" I asked Mother. She took my hand and hurried me along the hall. "You did more than O.K., Nancy. I think you bowled them over. I'm taking you downtown to buy you a new sweater and skirt. Maybe your own new coat. You don't want to look tacky in the sixth grade."

My skipping the remainder of the fifth grade was a mistake—one that raised Mother's self-esteem but diminished mine during the rest of my school years. From Stockton on through high school graduation, a few days after my 17th birthday, I was a year younger than my classmates—socially less sophisticated and physically less coordinated.

When school teams were formed on the playgrounds, I was invariably the last person left standing—my name called out amid groans from the team that had to take me. When girls formed cliques, I had the double disadvantage of being new *and* "too young."

I wasn't the brilliant child my test scores seemed to indicate, just a girl who had been coached well on how to take tests. I knew this but worked hard to survive the sixth grade, often feeling as if I had been dropped into school in a foreign land.

Both Mother and Daddy tried to be fair and grant me the same personal freedom as my older classmates. They bought me a reconditioned bicycle, and after school and on weekends I would innocently ask if Skippy and I could "take a little ride." Daddy was certain to say, "Sure," and Skippy and I would explore Stockton, riding to a pet shop across town to see the guinea pigs, to the dump to careen around unfilled craters and to a favorite underpass where, if we were lucky, we would huddle while a freight train roared past overhead.

Without plotting our agreement, neither Skippy nor I ever let our cautious parents know the full range of our explorations. Later, in high school, I learned a French phrase that summed it up: "Cèla va sans dire."

Sunny

We spent Thanksgiving and Christmas in Stockton because we were too far away to visit our grandparents at The Ranch. In February Daddy planned a trip to San Francisco for us. Even though he disliked big cities, this was to be a special treat. We left Stockton early one Sunday morning and took a ferry from Oakland across the bay to San Francisco. The ferry took us close to the San Francisco-Oakland Bay Bridge which was then under construction.

As we stood by the railing of the ferry and looked upward at the huge concrete piers Daddy explained, "This bridge was started in 1933. It will be eight and a quarter miles long." Later Daddy drove us around the steep streets of San Francisco and then to an outlook where we could see the Golden Gate Bridge, which was also being built. "That will be the longest single-span suspension bridge in the world," Daddy marveled.

Daddy told us that his mother, Grace Barnard Lockard, lived in San Francisco before her marriage in 1887 and that she studied painting there with William Keith, the renowned California artist. "After she became a minister's wife she didn't paint as much," Daddy recalled. "And, of course, she had five children to keep her busy." I recalled seeing some of my grandmother's lovely landscapes, but I did not remember her clearly. She died when I was ten years old.

Mother wanted to see more of San Francisco, but we were

to visit Aunt Rose in Berkeley that afternoon. Aunt Rose was Mother's father's sister. Her son, Paul, was a professor of economics at the University of California at Berkeley. His second wife was Dorothea Lange, the well-known photographer. Paul Schuster Taylor and Dorothea Lange collaborated on "*An American Exodus*," a book about the migrations of people from the land to the cities.

Aunt Rose's house in the Berkeley hills opened onto a lovely garden. The living room had a high, beamed ceiling, a stone fireplace, and a staircase leading to a kind of mezzanine floor with colorful Spanish shawls draped over the railing. Aunt Rose gave presents to Nancy and me: hand-embroidered blouses from the Philippines and copies of her book, "*The Last Survivor*," the story of Maria Lebrado, granddaughter of Tenaya, chief of the Yosemite Indians. We treasured the book but thought the blouses were tacky and never wore them. We liked Aunt Rose, though, and thanked her politely. Mother insisted on good manners, always.

We settled into Stockton as if we were going to be there forever. Daddy resisted any guesses as to the possible length of our stay there. Mother enrolled Nancy and me in dancing school and arranged for elocution lessons for Nancy, who had a slight lisp. I didn't worry about having to move, and none of us talked about it.

Sometimes Daddy would be away for a few days on a job, but he was always home on the weekends. On Sundays we walked around the port area or went on picnics in the surrounding countryside.

Church was not on our Sunday agenda. Even though Daddy grew up in a strict Scots Presbyterian household, like another Scot, John Muir, Daddy found inspiration in nature, and for him that seemed to be enough. Mother's half-hearted forays into the area of Christian Science were offset by her preoccupation with germs and her worried calls to the doctor when one of her children so much as sneezed.

Nancy

Murdock's Studio of the Dance was just around the corner from us, and Mother enrolled both Sunny and me in dance classes. Muriel Jo Murdock, the daughter of the owners, was my only friend from school, and her visits to our house might have given Mother the idea.

A thin girl with wispy brown hair and a vocabulary consisting mostly of "I couldn't say," Muriel came to life when she demonstrated dance steps in our living room. She could do the splits, tap dance, prance around trailing pretend veils and execute a full pirouette while curving her skinny arms daintily overhead. Her demonstrations usually ended with Skippy's rushing to center stage to do his sultry impersonation of Mae West's "Come up and see me some time," only to have it ignored in the wake of Muriel's talent.

Sunny and I didn't sing, dance or recite poetry, and our uncles on Mother's side of the family dismissed our intellectual achievements by describing us as "repositories of vast amounts of useless information." Clearly, in Mother's view, it was high time to give us dancing lessons.

Sunny chose ballet classes and began standing straighter and combing her hair severely off her face. The scarf that she claimed she wore tucked around her neck because of Stockton's cooler climate would flutter artistically behind as soon as she left the house. Her profile was classic, Mother's perfect nose having effected a genetic rescue on the Lockard one.

Muriel's mother started me in Sunny's ballet class but quickly advised mother that I might do better with children my age in "creative dancing." Most of the young creative dancers wore special tan suede dance slippers, but Mother felt I could dance in my socks as several of the children were doing. The slippers were expensive, and the lessons alone were straining her budget.

Often, when my class began, I discovered one of my socks had a hole in the end, so I tried to hide it by stretching the toe out and folding it under my foot, holding the fold in place with all five toes. As the pianist played "A Little Bit Independent," I would shuffle around the room performing the steps as well as I could with scrunched up toes. Before long Mrs. Murdock suggested I might do better in her modern tap dancing class.

At least in the tap class I could wear an old pair of school shoes to which the cobbler had nailed steel toe taps. The pianist still played "A Little Bit Independent," and I would tap away several beats behind my classmates, singing under my breath in off-key determination.

My tap dancing didn't come up to Mrs. Murdock's standards, but she had no place else to put me. There was her Spanish dancing class, but that was out of the question. A girl who barely moved her feet in rhythm could hardly be expected to click castanets at the same time.

I knew I was a flop, but Muriel said, "Don't let it bother you, Nancy. All that matters anyway is ballroom dancing. Sometimes we're short a girl in that class, and I'll get my mother to ask you to fill in. It won't even cost you anything." With the sang-froid of a professional she added, "I fill in all the time."

When Mrs. Murdock's pupils started rehearsing for a recital, I knew I wasn't proficient enough to perform on stage, so I thought of a handy way to avoid embarrassment. I told Mrs. Murdock our family was moving. Mother was surprised by my lie, but Sunny was indignant. "What about me? I have a big part in the Midsummer Night's Dream sequence! I'm going to carry a wand! All you're going to be anyway is a toadstool. I heard Mrs. Murdock say so."

So I sat on stage in my brown hopsacking toadstool suit with nothing to do but watch through the two eye holes cut in the mushroom's cap. My future visits to Murdock's School of Dance were only to fill in at the ballroom dancing class. Muriel was right, I decided as my young gentlemen partners and I "step together stepped" around the room to the same upright piano rendition of "A Little Bit Independent." Ballroom dancing was all that mattered anyway.

Sunny

The highlight of being in Stockton, for me, was dancing school, and it went to my head. I flounced and sashayed around the house—and even on the school baseball diamond—fancying myself a graceful Ginger Rogers gliding gracefully across a highly polished dance floor. I was glamorous and seductive in a softly flowing gown with thousands of tiny feathers which floated and fluttered and then settled against my body as I dipped and turned, guided into sensual embraces and backbends by attentive, suave, debonair Fred Astaire. My self-image improved, literally, by leaps and bounds. I no longer saw myself as skinny and scrawny, but as slender, even *willowy*, like a dancer should be. I sat up straight in chairs, held my head high when I walked and gestured gracefully— so I thought—when I talked. By April I had not only ceased to dread current events on Fridays but I actually welcomed walking to the front of the class with my new-found grace and composure. I *loved* Stockton. I was thirteen and a half. *I was growing up*.

Nancy

Other memories of Stockton are fragments. Skippy's turning the garden hose on a nosy neighbor as she peered through a knothole in our backyard fence. Catching a baby jack rabbit in the front yard and letting it go in a field out of town when it was grown. Daddy's taking a bath with the upper part of the bathroom window uncurtained and receiving a letter from the "shocked" tenant in the second floor apartment next door.

"If she's so shocked she doesn't have to look," Daddy muttered as he installed a green window shade.

Daddy's building new front steps and painting them gray to match the worn paint on the house. Our landlord's hinting for that family dinner that Mother had half promised. "I'm not doing much real cooking here until I get used to that kitchen stove," she lied, handing him the rent check. "But when I make my angel food and sponge cakes, I'll save a piece for you."

We were settling down in Stockton, but I knew that any day I might come home from school and find my suitcase open on my bed. I was lucky, though. Our family lived in Stockton for the rest of the school year. Daddy didn't receive orders to move again until mid-June, 1936.

CHAPTER 8

Our First Dates

Sunny

Even though Daddy always cautioned us not to get too settled, Mother, Nancy and I were jolted by the news that we were moving to Bakersfield in the southern end of the San Joaquin Valley as soon as school was out.

Mother thought of Bakersfield as a suburb of hell—a hot, arid boom town of the roughneck mentality fostered by tough oil men in the not-so-distant discovery of oil days.

After the initial impact wore off, however, Mother tried to look on the bright side. "Why," she said, "we'll be close enough to The Ranch to go there on weekends! And maybe we can even get to Lynwood to see old friends!"

Roy was able to transport Nancy's bicycle and Mother's sewing machine in his pickup. Early on Sunday we left for the long drive to our next home, 225 miles away down Highway 99, through Modesto, Merced, Fresno and Tulare to Bakersfield.

It was unusually hot in the San Joaquin Valley for June, bringing out the hordes of airborne bugs that smashed against the car's windshield and radiator. The trip was grueling. Skippy rode in the back seat most of the way because Mother wasn't feeling well. He wiggled and squirmed, pestered and poked

Nancy and me. When we retaliated, he would sit back and chant, " 'That's me all over' the bug said as it hit the car!"

The canteen of cool water was passed around frequently. Mother, suffering from her "neuralgia," kept a wet cloth on her forehead and fanned herself with a road map.

We made as few stops as possible and finally arrived in Bakersfield, everyone hot and tired, in the late afternoon. When we reached the auto court Mother went inside our cabin and collapsed on a bed, holding a wet cloth to her head. The cabin, which had been closed up because of a dust storm, was an airless oven. Daddy opened the windows, propped the door open and turned on the fan, aiming its meager breeze at Mother. This was the only time I can remember when Mother did not disinfect an auto court cabin before we were allowed to enter.

Daddy went out and got a block of ice for the icebox in our little kitchen. Nancy and I fixed a pitcher of iced tea and took a glass to Mother. Daddy said he'd take us all out for hamburgers and malts.

"You go ahead," Mother said. "I don't want anything."

"We can bring you something, Hon," Daddy offered.

Mother sighed. "Nothing. I just want to rest." She burrowed deeper into the bed pillow, which hadn't undergone her usual cleanliness inspection.

Baking in Bakersfield, where summer temperatures could climb over 115 degrees, was a joke we had already worn out. Nancy, Skippy and I shared Mother's mood. We children hadn't wanted to leave Stockton. In the eight months that we were there we had begun to put down roots in spite of Daddy's warning.

The next day, Monday, Daddy had to work, but he got up very early and cooked bacon, eggs and toast for all of us. Mother ate a little toast and went back to bed. "I don't feel like looking for a house today," she said weakly.

"You just rest, Honey," Daddy said. "That can wait." Turning to Nancy and me he said, "You girls take care of your mother and Skippy. I'll be back around 5:30."

Nancy and I washed the dishes and straightened up the cabin. We played games with Skippy, fixed peanut butter sandwiches for lunch and took glasses of iced tea to Mother. She said she was feeling better, but that we might have to go out for hamburgers again when Daddy came home. To us, that was a treat!

When Daddy came in from work he went directly to Mother, who was sitting up in bed, reading. "Well, Hon, you look better!" he said. "Ready for the news?"

"*News?*" Mother replied, looking alarmed. "Don't tell me . . . ?"

Nancy and I gathered around the bed to listen. We knew a tone of importance when we heard it.

"Well, Hon, we're moving."

Mother sat bolt upright. "Good Lord!"

Now, Mother *never* took the Lord's name in vain. Not because she was religious, but because it wasn't "ladylike."

Then Daddy said, with a broad smile, knowing Mother would be pleased, "We're going to Long Beach!"

"*Long Beach!*" Mother gasped. "*Long Beach!* I don't believe it! Is it true?" Mother held her hand over her heart as if it might flutter away.

"Yep, it's true," Daddy assured her. "We should leave tomorrow. Do you feel up to it?"

Mother sprang out of bed and grabbed her robe. "I'll be fine tomorrow! When we hit that ocean air I'll be completely recovered, you'll see! *Long Beach!* God's country! I'll just have a bath, and then we can all go out for hamburgers!"

The trip to Long Beach was a happy one. Nancy and I sang *"Three Blind Mice"* and Daddy, then Skippy, joined in. Finally Mother laughingly asked us all to stop.

On our trips Daddy usually had us play a game which involved who could spot something first, like the ocean, or a lake, or some landmark. I suppose this was to keep us alert and interested in where we were going. As we climbed towards the Ridge Route summit Nancy challenged, "Who's going to see the ocean first?"

"You won't see the ocean from the Ridge Route," Daddy said. "It's too far away, and it's not clear enough. Instead of that, let's see who will be the first to feel cooler air."

Mother said, *"I'm* going to win this one!"

"No, *me!"* Nancy shouted.

We were all so thrilled to be going to Long Beach that the car and trailer seemed to float effortlessly over the tortuous turns and steep downgrades of the Ridge Route. When the air cooled we all yelled "Cool air!" together, and nobody won the contest. It seemed no time at all before we began to descend into the San Fernando Valley.

In the 1930s, Long Beach, 14 miles south of Lynwood, was a resort town catering to wealthy easterners who rented airy apartments or tile-roofed cottages by the sea for their vacations. It was also a health resort, obsessed with the functions of the digestive tract. Signs offering "colonic irrigation" alternated with well-stocked health food stores promoting cures for the sluggish colon. People came to Long Beach for the healthful benefits of sunshine and sea air as well as for the year-around availability of fresh fruits and vegetables.

Orange, grapefruit and lemon trees flourished in Spanish-style patios and the scent of jasmine filled the air. Geraniums and bird of paradise plants bloomed under the palms.

While Long Beach catered to the physical body—especially the nether regions—a few miles to the north, in the Echo Park area, a charismatic evangelist, Aimee Semple McPherson, served up a feast for the hungry soul. In her 5,000-seat Angelus Temple, under a proscenium arch designed by Charlie Chaplin, using attire from The Western Costume Company and with a full orchestra (which included young Anthony Quinn on the saxophone), Sister Aimee dished up soul-saving and faith-healing extravaganzas characterized by her critics as "supernatural whoopee." In her illustrated sermons, which rivaled any Hollywood performance, the evangelist fought off horned, pointy-tailed red devils which emerged from boiling cauldrons, welcomed angels descending from the Temple dome or urged sinners (hired acrobats) to leap into the net of salvation.

In search of better health, renewed youth and the good life, a half million immigrants from the Middle West settled in southern California in the early 1930s. Tired of the Calvinistic gloomy view of hell and damnation with which they were raised, many of these immigrants sought Sister Aimee's joyful emphasis on miracles and heaven, which seemed more consistent with the balmy climate and the glamour and excitement of the entertainment industry.

Aimee Semple McPherson maintained open kitchens to feed people of any creed or color who were hungry, never requiring Bible study or attendance at her sermons in return.

We moved into a white board-and-batten duplex just 12 blocks from the beach. I loved the rooms on different levels, the bathroom two steps up off the hall and the back bedroom two steps down. Floor-to-ceiling sliding doors could be drawn to separate the living and dining rooms, and we children almost wore them out. The window seats beneath the front bay windows were padded in faded chintz decorated with peacocks and exotic flowers, and, when I lifted the seats up, I found stacks of music, now crisp and brown around the edges.

One Saturday we visited Daddy's sister, Aunt Maisie, and her husband, Uncle Bert. They lived in the Silver Lake district of Los Angeles on a long, sloping lot, the back of which hung like a rocky precipice over a busy boulevard. As we walked up the driveway of their big house in front—which was rented to a large Italian family—and then climbed a flight of slippery flagstone steps to the small cottage in the rear, I was already tasting the raviolis I knew we'd have for dinner.

"I suppose we'll have raviolis again," Mother said in the car on the way to Aunt Maisie's. "I don't think she ever does any *real* cooking."

In defense of his sister Daddy replied, "The cactus business takes most of her time, and she loves being outdoors." Aunt Maisie raised various types of cactus which she potted for sale in the colorful Mexican stalls on Los Angeles' Olvera Street.

Uncle Bert burst out of the big storage room underneath the cottage and greeted us with an expansive "Hello, folks! I'll be right with you. Maisie's in the backyard." With the exception of Mother, we all liked Uncle Bert. He was a tanned, lean man with quick, darting movements and a ready smile. When he laughed, which was often, long crinkly lines formed on his sun-beaten but still good-looking face.

Uncle Bert dashed back into the storeroom and came out carrying a jug of red wine. Motioning to another steep flight of steps which wound around the side of the cottage to the main entrance in the rear he said, "Just a few more steps!"

We children charged up the steps while Mother puffed her way up one step at a time, her right hand gripping the wrought iron railing. Daddy lingered behind and exchanged a few words with Uncle Bert.

When Aunt Maisie saw us she took off her gardening apron, wiped her hands on it and hugged me, Nancy and Skippy each in turn. Skippy twisted loose from her embrace and ran up the stone stairs to the top of the terraced back-yard. "Where are the spiders?" he yelled. "Nancy said there were spiders!"

"Later, Skippy," Aunt Maisie laughed. "Uncle Bert will show them to you." She patted a few strands of hennaed hair back into place, hair which closely matched the vivid color of the flowers on her embroidered Mexican blouse. As she turned to Mother, her long silver earrings caught the late afternoon sun. "Dorothy, you look done in. Let's go inside."

At the door Aunt Maisie kicked off her gardening clogs, slipped into a pair of huaraches and held the screen door open for Mother.

Mother, still wheezing from the climb up two flights of steps, fell into the nearest chair, picked up a piece of news-paper and fanned herself. "I can see how you keep your fig-ure, Maisie, going up and down those steps every day."

Like Uncle Bert, Aunt Maisie smiled a lot. She was pretty in a way, and would have been prettier if she hadn't inherited a good share of the "Lockard nose." I liked her style in spite of the fact that Mother called her mode of dress "outlandish."

Aunt Maisie handed Mother a glass of water. "I'm used to the steps, Dorothy." Aunt Maisie had always led an active life and she was very trim. When she was growing up she and Daddy worked on their parents' dairy farm, rode horses in the mountains around Santa Barbara and sailed Daddy's home-made boat along the coast. Aunt Maisie and Uncle Bert took frequent camping trips to Baja California to fish and hunt, and Aunt Maisie was used to scrambling over rocks and down cliffs to get to the best fishing spots.

Daddy and Uncle Bert came in. When Aunt Maisie and

Daddy exchanged hugs I could tell they were fond of each other by the way their faces lighted up. "Good to see you, Bruce," Aunt Maisie beamed. "It's been a while."

Uncle Bert went into the kitchen and poured red wine into four tumblers. "I'll water some down for the kids," he said, passing glasses to the adults.

Mother objected. "None for them, and water's enough for me, thank you. Those steps made me dizzy enough."

While my parents, Aunt Maisie and Uncle Bert talked I wandered around the living room looking at the *wonderful* things that Aunt Maisie had brought back from Mexico. There were broad-brimmed sombreros and retablos hanging on the walls. Pottery with Aztec designs sat on open shelves. A huge Mexican market basket heaped with crepe paper flowers of every color occupied the table under the picture window. Spread out under the basket was a bright green fringed rebozo. Striped serapes were thrown over the couch and chairs, little boxes of Mexican silver gleamed from end tables and a huge pottery toro, snorting and pawing the ground, dominated the coffee table.

Mother pointed to the toro. "Maisie, I'd feel better if you'd put that away before Skippy comes in. He gets rambunctious and I can't watch him every second. By the way, where is he? I don't see him outside."

"He's looking for trap-door spiders," said Nancy.

"Nancy, go see what he's up to. I don't want him rolling down that hill above the boulevard."

"Don't worry, Dorothy," said Uncle Bert. "I built a fence up there since you were here last. Come on, Nancy and Sunny, we'll go find Skippy and look for spiders."

Nancy went out with Uncle Bert. I stayed behind because the things in Aunt Maisie's house interested me more than trap-door spiders. Also, I knew that Uncle Bert would take Nancy and Skippy to the storeroom and feed them bear jerky, which I found disgusting. The storeroom was gloomy and there were creepy things down there, like snakeskins and shark jaws.

Aunt Maisie picked up the toro and started to leave the living room. Curious, I followed her, hoping that she was headed for the mysterious room at the back of the cottage known as "Giovanni's room."

The cottage, built by Uncle Bert when it became clear that he and Aunt Maisie were not going to have any children, consisted of a kitchen and breakfast nook, a long, narrow living room with a window overlooking the large house below, a "dressing room" where Aunt Maisie kept her clothes and the narrow cot on which she slept, and a bathroom between the dressing room and Giovanni's room. The storeroom underneath the cottage was Uncle Bert's domain.

Now Aunt Maisie unlocked Giovanni's room and went inside, placing the toro on the floor. Then she closed and locked the door. The brief glimpse I had of the dark room revealed a large bed with a light-colored spread, a dresser, a straight chair and some pictures on the wall. I was curious, but polite. Mother didn't tolerate nosy questions unless she asked them herself.

Aunt Maisie put an arm around me. "How about raviolis for dinner? I'll just call down to Giovanni's."

Raviolis from Giovanni's. Giovanni's room. More mysterious than ever.

Skippy, Nancy and Uncle Bert came in, all of them chewing on something. Bear jerky, I thought. Ugh.

"Don't eat too much of that stuff," said Aunt Maisie. "We're having raviolis for dinner."

"Let me make a salad," said Mother, getting up and going into the kitchen.

"I'll get some fresh greens from the garden," said Aunt Maisie.

Daddy and Uncle Bert talked about fishing, hunting and

Uncle Bert's plumbing business. Mother didn't have much to say until we were in the car and on our way home.

"I hope I *never* have to climb those steps again," she sighed. "And I think I'm getting a stomachache from those raviolis."

"You should have had a glass of wine, Hon," Daddy said. "Good for what ails you."

"Uncle Bert has a bottle of wine with a *worm* in it!" Skippy exclaimed.

"*A bottle of tequila from Mexico with a worm in it,*" Nancy corrected.

"What was he feeding you?" Mother asked. "Heaven only knows what he has down in that room."

"That's where he keeps his tools and his fishing and hunting equipment," Daddy said in Uncle Bert's defense.

"Uncle Bert sleeps there, too," said Nancy. "I saw a bed."

Neither Mother nor Daddy commented. After a short silence I ventured, "Who's Giovanni?"

Daddy stared straight ahead and didn't move a muscle. Mother sniffed. I hadn't heard her sniff like that since we went to visit Daddy's other sister, Aunt Gladys, and were introduced to a tall man named Jeff with slick dark hair who was wearing riding britches and puttees. Nancy and I were told that we were not to call him "Uncle" Jeff.

"Giovanni?" Mother echoed. "Giovanni makes raviolis." And that was the end of that.

Our duplex was walking distance from the popular beach amusement zone called "The Pike." Sometimes on balmy nights we would all walk down to The Pike and Daddy would buy us cotton candy or salt water taffy. Once in a while I was able to talk Daddy into taking me for a ride on the roller coaster. The Pike's attractions included The Man Turned to Stone, The Bearded Lady, The Snake Lady and The Wild Man from Borneo.

It was this last "attraction" that frightened me so much that I would walk on the opposite side of the walkway, as far away as possible from the "The Wild Man." Of course I knew that this creature wasn't really from Borneo, and that he was only pretending, but his filthy, disheveled, maniacal appearance, his insane shouting and violent shaking of the bars of his cage were, to me, bone-chilling. I was always careful to walk so that Daddy was between me and the "The Wild Man," and I fervently hoped that he would never break out of his cage.

When Mother saw the piano in our furnished duplex she immediately decided that I was to have lessons. She and I toured the local piano studios where instructors demonstrated samples of the music I would be taught to play. Finally, rejecting the "play-by-ear" method in favor of learning to read the notes, Mother selected a teacher.

In Long Beach there were day trips to the beaches on the weekends, barbecues, picnics and visits to or from old Lynwood friends. I found my piano lessons boring. One evening Mother announced, "I got a note from Mrs. Stanton. She's coming by tomorrow with Cora Sue and Daniel."

Cora Sue Stanton had been my best friend in Lynwood, and I had not seen her for a year. After saying hello and uttering a few polite words we sat in silence, listening to Mother and Mrs. Stanton talk. Cora Sue's little brother, Daniel, had gone to the back room with Nancy to look at her guitar. Noticing our silence Mother said, "Sunny, why don't you play something for us?"

What did she mean, "play something?" I had been studying piano for six weeks, and I couldn't even play chopsticks. I wasn't going to make a fool out of myself in front of Cora Sue, who had studied piano since she was able to sit up on a piano stool and reach the keys.

Mother insisted. "Wasn't that a little waltz you were practicing the other day? Play that one."

"I don't have the music," I lied. "Besides, Miss Barbieri says our piano is out of tune." Another lie, but necessary, I thought, under the circumstances.

"How could the piano be out of tune?" asked Mother. "We had it tuned when we moved in. And if you don't have that music, play something else."

"I don't know anything else." This time I was telling the truth. I wasn't going to the piano, no matter what. *Not in front of Cora Sue!*

Mrs. Stanton smiled and said, "Cora Sue will play something, won't you, dear?"

Cora Sue dutifully went to the piano. Her fingers ran expertly up and down the keyboard a few times. Turning to Mother she said, "It's really not out of tune, Mrs. Lockard. It's just that . . . well, it's an *old* piano."

Mother laughed apologetically. "It was here when we moved in, you know."

Cora Sue announced each piece before she played it. First was "*Für Elise*," by Beethoven, followed by Dvořák's "*Humoreske Op. 101, No. 7.*" She finished with "*Chopin's Nocturne Op. 9, No. 2.*" She played beautifully, without missing a note. Of course, if she had missed a note I wouldn't have been able to detect it, given the stage of my own musical development. Cora Sue returned to her chair, looking pleased. She had a right to be pleased. She was *good*.

That was the last time I ever saw Cora Sue, for our family never again lived outside of the San Joaquin Valley. She and I exchanged a few short letters, then we dropped our correspondence, such as it was.

Nancy

The reputation each of us children had in the family was reinforced in our new surroundings. Sunny was ladylike. Skippy was precocious. I was awkward and outspoken.

Cultural experiences were not to be denied me although lessons in Stockton proved I was not cut out for the world of dance. Mother and Daddy, trying as always to be fair, signed me up for guitar lessons from Mr. Sanger, who taught the "Eddie Peabody" method.

Once a week I walked the eight blocks to town for my lesson, at first proudly carrying my rented guitar in its black cardboard case. Mr. Sanger and I never progressed further than "*The Dutch Girl Waltz*," though, because the strings, frets, written notes and above all, the rhythm eluded me.

I began to slink to my lessons with less and less pride, then with apprehension and finally dread. Maybe my grandmother Mama Dot was right. Proud of the polite applause after my elocution readings in Stockton, I had decided, "I want to be an actress!"

Mama Dot, who was visiting us, glared at me. "Nonsense!" she said. "You can't carry a tune, you can't dance, you're clumsy, and you're going to grow too tall. You could never be an actress."

In later life I noticed that Ingrid Bergman didn't sing or dance in her films and appeared to be tall and not at all dainty. I felt Mama Dot had crushed my dreams unfairly.

One Sunday afternoon Sunny's friend, Cora Sue, and her mother came to visit, bringing Cora Sue's younger brother, Daniel. Daniel, who had never had a guitar lesson, picked up my guitar, hummed a little and began playing "*Oh, Susanna*."

Listening to Daniel bring my guitar to life, I got the same "clunk" feeling I felt in dancing school. I *knew*. I knew Daniel had talent and I was hopeless. Mr. Sanger knew it, too, because the next week he sent me home without the guitar and carrying a sealed note to Mother. She opened it and read aloud, "Dear Mrs. Lockard, I can't take any more of your money. Trying to teach Nancy to play the guitar is a waste of time."

Sunny smiled smugly, tilted her head and walked gracefully to the piano where she launched into the only tune she knew, wrists held correctly, of course. Skippy's version of "So there!" was to wrinkle up his nose and put his fingers in his ears. Daddy eyed me sympathetically, but I could tell he was trying to conceal a smile. I knew that smile was on my side, though, and that he valued me for the things I *could* do—tomboy things like climbing trees and building forts with Skippy.

With a smile of resignation Mother waved the note in the air. Seeing her amused was such a happy surprise that I grinned. Daddy joined in with a chuckle. What a relief! No more guitar lessons!

Sunny

This was the summer I fell in love—hopelessly, desperately, head-over-heels in love. The object of my affections was Bobby Wilson, the nephew of Fred Wilson, a geophysicist who had been hired to work on the doodlebug party after Daddy put in a good word for him. Bobby and his 13-year-old brother, Jimmy, had come to Long Beach from Texas to spend the summer with Fred and his wife, Edna, in order to learn something about doodlebugging.

Fred, Edna, and the boys occasionally dropped by our house in the evenings. We would all walk down to The Pike together or Bobby, Jimmy, Nancy and I would play cards while the adults talked. Bobby was 16, with dark good looks and a soft, masculine Texas accent. And, he could drive a car. I did not really expect that my love would be requited. After all, I thought, how could a boy of 16 feel romantic about a girl who was only 13 1/2? A gangly girl with a big nose and corkscrew hair who wasn't allowed to wear makeup, stockings or high heels?

And then, out of the blue, Bobby asked me for a date, an *actual date*. It was the second week of August, a few days before we were to leave on Daddy's annual two-week vacation. Fred, Edna and the boys dropped by for an evening visit. Bobby asked me to go out with him that coming Friday evening. I was *stunned*. My wildest dream had come true: a date with Bobby, my true love! This wasn't a crush like I had on Matt in the fifth grade, the boy who could throw a baseball higher then any other boy in the class, nor was it little-girl admiration for Jack, who could kick the can and run faster than the other boys in our Lynwood neighborhood. No, this was LOVE, no doubt about it. Now I could hold out the hope—be it ever so faint—that Bobby might care for me.

Mother and Daddy were nodding their approval. Then Edna said, "Why not take Nancy along, Bobby? And Jimmy could go, too." Bobby replied, "Sure! Good idea."

Now my cherished date with Bobby had degenerated into a foursome, consisting of my little sister and Bobby's little brother, a couple of kids! My heart sank. Well, I thought, at least I'd be out with Bobby, and it mattered that he had actually asked me.

Nancy

I had just turned 11 and Skippy would soon be five. With an older sister and a younger brother, I could prolong my childhood by playing with Skippy or sample my forthcoming teen years by horning in on Sunny's activities. Skippy was thrilled when I helped him with his Erector Set or took him for a ride on my bike. Despite our pokes, jabs and faces at each other, he was my little buddy, and we kept many secrets from the rest of the family.

Entering Sunny's world was a different matter. She didn't want an awkward little sister slipping in behind her as she stepped through the magic coming-of-age portal. It was as if she kept looking behind her to say, "Nancy, you're too close. You're not ready. It's my turn to be a princess. Don't spoil it for me."

Toward the end of our summer in Long Beach, though, I was pushed into sharing a significant event in her life, one that left me vowing to grow up quickly and her crying the whole night through.

Sunny was in love with Bobby Wilson although she had only seen him when the Wilsons came by to visit. I admired him too, but, for now, an occasional sigh over Johnny Able's redwood plaque was the extent of my interest in romance. I was gawky, flat chested and still ran around with Skippy in the backyard playing cowboys and Indians.

Sunny was beginning to grow breasts, and she locked herself in the bathroom while she checked their progress and tried to tame her curly hair with gooey wave set.

When Mother and Mama Dot told me that Sunny was going out with Bobby Wilson, I was surprised. But I was flabbergasted when they told me Bobby's younger brother Jimmy would be along, and I would be Jimmy's "companion."

Immediately Mother and Mama Dot began hovering around me like Cinderella's fairy godmother. They worried about what to do with my hair and what kind of new dress would be suitable. I was excited but confused. Perhaps Mama Dot, who always criticized my table manners, skinned knees and uncombed hair, saw this as a chance to make a lady out of me.

Maybe I was to go along to insure that Sunny and Bobby didn't have any time alone to "neck." Sunny thought her crush on Bobby was a secret, but she had been mooning around ever since she met him.

Mother and Mama Dot's zeal in transforming me from a tomboy into a young lady was ill advised, as they must have realized later. How could you keep a girl "down in the San Joaquin Valley" after she's seen the moonlight on the bay in Long Beach?

Still, I fell in with the "date" preparations. Mama Dot took me to Long Beach's best department store where she selected a dark blue rayon dress for me. It had a tasteful small flower print, a Chinese-style collar and a narrow sash of the dress material lined in pale green. It was a dress any girl five years older than I would have been proud to wear. It was expensive and grown up, and I loved it.

She bought me flat patent leather pumps to complete the outfit. Over Sunny's protests, Mama Dot borrowed Sunny's best navy blue nubby sweater for me to "throw over my shoulders" if the night got cool.

She insisted I have my straight hair done at a beauty parlor the day of the outing. The hairdresser combed wave lotion into my straight hair and used her index finger to hold one row down while she swirled the hair underneath to one side. Then, holding the swirled row, she would reverse the process.

When I emerged from the dryer and the beauty operator ran a comb through my hair, it bounced into zigzags which Mama Dot pronounced satisfactory.

Mama Dot's final words were, "Now don't just put the sweater on as if you were going to school, Nancy. That would look tacky. If you get cold, just drape it over your shoulders, casually. And keep your legs crossed when you're sitting down. If you act like a lady, you'll be treated like a lady."

Sunny

It seemed an eternity until Friday, but the appointed time finally arrived. Mama Dot gave Nancy and me some final instructions on proper behavior for young ladies while Mother fussed over what I was going to wear. I don't remember what I wore. I only remember being *in love*.

I sat in the front seat with Bobby, and Nancy and Jimmy were in the back. I don't remember anything about Jimmy because I was totally focused on Bobby. We went to The Pike, walked around for a while and rode on some of the tame rides like the merry-go-round and the ferris wheel. We didn't see The Wild Man from Borneo. It might have been his night off. Too bad, I thought. The screams of The Wild Man would have given me a good excuse to hang on to Bobby's arm more tightly.

When we came across the electric boats, the boys were eager to take a ride. The battery operated, covered boats each held two people and were guided around the bay with a steering wheel. Nancy and Jimmy took one boat and Bobby and I took another. We rode around the lagoon for an hour or so. The reflection of the moonlight on the water, the sparkle of city lights, the music from the carousel on the pier, Bobby sitting next to me guiding the little boat with his strong hands—it was magic. Being alone with Bobby was so romantic and I was so much in love that I thought I was going to expire.

Nancy

My partner, Jimmy, had sandy blonde hair, hazel eyes and the promise of a solid masculine build. Self-assured in his tan slacks and sports jacket, he indeed treated me like a lady. He took my elbow when he helped me into Bobby's uncle's car and sat a respectful distance from me in the back seat. We joked as the four of us walked around the Pike, and I was grateful that no one suggested we ride the scary roller coaster. When Sunny could take her eyes off Bobby or her arm out from under his, she treated me like a girlfriend instead of a little sister.

Jimmy, in no danger of being seen by his school friends in Texas, made me feel like a real date instead of an 11-year-old. I was grateful to him and, at the same time, felt that he was surprised that I was so mature and interesting. I knew he was having a good time too. I was in heaven.

As we strolled, the evening turned to night and the colored lights of the amusement park reflected in the ocean made way for the moon as it rose over Long Beach. The smell of the sea mingled with the odors of popcorn, hot dogs and salt water taffy. Even though I was getting cold I followed Mama Dot's instructions and threw Sunny's sweater casually over my shoulders so I wouldn't look tacky.

When Bobby and Jimmy rented the two-seater boats so we could putt around in the bay, there was so little room in our boat that Jimmy and I couldn't help touching. "Aren't you cold?" Jimmy asked, taking off his jacket and wrapping it around me.

I shook my head, no, but he laughed. "You lie, you know." Jimmy's arm was still around my shoulder from adjusting his jacket. His jacket was warm and a clean male smell clung to it.

"Look," he said, gripping the steering wheel and rocking our boat slightly. "You're a nice girl, and I'd even say you're very special. When you're sweet sixteen you'll have your pick of the varsity. Believe me."

The rest of the evening was a delirious romantic blur. I didn't fall in love with Jimmy, but I fell in love with love. This kid stuff, this running around in the backyard and building forts or daydreaming about Johnny Able, was over. Naively, Mother and Mama Dot had opened a door and pushed me through it. I wasn't going to turn around and go back. I could hardly wait to grow up.

Sunny

Bobby drove us home. There was no goodnight kiss, no hand holding, nothing of the sort. Bobby was very polite, but no different than he had been while visiting at our house. Nancy and I thanked the boys for a nice evening, as Mama Dot had instructed us to do. Then Bobby said to me, "I'm going home tomorrow. Back to Texas."

I don't remember if I answered him. I was devastated. I was so deeply in love and the object of my love was going away the very next day! I ran into the house, bolted past Mother, who was waiting in a chair by the front window, and went straight to my bedroom. I was sharing my bed with Mama Dot, who was already asleep, snoring. I tore off my dress, threw my shoes in a corner and climbed into bed, my whole body shaking. Then the sobs came. I cried and cried until the bed rocked like our little electric boat on the bay. The more I tried to hold back my grief the more intense my sobs became. Mama Dot awakened and shook me, saying, "What's the matter? What's the matter?" I couldn't answer. Mama Dot fell asleep again and eventually, totally exhausted, I fell asleep, too.

Nancy

That night when I climbed into bed and put my head on the pillow, I felt my finger-waved hair, softened by the sea air, spread out and make a magic nest for my head. I wasn't thinking about my first "date," only feeling. Feeling Jimmy's arm around my shoulder and hearing his words, "You're very special."

I could still smell the salt air, hear the water lapping against our little boat and see the moonlight mix crazily with the colored lights on the water. I thought I heard Sunny crying in the next room, but soon I fell asleep.

Sunny

The next morning when I appeared at the breakfast table with puffy cheeks and swollen, red eyes nobody said anything to me, not even Nancy. After breakfast Daddy said,

"Sunny, want to come with me when I take Mama Dot to the train station? We'll leave here at ten, and you can pack when you get back."

I had almost forgotten about our family vacation. This year we were driving up the coast to spend two weeks with our friends, the Flanagans, who lived in Ventura, about eighty-five miles north of Long Beach. The Flanagans owned a beach cottage on the Rincon, a stretch of beach north of Ventura, and they had invited us to stay with them at the cottage. I had looked forward to this vacation, but now it didn't matter. I was too much the Tragic Heroine to care what happened to me after Bobby Wilson left town.

When Daddy and I returned from taking Mama Dot to the train station I found that Mother had already packed my bag.

"All set!" Mother said cheerfully. "I'm certainly looking forward to seeing the Flanagans."

"Yes," Daddy replied. "They're always good company."

"And wasn't it thoughtful of the Wilsons to plan such a nice outing for the girls? They're nice people, and it was a clever way to show their gratitude for your help in getting the job for Fred."

Daddy looked at me, then turned to Mother and remarked, "I'm sure it was more than that, Hon."

I grabbed my suitcase and took it out to our car. It was more than that, a lot more. Nothing was going to spoil my magic date with Bobby Wilson!

CHAPTER 9

Rincon Vacation

Nancy

As our family drove along the coast toward the Flanagan's beach cabin on the Rincon north of Ventura, Sunny's periodic sighs over the end of her make-believe romance with Bobby Wilson blended in with the sound of the waves. Soon we passed Manhattan Beach, Santa Monica and Malibu. Skippy, whom Sunny in her "nothing-matters-now" mood had allowed to sit by the window on the ocean side, amused himself by sticking his left hand out the window and arranging his fingers in different positions to test the air flow. Ordinarily Mother would have warned him, "Bring that hand in, young man, or a truck will come by and rip it right off," but she was in a good mood. She loved visiting our friends, the Flanagans.

As I breathed in the salt air that Skippy's fingers were beckoning into the back seat, I was enjoying my own love affair—one that will last all my life. I was in love with California's Pacific Coast Highway, affectionately known by Southern Californians as "PCH." With few exceptions (where Highway 1 briefly joins 101 or skirts a rocky promontory), PCH runs along California's spectacular coastline from Orange County to Northern Mendocino County, passing by Morro Bay, Santa Barbara, Big Sur, Monterey, San Francisco and Fort Ross.

Driving along the coast starting out on a family vacation held the same magic for me as driving up through the Sierra Nevada foothills headed for Yosemite or Sequoia or Kings Canyon. The road briefly took us a mile or so inland, and I knew that as soon as it outlined the coast again we'd be close to the Rincon. I could hardly wait.

Maggie and Pat Flanagan were warm, sincere and constantly smiling. They looked enough alike to be brother and sister. Both were on the short side of average and slightly plump with smooth, rosy cheeks. "Aunt" Maggie's Norwegian ancestry was evident in her mouth-watering coffee cake and cookies, and "Uncle" Pat's Irish charm made him well liked in his city administration job. As we all greeted each other, Mother hugged Aunt Maggie. "I've brought an angel food and a sponge cake, but I didn't bake cookies because I can't top your Norwegian ones! I fried six chickens, and we can have that and some potato salad I made for dinner."

Before Aunt Maggie could protest Mother went on, "I thought fresh peas would be good with the chicken, and that box is full of a variety of Campbell's soup and saltines and cheese for our lunches. I've deviled three dozen eggs, and Bruce picked out a good watermelon at the market on the way up. The grocer plugged it, and it's juicy and sweet."

"My goodness," Aunt Maggie said. "We're certainly going to eat well! I cooked a ham and baked some rye bread, and Pat got a lug of local oranges we'll keep by the back door in case the children want to snack."

Sunny's love sickness didn't last long at the Flanagans. The cottage was rustic with three small bedrooms without doors or closets. There was a two-burner gas stove in the kitchen, a small ice box, a drinking water stand, smelly sulfur water piped into the sink, electric lights in the kitchen and living room only and a two-seater outhouse.

We kids loved the cottage because we didn't have to be careful of anything. The walls were unfinished, there were no rugs on the floor, and there was no furniture that mattered. We could hear the wonderful sound of waves breaking day and night.

Uncle Pat put down a suitcase he was carrying in for us and picked up several oranges which he juggled expertly before tossing one to me, Sunny, Skippy, his daughter Cathy and his son Terry. Cathy and Sunny ran off giggling, and I suspected that Sunny was already talking about her date with Bobby Wilson, no doubt embellishing it for Cathy's benefit. I could hardly wait to tell Cathy I had been on a date, too! We three girls would sleep together that night, and it would be just like a slumber party.

Cathy was closer to Sunny's age than mine, a petite girl, not gangly like Sunny and me but compact and already curving out in her bathing suit like the "Petty" girls in *Esquire* magazine. Her disposition was as sweet as her parents', and later I heard Daddy whisper to Mother, "When she's 16 every young blade in Ventura will be standing on the Flanagans' doorstep with a bouquet in one hand and a box of candy in the other."

Mother's retort was, "Well, she'd better be careful not to eat those chocolates. When a girl fills out too soon she's liable to develop a weight problem."

Terry was slightly younger than I was and looked exactly like his father. As amiable as the rest of his family, he was happy digging in the sand with Skippy or playing "Snap" or checkers with us girls. Still, as Terry and I ran off with our oranges, I tried to ditch Skippy, but he was an expert in locating ditchers. He joined us on a rock near the water, and by the time we had finished our oranges the tide had risen, and we had to wait for the water to gurgle down to its low phase before we could scamper off the rock and run back to the cottage. Without being told, all three of us deposited our orange peels in the garbage can outside the back door. Our parents had taught us well.

To my surprise, Daddy, who seldom drank anything alcoholic, was having a beer with Uncle Pat. "There's time for a swim before dinner," he said, draining his glass. "Why don't you children get your suits on?"

Mother didn't go in the water, and Aunt Maggie and Uncle Pat seemed content to sit in the cabin and talk, plan meals or work the big jigsaw puzzle that was always in progress on a low table by the day bed under the front windows. When it was high tide the ocean came so close to the cabin that I couldn't see the rocky shore at all, and I loved to look out those windows and pretend I was in a boat. But there wasn't time for that now. Pleasures were offered up all around me like chocolates in a just-opened box of See's candy. I didn't know which to pick first. I ran to find my bathing suit and towel.

Skippy and Terry had just started a game of Snap, so Daddy, Sunny, Cathy and I started off toward the swimming area, about 20 cabins south of us, that was sandy instead of rocky like most of the shore. I jumped from rock to rock, chasing the water as it receded and squealing when the cold foam swirled up around my knees with the inrushing tide. There was time to poke my finger gently into sea anemones or dig up a handful of squirming sand crabs or skip a flat rock on the water. "Two skips!" I yelled.

"Three for me," Cathy answered, "but then I get to practice a lot."

Even Sunny, who had been trying to look world weary, picked up a stone and skipped it out over the water. Daddy skipped one too, and his bounced four times, but he didn't comment on it.

When we reached the swimming spot, we spread our towels out on the warm sand, anchoring the corners with driftwood. Then we headed out for a swim. Daddy dived right into the shallow surf, came up with water streaming down his hair and body and shouted, "Brrr!" Swimming out past the breakers, he floated on his back like a sea otter. "Come on out," he encouraged with a wave. "The water's great!"

Cathy was already out to where the waves were foaming around her waist, but Sunny and I hung back in water up to our knees, waiting for our bodies to get used to the cold, inch by inch. I was usually the last one to get completely wet, and the final dunking was seldom voluntary. As Sunny caught up with Cathy, I waded slowly forward, keeping a careful eye on the line of breakers. At mid-thigh point the white turmoil of just-broken waves engulfed me, almost knocking me over. I turned sideways as Daddy had taught me, and the next assault hit me with less force but left only my head dry.

Now my job was to get past the breakers to the swells where Cathy and Sunny were jumping and laughing. This was the scariest part for me. If I kept walking out and timed it just right, I could dive through an oncoming wave then swim like crazy out to the swells. If a big wave caught me, though, I would go under, salt water would rush up my nostrils and my body would be tossed over and over and carried back to shore. Not only was this humiliating but it meant having to wade out toward the breaking waves all over again.

I watched. The swell almost upon me was gathering height to crest, another swell was rolling in close behind it, and a gigantic swell loomed up behind that. I turned sideways and jumped as high as I could, just managing to ride the top of the swell as it floated past. In a second I heard it roar and crash, heading for shore. Then I swam toward the oncoming swell. Again I jumped as it peaked, and my body was carried up high then gently dropped down before the swell turned into another crashing wave. Now I was in a calm trough and could touch bottom again. But all my attention was focused on the gigantic swell that was moving slowly toward me. I looked for Daddy. He was still floating on his back out in the deep water but I could tell he was keeping an eye on me. "You'll do okay," he motioned, apparently unconcerned.

I had planned on jumping this giant swell too, but it was curling early and fast. Facing it, my heart pounding, I saw a rising wall of transparent green. The water was strangely beautiful. The sun shone through it silhouetting three leaves of sea weed. Water fizzed high on its edge sending white mist out against the blue sky. I was scared. Diving through this powerful wave was out of the question. Letting it break on me would be like standing out on the Southern Pacific tracks across the highway from the Flanagans' cottage. I held my nose shut, closed my eyes and sank to the bottom.

While I swirled underneath, I wondered if I could hold my breath long enough for the wave to rumble past. I waited below while tons of water crashed directly above me. It seemed a long time before the tumult ended and I felt the wave dissipate toward shore. I surfaced, gulped a deep breath and swam quickly out past the swells into the calm water next to Daddy.

"Good choice, Nancy," he said, moving his arms slightly under the water to float nearer to me. "I do that sometimes. Diving directly into a strong wave could be dangerous."

I turned on my back to float and rest. The top few inches of water were tepid from the sun. Several summer clouds evaporated as I watched them. The beach cabins on shore looked like toys. I was in heaven. Suddenly Cathy yelled, "Hell divers. Nine of them!"

The sea was my pillow as I watched a string of brown pelicans 20 feet overhead cruise the shallow waters for schools of fish. Suddenly the lead bird stretched his feet under his tail, flattened his wings back tightly and pointed his bill toward the blue-green water, making an arrow of his plunging body. As I watched him splash into the water, I could barely see him open his expandable pouch beneath it. When he surfaced, facing the breeze, water was draining from his mandibles and he was positioning squirming minnows so he could swallow them head first.

I watched the other pelicans as they spotted fish and dived too, filling their stomachs before returning to the Channel Islands, San Miguel, Santa Rosa, Santa Cruz, Anacapa and Santa Barbara, offshore. Cathy's name for the pelicans, hell divers, was her own, but it was apt, and it gave us children a chance to use a forbidden word without risking a reprimand from our parents.

"The pelicans will probably fly back to Anacapa Island this evening," Daddy called out, unable to resist a chance to educate his children, even while vacationing flat on his back in the Pacific. "That's their favorite nesting ground."

Sometimes I wished Daddy's lectures would take a vacation, too, but I respected his knowledge. Looking out at the islands, I was reminded that he had built a boat when he was a boy in Santa Barbara and sailed it to those shores—a dangerous trip in uncertain weather.

For the rest of our visit we swam morning and afternoon, with Daddy giving Skippy lessons whenever he joined us. Soon I was looking for the biggest swells to jump just in the nick of time and waves that were perfect for body surfing. Unless there was a storm or the riptides were active, the Rincon was a safe place to swim. The beach was generally rocky, sand fleas hopped over wet kelp and naturally occurring seeps offshore deposited tar on the sand, but it was all part of the Rincon, and there was a sense of camaraderie as we sat on the cabin deck at the end of the day and cleaned tar off the soles of our feet.

There was also a sense of camaraderie making the trip to the outhouse. Sunny tells that story best.

Sunny

A little distance from the rear of the cabin was a cluster of outhouses, each one belonging to a particular cottage. The Flanagan outhouse was a two seater which meant that two people at a time could enjoy its benefits. The procedure for using the outhouse required one to first obtain the key, which was attached to a wooden paddle about five inches wide and three feet long and kept hanging near the rear door to the cabin. If the key was missing, the outhouse was assumed to be occupied. The large piece of wood attached to the key ensured its safe return. There were many jokes and comments about the outhouse, which amused everyone. There was always a small bag of clothespins hanging near the outhouse key, and Nancy and I would pretend to clip one on our nose as we made our way out back. Once Skippy took the clothespin joke literally, and it took several days for his freckled nose, already sensitive from sunburn, to recover from the pinches.

One night before going to bed, Nancy and I took the key off the hook and headed for the outhouse. It was late and very dark. We had played cards with the Flanagan kids until almost midnight. As we approached the outhouse we saw, a short distance away, a small bonfire near the back of one of the unoccupied cottages. We could see the dark figures of three men sitting around the fire warming their hands. When we returned to the cottage, we told our parents and the Flanagans what we had seen.

Daddy and Uncle Pat put on their jackets, grabbed flashlights and went out to investigate. They came back about 10 minutes later and told us that the men were out of work, that they were on their way to San Francisco to look for jobs, that they had no money or food and would leave in the morning, walking or thumbing rides or riding the rails. As soon as they heard this, Mother and Aunt Maggie went to the kitchen and fixed food for the men: thick ham and cheese sandwiches, mugs of steaming soup, big chunks of apple pie, a pot of hot coffee. Daddy and Uncle Pat took the food to the men and sat and talked with them while they ate.

Seeing homeless, jobless men on the road was not an uncommon sight during the years of the Great Depression.

These casualties of a collapsed economy rode the rails, traveling from town to town, city to city, looking for work or a handout, trying to stay alive. Some gathered in hobo camps near the railroad tracks and shared food and information. Others walked through neighborhoods, knocking on doors and asking for food.

I remember tramps coming to our back door several times when we lived in Lynwood. Mother never turned anyone away without food. Many delicious meals and mugs of strong coffee were handed out through our back door to the less fortunate. Although the hobos were always grateful and never caused us any problems, Mother nevertheless warned Nancy and me to keep our distance. We were taught to say, "We don't want any, we don't have any," or "I'll get my mother," whichever seemed to fit the circumstances. Under no conditions were we to open the door to a stranger—never.

One incident that occurred on Thanksgiving in 1933 made such an impression on me that it remains vivid to this day. Our family was seated at the dining room table enjoying a bountiful dinner. With us was my grandfather, Daddy's father, the Reverend Earl Tubbs Lockard. My grandmother, Grace Barnard Lockard, had died the previous year. Mother seated me next to my grandfather in spite of the fact that I had complained to her, "Granddaddy dribbles food all over his white beard, and he makes funny chewing noises."

Daddy had nearly finished carving the turkey when we heard a loud knock at the front door. "Sunny, go see who that is," said Mother.

I went to the screen door and saw a huge dark figure of a man in an old cap and ragged clothing. "Can you spare some food?" the man asked in a hoarse voice.

My 11-year-old mind searched for the proper thing to say. "I'll get my mother," wasn't it because Mother had sent me to the door. He wasn't a salesman, so "We don't want any" wouldn't do. All that was left was "We don't have any," so

179

that's what I said. The big man turned around and walked slowly down the steps and into the driveway. I went back to the table where Granddaddy was telling one of his long stories.

"Who was it?" Mother asked when Granddaddy finally finished.

"A big man who wanted some food," I replied.

Mother stared at me, her fork poised in midair. "Why Sunny, we have plenty of food. We certainly could have given him something, especially on Thanksgiving."

My grandfather mumbled something from the Bible about charity. I put down my fork and hung my head. I couldn't eat another bite. I had turned a hungry man away from our house, and I felt like a criminal. I asked to be excused from the table. Mother said, "No." Tears ran down my cheeks and splashed on my plate. I got up, ran to my room and shut the door. About an hour later Nancy brought me a piece of pumpkin pie, but I sent it back. That was a Thanksgiving that haunts me to this day.

Nancy

A highlight of this particular visit to the Flanagans' cabin was the grunion run. One night during the second week of our stay, the nine of us had just finished a Spanish rice dinner with avocado salad, and Mother was cutting a pineapple upside-down cake she had made that afternoon in Aunt Maggie's cast iron skillet. Skippy was whipping the cream for topping with an eggbeater. "Whoa," Daddy said. "That cream will turn to butter if you keep on beating, Skippy."

"Yeah! Let's make butter," Skippy said. He assumed his "little demon" look as he speeded up his beating, his red curls bouncing up and down with the rhythm.

"None of that," Mother said, taking the bowl from Skippy and adding two tablespoons of sugar. "Here, Skippy. Beat this five more times for us then you can lick the beater." Naturally Skippy scooped up as much whipped cream as he could when he removed the beater, but Mother managed to tap it against the bowl several times before he took any licks. Skippy put on his "foiled-again" look. After Mother had dolloped whipped cream on everyone's cake, she gave the bowl to Terry to scrape clean with a spoon.

As I took a bite of my cake, carefully getting the right combination of whipped cream, pineapple and crusty brown sugar-soaked cake on my fork, I had a fleeting feeling of there being a penalty for growing up. Licking the bowl or eggbeater after Mother put a cake in the oven had always been special to me. Now the two youngest children in our group were enjoying the honor, and I was supposed to be as grown-up as Sunny and Cathy and not care about such things. I could feel myself letting a part of my childhood go, like setting a balloon adrift in the sky, but, at the same time, I wondered if this loss made me eligible for some grown-up privilege as yet unidentified.

"Don't anyone eat too much," Daddy warned. "The moon is almost full, and if we catch enough grunion tonight, we'll have a midnight fish fry."

"I don't have a fishing pole," Skippy said eagerly. "Can I make one?"

"Oh, you won't need a pole," Daddy said. "The grunion come in on a wave to spawn, and when you see a silver body flashing, you just go pick the fish up. All you need is a bucket to put it in."

Skippy looked all around the room to see if we were playing a trick on him. The Flanagans were smiling as if they had a little secret, and Sunny and I started to snicker. All of us had caught grunion before, but tonight Skippy was ripe for teasing.

"Actually, Skippy," Daddy said, "there *are* grunion and they *do* spawn in California when the moon is full. They're called leuresthes tenuis. Now, can anyone find a couple of buckets for tonight?"

That night the adults sat out on the front deck in the moonlight sipping coffee, and we children, in our swimsuits and sweatshirts, darted for thrashing slivers of silver each time a wave came in. If we were quick, we could pick up one or two grunion before the next wave carried the spawning fish back to the sea. We yelled and squealed and got caught by the waves until our sweatshirts were soaked and our teeth chattering. But we filled two buckets with grunion and insisted that we would eat them all if the adults would cook them.

"They're pretty bony—not much meat," Daddy said. "Still, they are delicious. Tell you what. You kids clean them and I'll cook them. Roll them in flour and cornmeal and fry them just like rainbow trout."

Cathy and Terry wrinkled up their noses at the thought of gutting two buckets of fish. Sunny didn't seem eager either. But both Sunny and I knew how to clean trout, and I kept thinking about how good the fried fish would taste. "Come on, Sunny," I pleaded. "I'll start. Daddy, may I borrow your knife?"

Sunny and I chopped off grunion heads and slit open grunion bellies, and Daddy fried and fried. At midnight two vacationing families had a fish fry. Aunt Maggie's turkey platter was heaped with crisp fish, and she cut Ventura-grown lemons in half to squeeze on them. Mother made tartar sauce out of mayonnaise, chopped onion and minced pickles. While we feasted, Daddy shared a beer and fishing stories with Uncle Pat, and Mother and Aunt Maggie laughed over small glasses of wine. My paper plate was heaped high with grunion bones. Skippy had fallen asleep on the day bed. It had been a perfect day, but mostly I loved seeing my parents happy. I wanted to visit the Flanagans forever.

Daddy's boss had asked him to contact the main office a few times during his vacation, "just in case." Daddy had called in twice the first week, and there was no news. Halfway through the second week Daddy went into town to place another call. When he returned about an hour after lunch we kids were waiting with our swimsuits on and beach towels in hand. We were not allowed to go swimming without Daddy's supervision. Mother was knitting and talking with Aunt Maggie. Seeing the expression on Daddy's face, Mother dropped her knitting in her lap. "Where to?" she asked.

For a moment Daddy said nothing. Then he said, "Yep, Hon, sorry, but we're on the move again. I'm afraid we'll have to go home tomorrow."

Mother picked up her knitting with an air of resignation. She turned to Aunt Maggie and said with a sigh, "The routine is one day cleaning and washing, one day packing, and one day traveling." Then she asked Daddy, "Back to the Valley, I suppose?"

"That's right," Daddy answered. "To Tulare."

Sunny and I looked at each other in disbelief then exclaimed in unison, "*Tulare?*"

Driving back to Long Beach the next day, Sunny whispered, "Nancy, will Johnny Able be your boyfriend again when we move back to Tulare?" I knew that if she didn't have love secrets of her own now she would have asked me out loud. I looked out at the ocean bordering the Pacific Coast Highway. Tulare and the San Joaquin Valley seemed a long way away. I didn't have a smart answer for her. All I could say was, "I don't know."

CHAPTER 10

Back to the Valley

Nancy

As I registered for school again in Tulare, my only thought was how embarrassing it would be to see Johnny Able again. After all, I was a year older and had been out on a "date" at the Long Beach Pike. I had been "double promoted" in Stockton and had managed to lose, tear or stain my childish, straight-from-the-shoulder dresses that I belted with string in Tulare the year before. In Stockton I had taken ballroom dancing lessons and visited San Francisco.

Poor Johnny! I had outgrown him while he pined away for me in small-town Tulare. I couldn't bear the thought of his lovesick brown eyes lighting up when he saw I was back. I cringed just thinking about it. He would probably want us to walk home together. He would even ask me if I still had the plaque with the heart. What would I do? I took a deep breath. With luck maybe he wouldn't recognize me!

As I walked along the school corridors, I could feel myself blushing. Until now I had treasured my memory of Johnny. The plaque he gave me was a special keepsake like the punched ticket Sunny saved from her boat ride with Bobby Wilson at the Long Beach Pike. Hundreds of times I had taken the plaque out of its hiding place and run my finger over the perfect little heart between the initials N L and J A.

184

Now, as I stopped at my locker to try out the combination, I realized I liked the *idea* of a boyfriend a lot more than the prospect of a real one.

As I pulled the locker door open, I saw someone who must be Johnny's older brother two lockers down. But no, it was Johnny! A taller, well muscled Johnny. A Johnny with a wisp of neatly cut hair falling over his forehead. A Johnny holding a red-headed girl's books and smiling into her eyes. A Johnny who looked over at me and said, "Oh, hello, Nancy," and turned back to whisper something in the girl's ear.

Well, I thought, praying the stinging behind my eyes wouldn't develop into humiliating tears, I guess we *both* had grown up a little. I felt silly as I slammed the metal locker door shut. Silly wasn't all I felt. I was jealous. And sad.

Why did our family have to move all the time? I was sick of always being the new girl.

Sunny

It was the first school day after Labor Day. The admissions clerk in the Tulare High School office studied Mother's note, my ninth-grade report card and a transcript of record from Stockton High School which Mother had enclosed in the envelope. "Of course we'll have to send for an *official* transcript," the clerk said. "In the meantime, Miss Palmer will assign your classes."

Miss Palmer enrolled me in Spanish II, Plane Geometry, English II, physical education and Art I, but not until she had remarked on my age. "You're thirteen?" she asked, doubtfully.

"Yes," I replied. Oh, here we go again.

"A little young for the tenth grade," Miss Palmer added, peering at me intently over her glasses on the end of her nose.

"I'll be fourteen in October." I hoped that would reassure her.

"That's better, but . . . did you skip a grade?"

185

"Yes."

"Ummm. Some children do, of course. We hope you stay in Tulare longer than you did last time. How long will you be here?"

"I don't know. Until my father gets transferred, I guess."

"Well, we hope you'll be here all year. We like to keep our *good* students. Enjoy your classes!"

"Thanks, Miss Palmer, I will." Some children were taught to address adults using "sir" or "ma'am," but Mother had strictly forbidden us to use these terms because she regarded them as subservient. We were to be polite and courteous, use "Mr.," "Mrs.," and "Miss," but never "sir" or "ma'am."

Mother found a two-bedroom frame house just a few blocks from the house we had rented in Tulare a year ago. We went back to our old neighborhood and found out that Billy Martin, our neighbor on one side, had moved away and that Mr. Cavendish, our neighbor on the other side, had died. Mother said that she could see that the muslin curtains she had made were still up in our former house.

I settled into my classes at school, thriving especially on Geometry and Spanish. Some of the kids looked faintly familiar, but I didn't clearly remember anyone from a year ago nor did anyone seem to remember me. The teachers were different because I was now in high school, not in junior high as I had been when we came to Tulare the first time.

I wasn't nervous about school. I went to school every day, did my best, went home, helped around the house and did my homework. I didn't expect to make friends at school right away, so I wasn't disappointed when the kids didn't seem overly friendly.

Three weeks after I had enrolled in Tulare High School I was back in Miss Palmer's office. "I'm sorry, Miss Palmer," I said, handing her a note from Mother. "I have to check out of school."

Miss Palmer gasped. "So soon? Gracious! You've only been here three weeks! Don't tell me your father got transferred?"

"Yes, he did."

"You were here in junior high only five weeks last year! You certainly lead a nomadic life!"

As a regular reader of *National Geographic* I knew what "nomadic" meant: desert, tents, Arabs, camels, sand. So I thought I'd make a little joke to lighten the atmosphere. "We don't have any camels, though."

Miss Palmer looked up from Mother's note and stared at me. Maybe she wasn't sure whether I was joking or being insolent. So I smiled, and Miss Palmer relaxed. "Well," she said. "I'll send copies of your records on to Fresno High. That's where your mother says you're going. And I'll have a letter ready for you to take along, if you'll come by my office on your way home today."

"Thanks, Miss Palmer." I used my nicest voice and smiled my nicest smile.

"By the way, dear . . . just what *does* your father do, to cause you to move around so much?"

"I'm not supposed to tell," I replied. "It's a secret."

Miss Palmer leaned forward and looked me in the eye. "I understand, dear, but you can tell *me*. We have lots of secrets here!" Then she smiled *her* nicest smile.

I was trapped. I don't know what made me do it, but I did it, and I didn't feel any regrets afterward. "Miss Palmer," I said in a low, confidential tone, "please don't tell anyone."

"Oh, I won't!" She leaned farther forward, bristling with anticipation.

"My father," I whispered, "is with the F . . . B . . . I. . . ."

Miss Palmer's eyes widened as she sprang back in her chair. "Oh! My goodness! What a dangerous life you must lead!"

"Oh, yes," I said. I resisted the temptation to embellish the confidence, thanked Miss Palmer and went to class. After school I picked up the letter she had written for me. It was a wonderful letter, full of praise for my courtesy, neat appearance and academic ability.

Miss Palmer patted my hand and said, with a wink, "Now, you take care of yourself! We wouldn't want anything to happen to you!"

CHAPTER 11

Blue Blood and Bad Advice

Sunny

Coming into Fresno on U.S. Highway 99 we passed miles and miles of vineyards. Trucks full of grapes bounced along the side roads while straw-hatted workers bent among the vines or carried boxes down the rows.

"Ummm, smell those grapes," said Daddy, inhaling deeply. "It's harvest time, girls."

We pulled into an auto court next to a walnut grove on the outskirts of town. The grounds were neatly planted with flowers and shrubs. The little cabins boasted a coat of fresh white paint.

"This will do," Mother said in a tone of semi-approval. "It looks clean on the outside, at least."

Daddy parked the car and trailer and went into the auto court office. He returned with a key which he gave to Mother. "It's number five," he said. "The manager says we can leave the trailer here when we go to dinner. You can do your inspection while I park the trailer and unhitch it."

Nancy, Skippy and I followed Mother to the row of cabins farthest from the highway. Under her arm Mother carried a wrinkled paper sack stuffed with clean rags and a bottle of Lysol. She unlocked the door of number five. "You children

189

stay outside until I tell you to come in," she ordered. "Stay right here by the front of the cabin."

Daddy backed the trailer into the shed next to number five. "Come on, Skippy," he called. "Help me unhitch the trailer." Skippy bounded over to Daddy, thrilled to have a grown-up assignment.

The hygienic odor of disinfectant drifted in waves out through the screen door of number five. Finally Mother came outside, drying her hands on a clean towel. "Girls, you can bring in your suitcases now. We'll have time to freshen up before going to see Uncle Clay and Aunt Jewell."

I was excited about having dinner with Uncle Clay and Aunt Jewell. They were fun to be around, and they were *family*. Uncle Clay was a salesman. His company, which made White King soap, sent him to Fresno from southern California to establish a sales route in the San Joaquin Valley. When Mother heard that we were going to be living in the same town as her favorite brother, she was ecstatic.

Nancy and I washed our faces and hands, combed our hair and put on clean dresses and clean socks. Skippy was scrubbed clean and dressed in new shoes, navy blue short pants and a white shirt. Mother put on one of her best dresses, a delicately flowered black and white print and added a touch of rouge to her cheeks. Daddy wore light tan slacks and a cotton plaid shirt.

"Let's see a little of the city," Daddy said. "We have time."

"I don't want to be late," Mother objected. "It's annoying when people are late for dinner."

"On the other hand, being too early isn't a good idea," Daddy replied. He drove slowly around the main downtown area and through some of the residential streets.

I had a good feeling about being in Fresno. It was a much bigger town than Tulare. Tall magnolia, sycamore, valley oak and pepper trees were plentiful. The houses I saw on our drive were big ones with huge shaded front porches, bright potted flowers and expanses of cool green lawn. The downtown had all sorts of buildings, some of them four or five stories high, and interesting shops. It would be fun to go downtown with Mother and look around.

Maybe we could live in one of those nice houses with a big front lawn. As we headed towards Aunt Jewell and Uncle Clay's apartment I hoped we'd stay in Fresno a long time. I might even make friends at school.

Nancy

While Mother, who felt isolated in the smaller Valley towns, was looking forward to spending time with her brother and his wife in Fresno, Daddy was less enthusiastic. His disdain of Clayton's get-rich-quick schemes and Jewell's effusiveness was evident as Daddy backed our car into a parking space in front of their apartment.

"I suppose Clay will describe his latest pipe dream invention and Jewell still has those darn Pekinese dogs," Daddy muttered, cramping the steering wheel. "What are their names? Chang and Pekie?"

Mother chuckled, enjoying this rare chance to gossip with Daddy. "*Ming* and Pekie," Mother corrected. "Those dogs *are* disagreeable little things. As for Clay's inventions, Bruce, some of them are very good ideas."

"Well, I wish he'd invent something to calm those dogs down," Daddy retorted. "The way they growl and snap, I'm concerned one of them will bite Skippy."

"I'll bite back!" Skippy declared as he jumped out onto the curb and bared his teeth. Biting had been one of Skippy's weapons when he was younger, and I thought I saw Daddy smile as he imagined Skippy's teeth sinking into one of Ming's floppy ears.

"Jewell treats those dogs just like the children she'll probably never want," Mother said, keeping the gossip going.

"Well, we don't know about that," Daddy said as he locked the car. I knew he was uncomfortable criticizing anyone, even Aunt Jewell. Sunny and I suspected, though, that he considered her to be frivolous with her two fashionable lap dogs, touched-up auburn hair, French perfume, fur-trimmed coats, antique furniture and frequent references to her blue blood.

"See these veins in my wrist?" Aunt Jewell would ask, turning her manicured hand over on a nesting side table. "Blue blood is running in them, isn't it? That proves I come from an aristocratic family!"

When Skippy and I would examine our wrists, she would exclaim, "See! It's in the family. Aren't you fortunate! You have blue blood, too!"

Sunny would sniff as if she knew better. Still, Sunny confided to me that she always hoped Aunt Jewell would cut herself with her kitchen paring knife just enough to bleed a few drops of blood that Sunny could inspect.

As Mother smoothed her hair and adjusted her dress, Daddy warned us, "Be careful of that antique furniture up there. If you see needlepoint anyplace, don't sit on it." Muttering, he added, "I don't know why that woman doesn't put a rope across the chairs we can't sit in."

"Now, Bruce," Mother said, "you know you like Jewell's enchiladas, and I'll bet that's what we're having tonight. I think I can smell them clear down here."

"Probably a lime Jell-O salad with marshmallows to go with them," Daddy said, uncharacteristically grumpy. In grade school in Santa Barbara Daddy had traded lunches with his Mexican schoolmates, and he liked his Mexican food on the authentic side.

Just then Ming and Pekie bounded down the stairs barking and yipping, followed by Uncle Clay, calm, smiling and handsome. Aunt Jewell was just behind, her cheeks rouged in perfect circles and her frilly apron spotless. "Yoo hoo, yoo hoo," she cried, "Welcome to Freeze No! October and still 85 degrees!"

I liked Aunt Jewell although later in my life the first question she asked me about a new boyfriend was, "Does he drive a late model car, dear?"

Uncle Clay adored Aunt Jewell, loved Mother and us children and respected Daddy. Quiet and generous, he was indeed the "sweet man" Aunt Jewell often called him as she patted his knee.

In Fresno visits to our aunt and uncle's apartment always meant plenty of rich food and light-hearted conversation with Mother in good spirits and Daddy's putting up with Uncle Clay's salesman jokes and Aunt Jewell's self-centered but cheerful chatter.

When Ming and the other "bad-tempered little dustmop" would waddle over to Daddy and sniff his hand, Daddy would relent and reach down to pet the creature as if it were a "real dog." But, invariably the dog would growl, its little pushed-in nose vibrating while its lips curled back for a snap, and Daddy would retreat to the bathroom to wash his hands. To Daddy only a farm dog was a real dog. He was never cruel, but in his estimation, tiny dogs were either dustmops or drowned rats.

"Dorothy, why don't you look for an apartment here instead of a house?" Aunt Jewell suggested after dinner as she cut Mother a second piece of mocha cake and put it on a Wedgwood plate, adding a fresh sterling silver dessert fork. "You can get a much nicer apartment than a house for the money. I've written some addresses down for you," she added as she gave Mother another hand-embroidered linen napkin.

"Well," Mother hesitated, picking away at the cake, "I think I'd like an apartment, but Skippy needs a place to play. He has so much energy."

"That's what parks are for," Aunt Jewell said brightly.

"Still," Mother argued, "most apartment managers won't rent to families with children. Especially if one of them is an active five-year-old boy."

Aunt Jewell turned to Skippy, who had started doing somersaults on her Oriental rug to prove how active he was. "You're going to kindergarten here, aren't you dear? That will keep you busy and out of trouble." She leaned toward Mother and volunteered, "I'll take this young man to the park while you check out the places I've marked. Just introduce your two lovely girls to the landlord, and once you're settled in you can admit to this darling little redhead."

She got up, chucked Skippy under his chin and handed him a piece of hard candy before he could make his little-brat face.

Daddy was looking doubtful. He glanced at his pocket watch to see how soon he could remove Mother from Aunt Jewell's influence. But I was thrilled. I thought apartments were glamorous. I hadn't dared to hope we might actually live in one.

Yet, a week later Mother held a house-warming dinner at our new apartment on the fourth floor of the Ashtree Arms. The smell of rosemary and garlic emanated from a rump roast sizzling in the oven, yellow chrysanthemums and glowing candles brightened the table, and classical music played softly on the radio. Warm light from Art Nouveau wall sconces filled the apartment's combination living and dining room. Mother, pretty in a new persimmon crepe dress, was beaming and even wearing a trace of makeup.

There was a pop as Uncle Clay opened a bottle of champagne he had brought, and I held out my glass while he poured a few drops of the sparkling wine on top of the cider we children were having. "To our families, Freeze No and the Ashtree Arms," Uncle Clay toasted.

"Fresno means ashtree in Spanish," Skippy volunteered, holding up his glass too and repeating the educational tidbit Daddy had told him when we moved in.

Our laughter drowned out the knock on the door, but not the angry voice of Mrs. Scranton, our landlady, as she used her master key and burst into the room. "You folks have to move," she yelled, waving a folded paper in the air. "This is an eviction notice!"

Mother's face turned as white as our tablecloth. She set her untouched glass down. "What do you mean, Mrs. Scranton? We've just moved in. I paid you a month's rent the day before yesterday."

Mrs. Scranton pointed to Skippy. "I didn't know about *him* then."

Mother's voice was softer but still firm. "I told you we had three children."

"All I saw was those two girls," the landlady said, waving the eviction notice in Sunny's and my direction. "I didn't see that redheaded boy of yours. Everyone knows boys cause more trouble and do more damage. Already all those trips he takes in my elevator are running up my electric bill!"

Mrs. Scranton's expression turned crafty as she added, "I think you tried to put something over on me, Mrs. Lockard. But. . . ." She pulled another piece of paper out of her dress front. "If you'll pay more rent, I'll let you stay. I've got the new rental agreement right here."

Mother was hesitant. I knew she liked the apartment and didn't want to move again. I also knew that, on the advice of Aunt Jewell, she had let Mrs. Scranton think all her children were girls.

Aunt Jewell drew herself up on what Daddy called her "high horse" and focused an indignant stare on Mrs. Scranton. Aunt Jewell had been a saleswoman "in retail" in Los Angeles and could be a tough negotiator. I could tell she was all set to take over and shame Mrs. Scranton into a corner. But Uncle Clay took her arm and put his finger to his lips.

It was Daddy who stepped forward, took both pieces of paper, slapped them together and handed them back to Mrs.

Scranton. "We'll move out when the rent my wife has already paid you is up. Now I'm asking you to leave." He walked over to the door and held it open until the woman, sputtering and brandishing her papers, left, warning, "If that boy does one bit of damage, you'll have to pay. And keep him out of my elevator!"

I was proud of Daddy, but when I looked around at Mother, she was crying. "I just don't know where I'll get the energy to look for another place," she told him.

Daddy, considerate but seldom demonstrative, put his arms around her. "Now, Honey, we just can't let that old bat cheat us. We have a month to find a house. Meanwhile I'll change the lock on this door in case she gets nosy."

"Dorothy," Aunt Jewell said, "I think I might have been a little naughty advising you to play a trick on Mrs. Scranton. Who would imagine she'd be such a sourpuss over a precious child like Skippy?"

She sat down next to Mother and took her hand. "Clay and I were going to tell you later, but we're planning to take you and Bruce out to Omar Khayyam's restaurant on Van Ness soon. The food is fabulous. The children will be all right in our apartment for a couple of hours. Ming and Pekie are terrific watchdogs!"

Uncle Clay poured more champagne, and Aunt Jewell put on the impractical organdy apron she had given Mother for a house-warming present and served the dinner. Mother, usually the busiest person at mealtime, sat at the table and dabbed her eyes. But, as Daddy carved the roast, we were all laughing again.

After dinner Skippy asked Daddy, "Does it really take electricity to make an elevator go up and down?"

While Daddy hesitated, no doubt pondering how to translate the entire theory of electricity into an answer a five-year-old could understand, Uncle Clay made one of his famous wry comments, "Yes it does, Skippy. Just think of all those trips up and down it could take to move your toys out."

Skippy brightened. "I'll take one Tinker Toy piece down in her elevator at a time!"

"A fine idea," Uncle Clay said.

"One sock," I chimed in. "One shoe."

"Now you've got it," Uncle Clay said.

Sunny got into the act, mentally running up Mrs. Scranton's electric bill to the sky. "One bobby pin. One toothbrush!" When Mother joined in with, "One fork, one spoon," I knew she was going to be okay. We'd have to move again, but at least we'd still be in Fresno.

CHAPTER 12

What the Cat Dragged In

Sunny

By the time we reached Fresno Mother had fine-tuned her househunting method. Besides consulting newspaper rental ads, cruising desirable neighborhoods and talking to women who were outside working in their flower gardens, she added a new wrinkle. She visited the water company, the gas and electric company, the garbage collection company and the telephone company, often managing to charm the clerks into telling her where service was being discontinued.

Furnished houses that could accommodate two adults and three children were rare in the Valley towns in which we lived, especially houses in good neighborhoods. We did not compete for housing with other members of the doodlebug party, however. Most of the men were single, and they could make do with a furnished room or a boarding house. The few men who were married rented apartments. Daddy was the only man on the party who needed a house, and furnished rental houses were in short supply. Mother's clever house hunting method, her neatly dressed, well-behaved children, Daddy's title "Civil Engineer and Licensed Surveyor" on his business card and Mother's charm and powers of persuasion won the confidence of landlords and landladies time after time.

To banish any remaining doubts from the homeowner's mind Mother would, if it seemed expedient, offer to paint or wallpaper a room, sew or repair curtains, plant a flower garden or have Daddy fix the plumbing. To a prospective landlord who was single, Mother would offer a homemade angel food cake or one of her best Sunday dinners.

After the apartment episode Mother found a house for us. "Why on earth did I ever listen to Aunt Jewell?" Mother grumbled. The house was bigger and newer than any of the other houses we had lived in since we had started traveling with Daddy. It had freshly painted spacious rooms and new curtains on all the windows. There was a dining room and a large, cheerful kitchen with a breakfast nook. For the first time since we left Lynwood, Skippy had his own bedroom and a big backyard to play in. Also, the house was only two blocks from Nancy's school and six blocks from mine.

Daddy pronounced Mother "an A-1 House Finder." Mother replied, proudly, "Just a stroke of luck, really. I talked with a very nice lady at the gas company when I stopped by to pay the bill. I had Skippy with me, and she said she has a grandson that age with curly red hair like just like Skippy's."

Basking in Daddy's praise, Mother warmed to her subject. "I told her I was looking for a house to rent, and she said that her sister, Mrs. Blodgett, was moving to San Francisco temporarily and that she wanted a nice family to rent her furnished house and take good care of it. I went to see Mrs. Blodgett right away. I helped her hang new curtains, we had a chat over a cup of tea and I convinced her that we were that nice family she was looking for."

Uncle Clay and Aunt Jewell stopped by our house frequently, usually accompanied by Jewell's two Pekinese dogs who charged all over the house yipping and yapping. "Here come those darn mutts," Daddy would say when he heard Ming and Pekie scratching at our front door.

One Saturday as we were finishing lunch Aunt Jewell pulled up in front of our house announcing her arrival with two loud toots on the horn. Looking through the screen door from my place at the table I saw Aunt Jewell take a large box out of the car and start up our walkway. There was no sign of either Ming or Pekie.

"Here's Aunt Jewell!" I called to Mother, who was in the kitchen.

Mother came out of the kitchen just as Daddy got up from the table muttering, "I don't hear those pesky pups, thank heavens." He went into the back bedroom just as Mother opened the front screen door for Aunt Jewell.

Aunt Jewell was wearing a silky blue flowered dress with long sleeves, a perky blue felt hat with a swooping iridescent feather and immaculate white gloves. Draped around her shoulders was a fox fur, the tail hanging down from her right shoulder and the glassy-eyed little face from the left. A small gold chain across her breast connected the face with the tail.

"Dorothy!" Aunt Jewell exclaimed in her effervescent tone. "Wait until you see what I bought!" She placed the box on the couch, took off her gloves and very carefully removed a gleaming, slender glass from the box. Holding the glass up to the light she flicked a vermilion-enameled fingernail against it, producing a pure, crystalline ring.

"Champagne glasses?" Mother asked, looking surprised.

"Yes! Two dozen! And you won't believe what I got them for, Dorothy! Aren't they lovely?"

"Yes, they are," Mother agreed. "Very nice."

Aunt Jewell, ecstatic over her purchase, snapped her fingernail against the glass again and again, making a series of clear, ethereal tones.

Daddy came into the room. "Do I hear the ice cream wagon?" he smiled, looking toward the street.

Aunt Jewell laughed. "Bruce, you do like your little joke! What do you think of my new treasure?"

Daddy looked at the glass which Aunt Jewell held up for his inspection. "Won't hold much beer. Hardly a swallow in there."

"Bruce!" laughed Aunt Jewell. "What a tease!" Turning to Mother she said, "Such a bargain, Dorothy! Ten cents apiece, can you believe it? The decimal was in the wrong place in the ad. They should have been one dollar a glass. They're real crystal, you know. At first the manager refused to sell them to me for a dime each, but I stood my ground! I threatened to sue! Dorothy, we can go there right now and get some for you."

Daddy left the room, shaking his head.

"I don't think so," said Mother. "They'd just be something else to pack and carry around."

"I never could resist a bargain," said Aunt Jewell, gently wrapping the glass in tissue and putting it back into the box.

"Sit down, Jewell, and have some coffee," Mother offered. Aunt Jewell sat down, adjusting her finery as she settled. Nancy and I cleared away the lunch dishes and Mother poured coffee into Aunt Jewell's cup. "How about a sandwich?" Mother asked.

"No, Dorothy, but thanks. I'll eat lunch with Clay. I need to get back home and walk Ming and Pekie. Clay won't walk them, you know, because they peed on his trousers!" Mother and Aunt Jewell chuckled.

Skippy hadn't taken his eyes off Aunt Jewell's fox fur since she entered the house. He edged over behind her chair and gently ran his fingers over the fur at the back of her neck.

"Stop that, Skippy!" Mother corrected. "Your hands might be dirty!"

Aunt Jewell laughed. "Let me see your hands, dear." She guided Skippy around to the side of her chair and inspected his hands. "They look clean, so you can feel the fur one more time if you want to." Skippy stroked the fox's tail a couple of times and then stood back looking at it in fascination.

Skippy was unable to resist touching fur. Many times

Mother had jerked him away from a fur-trimmed collar, a fur coat or stole that the wearer suddenly realized was being petted by a little redheaded boy.

Skippy reached out to stroke the fox's tail again. "Just a minute, Jewell," Mother said. "I can fix him." She left the room and came back with a pair of black gloves, which she handed to Aunt Jewell. "Put these on your lap."

When Skippy saw the gloves he backed away slowly, then ran through the kitchen and out the back door.

Mother laughed. "Works every time. He's afraid of these gloves, so I put them near whatever I want to protect."

Aunt Jewell gasped. "Well, Dorothy, I never! Wait until I tell Clay!"

That evening after dinner Nancy, Skippy and I tried to make our empty water glasses ring like Aunt Jewell's champagne glass. Daddy joined our symphony for a few rounds, then Mother said, "Come on, girls, time to get those dishes done. And don't make fun of Aunt Jewell. She has good taste."

"She probably already has those glasses in a display case with a 'do not touch' sign," said Daddy. "Just like those two Louis-something-or-other chairs she has that nobody is allowed to sit in."

"Well," said Mother, "she was well brought up and she knows quality when she sees it. It must be hard on her not to have the kind of money she had before her father lost everything."

"Probably harder on Clayton," said Daddy.

I took the same classes at Fresno High School that I had been assigned in Tulare. I settled down to do my best work in school and the teachers paid more attention to me when they realized I was a serious student.

Mother always cautioned me not to make friends in a

hurry because the kids eager to befriend a new student would most likely be "undesirables." I was to keep to myself, be nice but not too friendly, and find out which kids were the "desirables." I usually obeyed Mother, but in Fresno I met a very nice, friendly girl and decided that Mother wasn't always right. Mother thought otherwise.

Darlene was pretty. She wore brightly colored clothes and flashy jewelry. She used makeup, nail polish and perfume. Her hair was touched up with henna. I was becoming interested in makeup, hair styles and fashion and was drawn to Darlene.

I was lonely. I hadn't made any friends, and Darlene made some friendly overtures. We talked together before school and ate lunch together. "I'll do your nails for you and help you fix your hair," she offered.

I replied, "Well, maybe." How could I tell her that Mother wouldn't approve? I wanted to do something with my appearance, but I didn't know how. I saw myself as too tall, with skinny arms and legs, impossible frizzy hair and a sharp nose. Why couldn't I be pretty like Darlene?

One day as I was starting home from school Darlene caught up with me. "I'll walk home with you. I have to go that way anyhow to my aunt's house. My mother went away for a while."

I looked at Darlene's crimson mouth, her dress with the splashy yellow-gold daisies and her bright green coat. My fascination with her was replaced with a shot of fear. What would Mother say? Maybe I could shake Darlene before we got to my house. Maybe Mother had taken Skippy with her and gone shopping. Maybe Mother would be busy and wouldn't notice.

The six blocks from school to my house seemed like six miles. Darlene stuck to me like stickers from a weed patch. I couldn't think of a polite way to put her off. With each block her lipstick became brighter, her dress splashier and her coat a more brilliant green. When we arrived at my house Darlene's coat had become so luminous that it glowed, and her lips had doubled in size.

Mother opened the screen door and walked to the edge of the porch, the floor of which was about three feet above ground level. She was wearing a flour-dusted apron and her hands were firmly planted on her hips. Her stare riveted on Darlene, Mother was an imposing tower of unrelenting scrutiny.

For a few seconds Mother said nothing. Then, turning to me, her words lashed out. "Sunny! I have some work for you to do. This isn't a good day to bring home a visitor."

Without a word Darlene turned on her heels and walked away, moving her arms in an I-don't-care swing. Mother's steady gaze lingered after Darlene's retreating figure, then she switched her attention back to me.

"Who *is* that girl? Look at the way she dresses! That awful green coat, nail polish, makeup, and her hair . . . ! She looks *cheap*! I don't want you to associate with anyone like that!"

As I well knew, it would be a mistake to argue with Mother. The unjustness of her reaction to Darlene settled like a hunk of raw dough in the pit of my stomach.

"What's the job you want me to do?" I asked weakly. I was angry and hurt, but if I showed it things would just get worse.

"Change your clothes and finish the laundry. Skippy's sick and I've been busy with him all day." Mother turned abruptly and went into the house, slamming the screen door.

I changed my clothes and went into Skippy's room. He was sitting up in bed sniffling and running a toy truck over the ridges and valleys of the bed covers. I handed him a Tootsie Roll that I had been saving for a special treat. "Here, this will make you feel better. Don't let Mom see you with this and don't tell her I gave it to you."

"Oh, boy!" said Skippy, tucking the Tootsie Roll under his pillow.

I went out to the back porch to finish the laundry. Sheets,

pillowcases, towels and dishcloths were soaking in one of the twin laundry trays. I punched them up and down a few times with a cut-off broom handle, drained out the soapy water and ran them through the hand wringer into the other laundry tray. I rinsed them and ran them through the wringer several times until all the soap was out. Then I put the laundry into a basket and went outside to hang it on the clothesline. It was then that the tears came.

Mother was so unfair. She didn't even try to get to know Darlene, to find out how nice she was, how friendly. One look at Darlene and Mother didn't like her. How would I ever explain things to Darlene? I had lost my only friend, and it was Mother's fault.

I finished hanging out the laundry and wiped my eyes on a wet pillowcase. I went into the house and put the clothes basket on the back porch. Daddy had come home, and I could hear Mother talking to him in the kitchen.

". . . a real little chippy," Mother was saying. "Really cheap looking. Not the kind of girl Sunny should have as a friend."

Daddy made no comment. Then he asked, "Do you want me to go get Nancy?"

"No. I'll pick her up. Keep an eye on Skippy. I'll be right back."

I went into Skippy's room, which was off the back porch. He had chocolate from the Tootsie Roll on his face but none, fortunately, on the blanket. I took some toilet tissue from the roll on the table near his bed, dipped the tissue in his glass of water and cleaned his face. I picked up the candy wrapper and stuffed it in my pocket. I wasn't in the mood for any more reprimands from Mother.

Mother thoroughly approved of my next friend, Helen, who lived in a big old house with her physician father and invalid mother. Helen always went home as soon as school was out, and I frequently went with her. She would go directly to her mother's bedroom to see if she needed anything, then the housekeeper would serve us cookies and milk in the living room. Mother didn't care if I was late coming home from school if I had been at Helen's. "That's the kind of girl you should be friends with," Mother pronounced. "She's a nice girl and comes from a good family." And, I thought, she doesn't wear nail polish or colorful clothing or do her hair like a movie star's. The fact that Helen's father was a physician was a definite plus in Mother's eyes. I imagined Mother writing to relatives and friends, "Sunny's new friend is the daughter of a prominent local medical doctor."

I didn't have to explain anything to Darlene. She *knew*. She smiled at me in the halls of the school but didn't approach me.

"How could you *possibly* befriend a girl like that?" Mother had asked me.

"I liked her," I answered. "She . . . well, she kind of reminded me of Aunt Irene and Aunt Jewell. The way they dress, I mean."

"Oh! There's no comparison!" Mother stated. "Girls who deck themselves out like Christmas trees before they even graduate from high school are just asking for trouble!"

Nancy

In Fresno, although I began junior high and liked having a different teacher for each class, it was harder than ever to make friends. Most of the girls Mother would want me to associate with belonged to tight cliques. Whenever I caught up with one of them to say, "Hi," or ask about homework, she would walk faster and join her crowd. Then they would all look back at me as if I were a pesky stray pup.

"You're just the new girl," Mother would say. "Keep trying. You'll make friends."

But, in each small, close-knit San Joaquin Valley town, I

was lucky to make one friend, and she was invariably a stray like myself.

In Stockton it had been Muriel Jo whom Mother tolerated because her parents operated a dance studio. In Fresno it was Memory. Memory was polite and earned respectable enough grades but always seemed to be coming down with a cold or recovering from one. Memory's mother wouldn't let her wash her hair when she was sniffling, so it stuck to her skull and forehead in oily brown strands. And, Memory was a whiner, something not tolerated at our house.

The first time I brought Memory home for cookies and milk after school Mother looked at her and pursed her lips. It was raining and drops of water stood out on Memory's hair with no hope of being absorbed. When Memory took out her handkerchief and blew her nose, Mother, ever on the alert for germs, could see there wasn't a clean corner left.

When my new friend looked up at Mother and whined, "I have another cold, and I haven't even got over my last one," I knew she had flunked Mother's suitability test.

But it was worse than that. When Mother described Memory to Daddy, she said, "Imagine giving that child a name like *Memory*! Everyone can guess what act it refers to. No wonder she creeps around like something the cat dragged in. I wish Nancy would make friends with some of the nice girls in her classes for heaven's sake!"

Mother didn't realize that the "nice girl" circles were closed to outsiders. In the thirties, the wives of "solid citizens" in the San Joaquin Valley towns were proud full-time homemakers very much involved in the community and their children's lives. At their "improvement" clubs, bridge parties and church gatherings they formed social sets and carefully selected their daughters' friends to fit in.

Families who pioneered in the Valley tended to stay put, and newcomers, such as our family, were not accepted until it was deemed, after years of community observation, that they would uphold all the local mores.

In Lynwood, Sunny and I were the center of our own clique. Mother joined the Parent Teachers Association as soon as Sunny entered kindergarten and was such a constant presence at school that many assumed she was on the staff. Judging by the photos of the little girls at our birthday parties wearing bonnets, organdy dresses and patent leather Mary Janes, Mother too must have selected our playmates to fit in with her idea of suitable friends.

Still, she never understood that this same closed social system was at work in Tulare, Stockton, Fresno and Delano. She seemed to blame Sunny and me for befriending the other outcasts—the girls like us on the periphery of their classmates' social life. And I blamed myself for not being accepted. Surely some flaw visible to everyone but me must cling to me like the Valley's tule fog.

That night as Sunny and I undressed for bed I asked her, "Does Mother call your friend Darlene 'something the cat dragged in'?"

"No," Sunny answered, snapping out the light. "She calls her 'cheap.' "

CHAPTER 13

The Ranch

Sunny

I was Mama Dot's first grandchild and she doted on me. I remember being the center of attention and receiving toys, clothes and dancing lessons which my parents could not have afforded.

Photographs taken of me in those preschool years, carefully hand-colored with special thin oil paints by Mother, show pretty, delicate dresses of voile or organza, shiny patent leather Mary Jane shoes and embroidered bonnets trimmed with lace.

I remember spending a lot of time at Mama Dot's house on Third Avenue in Los Angeles. The spacious interior of that two-story bungalow is as clear in my mind as if I had been there yesterday, and I can taste the juicy persimmons from the tree in the backyard. I often spent the night with Mama Dot and Granddad. Special occasions, like Christmas, were enjoyed there with the whole family.

Granddad was a salesman for Albers Brothers Milling Company. He was a soft-spoken, very sweet, easy-going chunk of a man who spoke fluent German. I remember him as tall and somewhat stooped, with large hands, a square, kind face and a full head of white hair. His parents had come over from the old country and settled in Wisconsin, where

Granddad grew up speaking both English and German. When we were little he often held Nancy and me on his lap and sang German lullabies to us. We loved the soothing foreign sounds of the songs and begged for more.

Granddad tried to teach us to count in German, and we repeated "ein, zwei, drei, vier, fünf." Sometimes we got all the way to "zehn." Unfortunately, however, neither Nancy nor I learned any German expressions, and we were not encouraged to do so by anyone else in the family. Counting to ten was as far as we got.

Mama Dot made fun of the fact that Granddad spoke German. In those days of the chauvinistic American melting pot assimilation myth people were anxious to shake off their foreign origins and become "true" Americans. Speaking a language other than English was not considered an asset. Also, the prejudice against Germans during World War I caused my grandparents to temporarily remove the "c" from their name—Granddad's last name was "Schuster"—in hopes that the name would seem less German.

Mama Dot was from New Orleans by way of Texas and Kansas. I have no idea what brought my grandparents to California. Family rumor had it that Mama Dot ran away from home in Louisiana at the age of sixteen to marry Granddad. Considering Mama Dot's adventuresome and often non-conforming nature, it *could* have happened.

When Mother was in her teens she sometimes came home from school to find a sink full of dirty dishes, a basket of unironed clothes and a note pinned to the wall which read: "Dear Dorothy, I've gone to visit Aunt Belle. Back in two or three weeks. M."

Aunt Belle, Mama Dot's sister, lived in the Bronx. Mama Dot loved to gamble, and on these trips to see Belle Mama Dot would go to New Orleans and take a boat to New York, gambling all the way. She returned to Los Angeles by cross-country train and, I suspect, may have enjoyed a few poker hands on the way back. While Mama Dot was away Mother had to cook and keep house for her father, two brothers and Uncle Buddy, who lived with them.

In 1930 Mama Dot and Granddad sold their home in Los Angeles and built a house on the Mojave desert ten miles west of Victorville, in Adelanto. Granddad had developed arthritis, and his stiff fingers could no longer write out the sales slips for Albers Brothers customers. It was thought that the dry climate and the hot summers on the desert would benefit him. In those days a change of climate or a long sea voyage was a common medical prescription for a variety of ailments.

My grandparents' desert home was named "Journey's End," after the James Earle Fraser bronze statue "End of the Trail," but we always called it "The Ranch." Daddy designed the house and supervised its construction. He often drove to Adelanto from Lynwood to talk with the contractor and leave instructions.

One Saturday I went with Daddy to Adelanto to see how construction at The Ranch was coming along. "I don't think we'll need chains to go over the Cajon Pass today," Daddy said. It was a clear, bright winter day. We drove from Lynwood over the San Gabriel Mountains and then up Highway 395 through Adelanto to The Ranch. The air was chilly and fresh. Patches of snow lay among the sagebrush and Joshua trees.

At The Ranch Daddy pulled into the long driveway and parked on the concrete apron in front of the double garage. "Let's hang this up," he said, unwrapping the wooden sign he had made with "Journey's End" carefully hand carved in script on a brown background which matched the trim on the house.

"Bring the toolbox, Sunny," Daddy said as we got out of the car. I took the toolbox out of the car, opened it and handed Daddy the tools he asked for. Soon the trim brown sign announcing the end of a long journey was hanging in the archway of the covered front porch.

Mama Dot never liked the sign. She thanked Daddy for making it, but later I heard her say to Mother, "That was nice of Bruce, but I can't say I like the message."

A pickup truck with "Gerald Potts & Sons, General Contractors" lettered on the side pulled into the driveway. Daddy said, "There's Mr. Potts now." A sturdy man with a desert-worn face got out of the truck.

Daddy walked over to the pickup and the two men shook hands. "Thought I'd find you here, Mr. Lockard," said Mr. Potts. "Ready for a look around?"

"We were just going to do that. This is my daughter, Sunny. She's eight years old."

I shook hands with Mr. Potts and we went inside. The house, a two-bedroom, one bath Spanish stucco, looked huge to me. "Looks pretty good," Daddy remarked.

"The trim in the bathroom and kitchen will be finished next week," said Mr. Potts. "Let's look at the room in the back of the garage."

We walked through the double garage and opened the door to what was to be Uncle Buddy's room. It had two big windows and an outside door which opened onto a deck. Daddy opened the door and walked out on the deck. "Nice job," he said.

"We'll put the stain on next week if it don't rain or snow," said Mr. Potts.

Daddy glanced at the chicken houses, which seemed to be quite a distance back from the main house. Mr. Potts appeared to read his thoughts. "You'll be glad they're that far back once you get the chickens, Mr. Lockard. Especially when the roosters start crowing."

Daddy laughed. "Well, that's for sure. Now, let's see how the bathroom turned out."

Mr. Potts shook his head. "Had quite a time with that. Plumber didn't believe the specifications, said there was mistakes, and refused to do it. I told him no, that you were an engineer, and that we had checked the figures several times. Finally I had to agree to take full responsibility."

Mr. Potts opened the door to Uncle Buddy's new bathroom. The child-sized toilet was very low. Both the wash basin and the valve handles for the shower were placed about three feet from the floor. "Exactly according to the blueprints," Mr. Potts emphasized. "You should've heard that plumber! He swore it was for kids, if it wasn't bad figuring."

Daddy said, "It couldn't be better, Mr. Potts. Mr. Douglas will be very pleased. It will make his life a lot easier. He'll really enjoy that deck, too."

"This Mr. Douglas . . . he's a relative?"

"Yes. My wife's uncle. He had polio when he was a child and lost the use of his legs."

"Don't he use a wheelchair?" Mr. Potts looked puzzled.

"No, he doesn't, and you'd be amazed at how he gets around without one. As long as everything is down low where he can reach it he does just fine."

Then I spoke up. "You ought to see Uncle Buddy! He scoots around all over the place!"

"Well, well," Mr. Potts remarked. "Imagine that. Imagine! Mr. Lockard, hope everything's to your satisfaction."

"It's fine. The Schusters want to move in four or five weeks from now."

"Can't see why not, Mr. Lockard, if it don't rain or snow. There's the deck and some outside trim, you see. And a whitewash on the chicken houses."

I was as pleased as Daddy was with Uncle Buddy's room, deck and special bathroom. Uncle Buddy was Mama Dot's brother. The polio he had as a child left him partially disabled. Parts of his body never grew normally. His head and hands were average size, but his chest was small and his legs useless. His thin, wiry arms were normal length and had grown strong in moving the rest of his body about. To outsiders he must have appeared grotesque, but to us he was just our Uncle Buddy, part of our family, and we were fond of him.

There was nothing wrong with Uncle Buddy's brain. He was smart. He kept up with events of the day by reading the newspaper and listening to the radio. He loved to play cards, especially poker and pinochle, and he was an excellent player. He was cheerful, optimistic, upbeat and always ready with a clever quip or joke.

Uncle Buddy got around the house on his own by using his arms to lift his body. He moved from his bed to a lower chair and then to the floor, where he scooted along quite well. He showered, shaved and dressed himself. The new bathroom would make these tasks much easier for him.

Mr. Potts said goodbye and left. Daddy closed up the house and we got into the car. "I'm hungry," I said.

Daddy started the car and backed out of the driveway. "Sunny, let's see if we can find a good place to eat the lunch your mother fixed. Maybe by one of those Joshua trees."

Nancy

I had been sent to our grandparents' home on the Mojave desert when I was nearly nine in the hope that the desert air would help me recover from an appendectomy. Mama Dot enrolled me in the fourth grade in the tiny town of Adelanto where the first to eighth grades were taught in one room, and one of my most vivid recollections was riding my Elgin Red Bird bike home from school in a dust storm.

For five miles I pedaled along the asphalt road in zigzags to miss the tumbleweeds as they careened through the Joshua trees and across the road with the sand. When I finally reached the foot of the driveway, I got off the bike and put my head down, squinting my eyes almost shut. Now the storm's force was hitting me head on, and I couldn't go any further toward the house. Although I knew I shouldn't get sand on the chain, I set my bike down and curled up like a tortoise, drawing my head and legs into the shell of my starched school dress. The sand hissed as it filled my hair and swirled up into my face, making it hard to breathe.

When I felt Mama Dot's hands on my shoulders, pulling me toward the house, I was surprised. Her usual style was to let me work out difficulties by myself. "Come on," she urged. "Leave the bike out here. Granddad will get it later. Hurry, child! It's only going to get worse."

Gratefully I took Mama Dot's hand, and together we struggled toward the house.

As soon as Mama Dot and I made it to the back door, I felt Granddad's strong arms around me. I knew he was trying to distract me and hide his concern at the same time when he said, "Those eggs down in the cellar need to be weighed, Nancy, and, as I recall, you're a pretty good egg weigher. The egg man's coming tomorrow, so we have to be ready. How about it?"

Sand sprinkled out of my hair as I shook my head in assent then followed Granddad down rough wooden stairs into the cellar under the kitchen. The small, concrete-walled room was cool and the air refreshingly damp. Granddad pointed proudly to four buckets of eggs he'd gathered from his spotless pens of white leghorns.

We each sat on an empty wooden box. A third box between us held the egg weigher, a balance scale with a weight on one end and a metal ring that held one egg on the other. First we cleaned each egg with a damp cloth to remove feed, straw or excrement. Then we set it in the oval ring.

"Remember," Granddad said, "if the ring sinks all the way down, the egg is a large one. If it balances evenly, it's a medium. And I guess you already know what the small ones do."

"Stay up in the air like Skippy on the teeter totter," I said while Granddad chuckled. Together we polished and weighed each egg, and I sighed with contentment, wondering how Granddad managed to run The Ranch when I was not around.

He was scrupulous about the weights, always moving a large egg back to the medium category if there was any doubt. We kept most of the small eggs for our own use, and I knew I could expect to eat plenty of fried eggs, scrambled eggs, hard-boiled eggs, egg salad sandwiches and omelets while staying on the desert. Mama Dot and Granddad always set a bowl of hot yellow peppers on the table to break the monotony of our menu, and Granddad would eat them whole without ever changing his expression. I ate them too, hiccuping, gulping iced tea and feeling sweat break out on my scalp.

After we had weighed all the eggs, Granddad and I went to visit Uncle Buddy in his room at the rear of the garage.

"Egg man's coming tomorrow," Uncle Buddy greeted us. "Won't see you much, Nancy Hanks, because we're going to Barstow." Uncle Buddy winked. "Probably see my sweetie at the Roadrunner Café."

The egg man, a distributor, had befriended Uncle Buddy when he picked up the eggs Granddad sold him. Once a week he lifted Uncle Buddy up onto the passenger seat of his truck and took him on his rounds. This trip, plus Mama Dot and Granddad's weekly poker games, were the high points in Uncle Buddy's life. Uncle Buddy's flirtation in Barstow was adding a twinkle to his eye. It didn't surprise me a bit that a woman would find him attractive. He was as full of charm as the rest of the men in Mother's family.

Granddad came out of Uncle Buddy's shower wearing clean work pants and a plaid shirt. As he ran a comb through his thick silver hair, he said, "Nancy and I are going up to the castle for dinner, Jake. Sis will bring your plate out in a bit." Granddad always reminded me that the chicken pens were his castle, and the house was Mama Dot's.

His close relationship to Uncle Buddy was evident by the nicknames they gave each other. Granddad often called

Uncle Buddy "Jake" or "Lone Star," and Uncle Buddy called Granddad "Ole" or "The Big Swede" despite Granddad's German ancestry. And, everyone called Mama Dot "Sis" much of the time. Being called "Nancy Hanks" made me feel like a special member of the nicknames club.

"I want to eat out here," I said. "May I?"

"Maybe we'll all eat out here," Granddad suggested, pulling a drop-leaf table over toward Uncle Buddy's daybed. But when he came back from the house, he had just three plates of fried chicken with sliced tomatoes and white bread on a tray. Of course, there were hot yellow peppers, too. "Sis isn't hungry." Granddad said, pulling up a couple of chairs. "Hey, Jake, see that you don't get into any trouble in Barstow tomorrow."

"Trouble is my middle name," Uncle Buddy bragged as he bit into a crusty chicken thigh and a yellow pepper at the same time.

When I lived at The Ranch, I tried to spend time with both Granddad and his polio disabled brother-in-law, Uncle Buddy, because I imagined they were lonely.

Because of the long hours each spent alone, it puzzled me that they seldom returned the offered affection of their small gray dog, Lobo, who seemed to be smiling at us whenever he folded his alert ears back.

"Don't get too friendly with Lobo," Granddad warned me whenever he saw me petting the dog. "He's part coyote. At night when the coyotes out on the desert start howling, Lobo will sit right out in the driveway and answer them."

It was true. I had heard their eerie chorus many times.

Uncle Buddy added, "Some full moon Lobo will hear a lady coyote and go trotting off to court her. You'll see."

Of course I adopted Lobo anyway and slipped bits of fried chicken off my plate into my pocket to give to him. Mama Dot's method of feeding little Lobo was to dip exactly three pieces of bread in the grease left in her big black skillet after dinner. Then she would open the kitchen door and throw a piece at a time high in the air to Lobo. Leaping to catch each slice, Lobo would gulp twice before positioning himself with quivering expectation for another piece. He seemed to know the third slice was his last, but he whined and wagged his tail and did a little dance every night before giving up.

I knew Lobo was always hungry, but I couldn't augment his meal much without arousing suspicion. My grandparents' table wasn't laden with food the way Mother's was.

One day a chicken was missing from the pens out back and the next day another was gone. Feathers and a few tell-tale parts clung to the diamond mesh chicken wire. The next day, Lobo disappeared. Uncle Buddy told me Lobo had gone to live with his coyote sweetheart, but I knew Lobo was dead. I had come across his stiff little body when I walked far out on the desert looking for him. I also knew that Granddad had killed Lobo with his 12-gauge shotgun.

I cried when I stroked Lobo's dull fur matted with spots of blood, but I couldn't hate Granddad. I knew the chicken ranchers' code: dogs that steal chickens have to be destroyed. Granddad didn't tell me what he'd done, but I knew he wouldn't deny it if I asked him. I never did. I just pretended I believed Uncle Buddy's story. Sometimes, though, I worried that my fried chicken tidbits had given Lobo his taste for white leghorns. And I wondered, when I heard a coyote cry at night, if Lobo had a sweetheart who missed him as much as I did.

From The Ranch I could see only one other house, that of the stocky, ruddy-faced German, Carl Braun, who had built a neat cement block house in the center of his vineyard. When Carl, in coveralls but no shirt, walked over to give Granddad a gallon jug of his homemade wine, he and Granddad would stand in the front driveway and visit, speaking in German.

Mama Dot would frown, give Carl a brisk nod and find something to do inside. Although she respected Carl as a farmer and good neighbor, she never invited him into her house.

Later, though, when Carl asked his mother in Germany to pick out a bride and send her to him, Mama Dot took pity on the young woman. She drove her into Adelanto and nearby Victorville to shop, invited her over for lemonade and helped her learn English. Hilda, younger and taller than Carl and quietly resigned to her arranged marriage, reciprocated by bringing over plates of German cookies. I didn't like the hard ones flavored with anise and was disappointed when I unknowingly selected one. I knew I had to eat it anyway and prayed Hilda wouldn't hand me another just like it when I said politely, "Thank you. That was delicious."

Although I was close to the two men on The Ranch, I felt distant from Mama Dot—barred from her approval for no reason that I could identify.

She seldom corrected me but didn't praise me either. She simply went on with her life when I was visiting, including me but never fussing.

I was even part of the Saturday night poker parties, taking the role of bartender, which consisted of carrying empty shot glasses to the kitchen and refilling them with bourbon. I was only allowed to return them to the players when cards were being dealt or shuffled as I could not be trusted to keep a poker face after I'd glanced at someone's hand.

One night in the kitchen I decided to taste the liquor, mumbling the often heard "Dealer takes one" as I downed a shot. The bourbon seemed to explode in flames in my mouth and throat. Deciding, as I coughed and gulped water, that bourbon was even more of a challenge than yellow peppers, I made my way to the sofa and fell asleep to the sound of cards being snapped on the table and poker chips scraped into piles.

I loved to read, but since there weren't any children's books in the house, I simply tackled whatever was in the bookcase or magazine rack. During the long afternoons in Mama Dot's living room, darkened with wine-colored velvet drapery heavily lined against the desert heat, I read Granddad's poultry journals, French novelist Emile Zola's *"Nana,"* and searched French satirist Anatole France's novels for the spicy sections the drawings promised. *"Penguin Island," "The Crime of Sylvestre Bonnard"* and *"The Red Lily"* were heavy going, though, and descriptions of a heroine in "black satin . . . scintillating with lights of flame" did not hold my interest long.

No doubt for my benefit, Emily Post's etiquette book sat on the coffee table, and I would flip through to determine when it was proper for a matron to leave a calling card or whether one would be in danger of outshining the bride if one wore a cream-colored dress to the wedding.

Upon opening one fat book, I found the center part had been cut out. Later I discovered one of Mama Dot's dashing sons had made good use of this "reading material" to accommodate a whiskey flask before the repeal of prohibition. I found another book, *"The Playthings of Desire,"* gone from the bookcase one day and imagined even broadminded Mama Dot had decided it was not for my eyes.

I tried out all of Mama Dot's lotions, from smelly turtle oil and green avocado lotion to fragrant Pond's cold cream. I bathed in Camay, "The Soap of Beautiful Women." I filed my nails with delicate little emery boards and plastered green wave set on my straight hair. I marveled at the midnight blue bottle with a crescent moon and star "suggestive of romance" as I dabbed my earlobes with "subtly enchanting Evening in Paris" perfume which Uncle Buddy called "Afternoon in San Diego."

I slept with my grandmother, and only once or twice during the night would we hear a car pass The Ranch and drive on into the desert night. The noise of the car's engine, like the whistle of a train, had a haunting effect as it grew nearer then faded away. Homesick, I would wish I were in the car with Mother, Daddy, Sunny and Skippy again.

Before we closed our eyes, Mama Dot would talk to me, once taking me on a pretend trip on an ocean liner leaving from New York. She advised me what to pack in steamer trunks, what to wear at the captain's party and how much to tip the stewards.

"Now," she said, staring at the ceiling. "Here's something to remember. Never let a strange man buy you a cocktail. If you do, he'll feel entitled to take advantage of you. You must always act like a lady."

Another night she said, "It's just as easy to fall in love with a rich man as a poor man. Love is highly overrated, but you'll always need money."

I had my own ideas of love, mainly formed by the movies. I would marry a dying poet and nurse him through his last days. Or, if I met a scalawag, I knew I could turn his life around with the purity of my love. If I married a soldier and he were killed after the first night of our honeymoon, I would enter a convent and never think of another man.

Without discussing her own marriage or the fact that she and Granddad had separate rooms, Mama Dot mused, "If you have plenty of money, there's no reason to marry at all. You can travel, live in Europe, do anything you want."

"What if you want a child?" I asked, pulling the covers up around me.

"Just find a charming wealthy man and have one," she said, flipping over to face the closet. Obviously Mama Dot wondered what the problem would be although I knew Mother's ideas were vastly different.

At The Ranch I usually woke up before Mama Dot and sat by the window to watch the sun come up from behind the purple mountain to the east. As the stars faded and light began to fill the sky, I always thought how different my mother was from her mother.

Sunny

We spent the Christmas of 1936 with Mama Dot, Granddad and Uncle Buddy at The Ranch. For several weeks before we left for Adelanto Mother was busy at her sewing machine making Christmas gifts. She made a nightgown for Mama Dot, a long nightshirt for Granddad and pajamas for everyone else, all out of thick, soft cotton flannel. She also made a shirt for Daddy, school dresses for Nancy and me and a sailor outfit for Skippy. Daddy gave Nancy and me some money for our Christmas shopping: white handkerchiefs for Daddy, notepaper for Mother, a toy truck for Skippy, Prince Albert tobacco and cigarette papers for Uncle Buddy, a pair of work gloves for Granddad and a perfume bottle encrusted with glass beads and gold leaves for Mama Dot. I bought Coty's bath powder for Nancy and she bought Evening in Paris cologne for me. Even though we knew what we were getting for Christmas, we still wanted everything wrapped up and put under the tree.

We loaded our car with food, bedding and Christmas gifts and drove from Fresno down Highway 99 through patches of low tule fog to Bakersfield. From there we climbed out of the tule fog and over the Tehachapi Mountains. We went through Mojave and Boron, turning right on Highway 395, which took us to The Ranch.

That year there was plenty of snow on the desert. Daddy stopped a couple of times to let Nancy, Skippy and me make snowballs, a rare treat for us, since we were strictly a summer sports family. The air was refreshing, the sky blue with bright sun. Our car had no heater, so the three of us snuggled under warm blankets in the rear seat. Skippy, up to his usual peskiness, sneaked a handful of snow into the car and tried to put some down our backs, but he was no match for two strong girls.

At The Ranch Nancy and I put all of the Christmas presents under the tree which Mama Dot had decorated with silver icicles and blue and silver ornaments. Then we went out to Uncle Buddy's room in the back of the garage to say hello.

"Uncle Buddy!" Nancy exclaimed excitedly. "Sunny and I just put the Christmas presents under the tree and don't you dare change the tags!" Nancy wagged her index finger at Uncle Buddy, who made a display of looking guilty. The three of us laughed.

"I'm going to stay up all night, Uncle Buddy, to be sure you don't creep in and get the presents all mixed up!" I warned.

Nancy and I knew, of course, that Uncle Buddy would not be able to go on his own from his room to the house to tamper with Christmas presents, but we pretended that it was possible. Uncle Buddy was very self-sufficient in his room, but he had to be carried into the house for the Saturday night poker games and any special event, like Christmas.

In the Los Angeles house Uncle Buddy's room was at the top of the stairs. This did not isolate him very much because, with his thin but strong arms, he was capable of going up and down the carpeted stairs. At The Ranch it was a different matter. Between Uncle Buddy's room and the main house there were expanses of rough concrete to negotiate, plus the possibility, at certain times of the year, of running into an unfriendly rattlesnake.

Nancy and I loved to joke with Uncle Buddy about the time he switched the cards on all the Christmas presents. This happened when we were at our grandparents' house in Los Angeles. One Christmas Eve after we had all gone to bed and were sleeping soundly Uncle Buddy worked his way down the stairs and switched the cards on the gifts under the tree. On Christmas morning when I opened one of my packages and found a can of Prince Albert tobacco, Mama Dot received a pair of flannel pajamas intended for Uncle Buddy and Daddy unwrapped *"A Child's Garden of Verses,"* we began to suspect something. Then the remaining presents were opened and given to their intended recipients, among much hilarity. Uncle Buddy thoroughly enjoyed his trick, and he chuckled about it for weeks afterward.

We heard the sound of boots scraping the doormat on Uncle Buddy's deck. "Here comes The Big Swede," said Uncle Buddy with a smile, lighting one of his hand-rolled cigarettes.

The door opened and Granddad came in. He removed the old wool cap from his thick mass of snow-white hair and took off his mackinaw. "Well, well, girls," he said, smiling at Nancy and me. "Here already. Well, well."

"Say, Ole," said Uncle Buddy, "can you imagine? The girls are afraid I'll switch the tags on the Christmas gifts! Now, would I do that?"

Granddad chuckled. "You've got to watch Lone Star over there," he said, pointing to Uncle Buddy. "No telling what he'll be up to next."

Uncle Buddy laughed. "Guess I've got quite a reputation!"

"So, Jake," said Granddad. "What have you been up to? Telling the girls some of those Texas tall tales?"

"Would I do that?" protested Uncle Buddy, with a look of mock innocence.

"Uncle Buddy!" I said. "Remember how you used to tell us that you were only nine years old?"

All four of us laughed. Granddad pulled a chair over to the window, took out his pipe, filled it with tobacco and lighted it. There was a tap on the door leading to the garage, then Mama Dot entered with Uncle Buddy's dinner tray. "Dinner in half an hour," she said. "You girls come on in and let Uncle Buddy eat his dinner."

"Thanks, Sis," said Uncle Buddy to Mama Dot. "Smells good."

"Dorothy brought a chocolate cake. I'll bring you some

later." With that, Mama Dot turned on her heels and went out.

Granddad stood up. "Guess I'd better get cleaned up. Some pinochle after dinner, Jake?"

"Sure 'nuff," replied Uncle Buddy, taking the dish towel cover off of the tray.

As Nancy and I followed Mama Dot out of Uncle Buddy's room and through the garage we both paused for a moment and looked at the rough wood supports which held up the roof and separated the two sides of the double garage. Although Nancy did not say anything, I knew that she was thinking, as I was, of the time several years ago when Daddy had a bad accident in the garage, and how, although we children did not realize it then, we came close to losing our father.

I was 11-years-old when it happened. One Saturday morning we drove to The Ranch from Lynwood. The next morning before the sun was up Mother and Mama Dot roused Skippy, Nancy and me from our warm beds and put us into the car in our pajamas. When Daddy got into the car and sat sideways in the front passenger seat I knew that something was wrong. Mother said, "Girls, take care of Skippy." Daddy was miserably silent while Mother drove directly to a hospital in Los Angeles.

While Daddy was in the operating room Mother told Nancy and me what had happened. "Your father went to the garage last night to get the army cots for you children to sleep on. You know how we always put you in the big beds at The Ranch and move you to cots when we turn in.

"Well, Daddy stepped on the bumper of Mama Dot's Nash to reach the cots, which were overhead in the garage. He should have used a stepladder, but he didn't. His feet slipped and he fell backwards against the rough wood supports in the garage. A large pointed piece of wood broke off and went into his back. It was just like someone stabbing your poor father with a dagger.

"I drove Daddy ten miles to the nearest doctor, in

Victorville. It was about midnight when we got there, and I had to pound hard on the doctor's door to wake him up. The doctor took the piece of wood out but he said that he couldn't get all the splinters. He told us to go to the nearest big hospital as soon as possible because your father would need surgery to get all the splinters out."

Nancy and I, in our pajamas, sat next to Mother. Skippy was asleep on a couch on the opposite side of the waiting room. The first warm rays of the early morning sun slanted in through the windows.

Mother reassured us. "Don't worry, girls. Your father was badly hurt but he'll be all right. Look, here comes the doctor now."

I was concerned about Daddy, but I wasn't worried. It didn't occur to me that my father, who was such an important constant in my life, could die.

The doctor smiled and patted Mother on the shoulder. "Mr. Lockard's doing fine. One splinter was close to the right lung, but we got them all. He's had quite a shock, but he'll recover well."

Mother breathed a sigh of relief. "I'd better get these children home," she said.

Dinner at The Ranch was always the same: a platter piled high with fried chicken, a heaping bowl of mashed potatoes, chicken gravy, sliced tomatoes, hot yellow chili peppers, string beans or peas, bread or biscuits and one of Mother's special cakes. The aroma of fried chicken coming from the kitchen caused Nancy and me to quicken our pace, run across the driveway and rush through the back door to our places at the dining room table.

"Granddad," asked Nancy, "can I help you grade eggs tomorrow?" She was chomping on a drumstick, her favorite piece.

"I'm not grading eggs tomorrow, because it's Christmas Day. But in the afternoon you can help me feed the chickens. They have to eat no matter what day it is."

"Can I help too?" I asked, taking a second helping of mashed potatoes.

"*May* I help," Mother corrected.

Nancy and I liked to follow Granddad around when he was doing chores. We fed the chickens, watered the alfalfa patch, gathered eggs and helped clean and grade them. In retrospect, we probably weren't much help, but we liked being with Granddad. We sneaked into the shed where the chicken feed was stored and ate handfuls of chicken mash. When Mother caught us she was horrified. "Spit it out, girls! No telling what's in that stuff! It'll make you sick!"

"Granddad," I asked, "can we . . . may we . . . help you shoot jack rabbits?"

Mother, Mama Dot and Daddy laughed. "We'll see," Granddad replied. "I haven't seen too many jack rabbits around lately."

Granddad had planted a row of young trees along the road on the edge of his property. He carried buckets of water to the trees because he didn't have a hose that would reach that far. Sometimes at dusk jack rabbits would come out and gnaw on the tender trunks of the little trees, often killing them. Granddad had lost several trees to the rabbits and he wasn't going to lose any more if he could help it. In the evenings after dinner he frequently sat on the porch under the "Journey's End" sign and shot at jack rabbits with his old 12-gauge shotgun.

Nancy and I liked to sit on the porch with Granddad and watch for rabbits. We were very quiet. Our sharp young eyes usually spotted a rabbit before Granddad could see it and one of us would whisper, "Over there, Granddad!" and the shotgun would blast away. We were too far away from the trees to actually hit a rabbit with the shotgun, but the noise frightened them away.

Granddad let Nancy and me each have a turn with the shotgun, but once was enough for us. "Hold the gun tight against your shoulder," Granddad cautioned Nancy, "or it could knock you out of your chair." When Nancy pulled the trigger the recoil sent her flying off the porch in a heap on the sand. Anticipating Nancy's reaction, Granddad had grabbed the gun as soon as it was fired.

Being older and stronger, I thought I could manage much better than Nancy. "Tight against your shoulder, now," said Granddad. I pressed the stock of the shotgun so tightly against my shoulder that it hurt. I fired. The kick of the gun almost sent me and my chair over backwards. Granddad, who had moved in behind me, steadied my chair and caught the gun. "Whew!" I muttered. I remembered a photograph of Osa Johnson standing upright after she had fired her gun. How did she do it?

Nancy and I cleared the table while Mama Dot made coffee and Mother cut the cake. "Sunny, take this to Buddy," Mother said, handing me a plate with a generous slice of rich chocolate cake.

"Sunny, tell Jake I'll bring him some coffee when I come out," added Granddad. Turning to the others he said, "I promised Jake a game of pinochle after dinner."

I took the cake to Uncle Buddy. "Didn't jump over any snakes, did you?" he teased.

"Only a couple," I replied, laughing.

"Glad you didn't drop my cake!" Uncle Buddy chuckled softly as he ground out his brown paper cigarette.

We both knew, of course, that rattlesnakes weren't out in the winter, and that in the late spring everyone would have to look out for them. They could be under piles of wood or debris, under a bush or tree, in corners of the garage or patio, under the car, in the chicken houses or the feed shed or lying on a warm driveway or road at night. There were harmless gopher snakes, too.

One summer at The Ranch I opened the back door to go outside and saw a snake slithering by. I had already started to take a step, so I quickly changed the step to a jump and leaped over the snake, landing on concrete and skinning a knee. I yelled for Daddy, who came running. When he saw the snake and then me sprawled, terrified, in the driveway he said, "It's only a gopher snake, Sunny! Won't hurt you." This is the incident Uncle Buddy teased me about.

All the locals had their snake tales. Carl Braun, who had a small winery just down the road, was bitten by a rattlesnake one day while he was picking grapes in his vineyard. He jumped into his pickup and drove 10 miles to the nearest doctor, in Victorville. Mr. Johnson, who lived on the edge of town, found a rattler curled up under his car in the garage, and Mrs. Bogarde, who sold fresh butter, found one in her cellar. You never went into dark places without a flashlight nor did you poke around in piles of *anything* without a long stick to do the poking. These were the rules in rattlesnake country.

"Granddad will bring you some coffee, Uncle Buddy," I said.

"Tell Ole to be sure it's good and hot!" he replied.

Back in the house everyone was eating chocolate cake. I sat down to eat mine.

Granddad said, "Did you tell Jake I'd bring his coffee?"

"Sure," I replied. "He said to be sure it's hot. What a big joker Uncle Buddy is! He teased me about that time I jumped over the snake!"

Everyone laughed. Nancy chimed in, "Uncle Buddy said we'd better watch out or he'd switch all the cards on the Christmas presents again!"

"He probably would," said Mother, "if he could get into

the house on his own. Remember that camping trip? He does like to play tricks." Everyone laughed again.

Granddad chuckled. He got up from the table, poured a mug of hot coffee for Uncle Buddy and went out the back door.

I would never forget that camping trip. It was a three-day trip, and we asked Mama Dot to go with us. She insisted on supplying the canned goods we'd need because she had so much on hand. It was her way of sharing expenses. We lived in Lynwood at the time, and it was just before Mama Dot, Granddad and Uncle Buddy moved to the desert.

When we reached our camping spot Daddy gave me the job of unpacking the canned goods. After I had removed a few cans from the box I yelled, "Mom! Daddy! Mama Dot! C'mere!"

The cans I had taken out of the box had no labels. We checked the remaining cans: none of them had labels. We could not tell whether a can contained corn, peaches, peas or spaghetti. The only can whose contents we could be certain of was the squat can unique to Dinty Moore Beef Stew.

Mother and Daddy looked stunned, then they both laughed. "Buddy struck again," said Mother.

"I didn't look inside the box before I packed it," Daddy said.

"I should have known better," said Mama Dot. "I packed the box on the floor of the back porch and left it there. That's how Buddy got to it. He gets down those stairs pretty well, you know."

I was worried. "What are we going to do?"

"Well, well," said Daddy. "We'll play a little game." He took a pencil out of his shirt pocket—which was always filled with neatly lined up drafting pencils—and found a piece of paper. "Before each meal we'll select some cans, guess what's in them and the one who wins gets a prize."

Nancy jumped up and down. "Oh, goody! What's the prize?"

"Do we have to eat whatever it is even if it's spaghetti for breakfast?" I moaned.

Daddy ignored this. "How about an extra piece of candy or not having to do dishes for a prize?"

"Goody, goody!" Nancy chirped.

"That's enough, Miss Goody Two Shoes," I growled, giving her a shove.

Nancy gave me a push in return. "Now, girls," Mother said.

Daddy wrote all of our names on a slip of paper except Mama Dot's. She lighted a cigarette, settled into a camp chair and said she'd leave the guessing to the rest of us.

"Nancy, you're first," said Daddy. "Pick out a can."

Nancy quickly picked out the can that we all knew was Dinty Moore Beef Stew.

"Not that one, Nancy," said Daddy. "We all know what that one is. Pick out another one."

Nancy selected a can, held it to her ear and shook it. "I think it's . . . pineapple," she said.

Daddy wrote down "pineapple" after Nancy's name and handed the can to me.

I turned the can around and around and shook it near my ear, but I could not get any clues. "I guess . . . corn," I said.

Daddy wrote down "corn" after my name. Mother guessed "peas" and Daddy guessed "string beans."

The mystery can turned out to be pineapple, and Nancy won. That's the way we selected the canned food for our meals on this trip, a few cans at a time. It was peas or string beans or spaghetti for breakfast or three cans of applesauce for dinner. "Thank heavens for Dinty Moore," Mother said. "At least that's one we can recognize without the label!"

Daddy's game, of course, was a device to get us to eat whatever the cans contained whether it was appropriate for the meal or not. Even if there had been a grocery store nearby, we could not have afforded to replace the cans with labeled cans. In spite of our inconvenience, no one was angry with Uncle Buddy. We didn't resent his tricks. In fact, we were all glad that his outlook was positive and playful.

On Christmas morning at The Ranch Daddy carried Uncle Buddy into the house so he could be there when the presents were opened. In the afternoon Nancy and I followed Granddad around while he fed the chickens and gathered eggs. A light snowfall drove Nancy and me into the house where we played checkers while Mother and Mama Dot cooked the turkey. After dinner we played rummy with Uncle Buddy, who let each of us win a hand.

The next evening—Saturday—was poker night at The Ranch, a much enjoyed weekly event. The players were Mama Dot, Granddad, Uncle Buddy, Mr. Johnson and a couple of other men who lived in the area. No women were ever invited because Mama Dot believed that "women don't know how to play poker."

I truly loved being at The Ranch when a poker game was in session. Daddy, Granddad or one of the men players went out to Uncle Buddy's room, carried him in and placed him in a special cushioned chair at the poker table. Uncle Buddy always "dressed" for the occasion. He was freshly shaven, his hair was slicked back and he wore a clean white shirt. An evening's supply of handrolled cigarettes filled his shirt pockets.

Mother and Daddy sat in overstuffed chairs by the wood stove. Daddy read a book while Mother knitted. Skippy had been put to bed in Granddad's room. Nancy and I settled quietly onto the sofa with our books and read quietly until we fell asleep.

The background of the Saturday night poker parties is part of my nostalgic memories of The Ranch. The shuffling and slapping of cards on the table, the tinkling of ice in the highball glasses, the clink of poker chips, the laughter, and the smell of cigarette and pipe smoke will even today bring these fond memories racing back to me.

Mama Dot took her card games seriously. The stakes were not high, but real money changed hands, and the winner purchased a new deck of cards for the next game. The seal on the deck was not broken until everyone was assembled. It was little wonder there were always plenty of used decks around Mama Dot's house for Nancy and me to play with. One of Mama Dot's favorite pieces of advice was, "Never draw to an inside straight." When I was little, I didn't know what that meant, but I know now. Mama Dot had a real knack for cards, something that didn't get passed down to me.

Like Mother, Mama Dot was a city person, but she dealt very well with the comparative isolation of her desert life. She steadfastly refused to "go native," as she put it. Even in the summer heat she wore stockings because "ladies always wear stockings." Every afternoon she bathed and dressed and drove the two miles into Adelanto, which then consisted of a gas station, a post office, and a grocery store. After she picked up the mail and groceries she paid social calls, buying butter from Mrs. Bogarde, chatting with Mrs. Rogers or stopping to exchange a few words with Mrs. Mullin. "A lady stays just long enough to drink a cup of tea or smoke a cigarette," Mama Dot instructed me, "not one minute longer." Keeping up appearances and maintaining a ladylike demeanor were important to Mama Dot. "A lady is *always* dignified," Mama Dot reminded me frequently, "*no matter what.*"

Mama Dot retained her dignity even when she was involved in a flirtation. Petite, pretty and impeccably groomed, but also self-sufficient and unflappable, she knew how to drop her handkerchief southern style when an attractive man was around. Mama Dot was "sweet" on Mr. Hartwell, a widower who was building a weekend cottage in Adelanto. When Nancy and I spent vacations at The Ranch Mama Dot would say, "Girls, let's go see how Mr. Hartwell's place is coming along. And when we get there, both of you beg me to take you to the movies."

It worked every time. Mr. Hartwell came by and took Nancy and me to the movies in Victorville. Mama Dot, of course, went along and sat next to Mr. Hartwell. Mr. Hartwell became a regular at the Saturday night poker games. Mama Dot was very animated around Mr. Hartwell, in a very lady-like way, of course.

Granddad, who liked Mr. Hartwell, didn't seem to mind. "I go to bed with the chickens and get up with the chickens," he said. "You folks go off and enjoy yourselves."

I've often wondered if there were other Mr. Hartwells in Mama Dot's past. However, I'm certain that she was always a lady, *no matter what.*

CHAPTER 14

Our Sixth School

Nancy

In January of 1937 our four-month stay in Fresno ended, and we moved south along Highway 99 some 65 miles to the small town of Delano. I was 11 and in the seventh grade. I no longer dreaded changing schools but didn't enjoy my classes the way Sunny, the family scholar, did.

Sunny almost cried when she told me how she got the news. She loved her art class and was carving a linoleum block when she looked up and saw Mother standing in the classroom doorway. All Sunny said when she and Mother got in the car with Sunny's half-finished artwork was, "Where to now, Mother?" and all Mother said was, "Delano."

I got by in most school subjects but was hopeless when it came to music. Standing among the altos in class, I would stare at the notes on the score and wonder how I could be expected to look at a dot on a piece of paper and produce its sound. When the teacher blew on her pitch pipe, the other students would begin singing while I hummed along, trying to make the same sounds as the children on either side of me.

Mother found a new elocution teacher for me in Delano and presented the private lessons to me as an advantage rather than a remedy for my lisp. Working with Mrs. Glendenning, I memorized humorous essays and gave readings at several local events.

One of these events, covered in the Delano paper under the headline, "Air Maneuvers Preparation for Peace, Not War," was a talk by WW I Ace Major E. W. Morris to the Delano Exchange Club assuring that, "The present maneuvers of the United States Army Air Force being conducted throughout the San Joaquin Valley are not preparations for any anticipated war but preparations for peace."

The United States may not have been anticipating war, but in 1937 Hitler was gathering his forces in Germany.

The newspaper article concludes with: "Prior to Major Morris' talk, Little Miss Nancy Lockard of Delano gave two delightful readings."

Delano, with its approximately 4,000 inhabitants, must have been hard up for a way to entertain the Exchange Club before the Major's talk.

Despite my "delightful readings" in Delano, both Mother and Daddy continued to reinforce the labels we children had been given. Sunny, scholarly; Nancy, practical; Skippy, precocious.

I soon turned my attention to exploring Delano on my bicycle after school. Our constant moving had made me cautious of seeking friends or joining in school activities. It had also taught me that one way to solve problems was to wait until we moved away from them. "It doesn't matter, we're going to move anyway," became my philosophy.

Sunny

Changing schools was beginning to seem normal to me. Delano High School was the fifth school I had entered since we left Lynwood in June of 1935. I was fourteen years old and in the second half of the tenth grade.

Mindful of Mother's warning about not making friends too quickly, I was polite and studious at school but not overly friendly. After all, I wouldn't want to bring home another Darlene and incur Mother's wrath. To my surprise, most of the kids in my classes were friendly. Even during my first week in school I was invited to walk to the next class with a group, to bring my lunch and eat with some of the girls, to join the Art Club and to participate in a dance program for the Spring Festival. It was no time at all before I felt accepted at Delano High School. I didn't realize it at the time, but the normal process of growing up and adjusting to our frequent moves had made me more outgoing.

There was one girl who was so friendly that she made a pest out of herself. Jane Horton, a junior, was in my art class. She was a large-boned girl, somewhat overweight and always in motion. She wore saddle oxfords and white bobby socks, flowered print dresses and a big floppy pink bow in her stringy, brownish hair. She had a large nose, freckles and a "hee haw" laugh. Jane was unable to stay with an art project for more than five or ten minutes. She would bounce out of her chair, run to the teacher's desk and ask silly questions or run around the room bothering the other students. The art teacher would get Jane back to her desk for a few minutes, then Jane would jump up and start roving again. I wondered how she ever got to be a junior if she couldn't sit still for more than a few minutes. Maybe the teachers passed her along to get rid of her.

The day I enrolled in Delano High Jane came over to me in the hall, playfully punched my shoulder and said, "Hi ya, New Girl!" In art class she would run over to where I was sitting, peer over my shoulder, then run off to look at someone else's work. In May, when the art teacher arranged an exhibit of our projects for Parents' Night, Jane had nothing to display because she hadn't completed anything.

During my first two weeks at Delano High Jane never

tired of pestering me. She would run up to me in the hall, poke me and say, "How ya doin'?" Outside on the school grounds she'd wave at me from a distance, then come running at me, back off, shout "Watch me!" and turn cartwheels. Or she'd run by me in the hall and give me a slight punch as she passed by.

One day Jane introduced me to her boyfriend. "This is Kenny," she said proudly, putting her arm through his. Kenny was a little shorter than Jane. He was pimply and skinny. He wore thick glasses and his hair stood on end. "He's *mine*," Jane said, squeezing Kenny's arm. "You can't have him!"

She's welcome to him, I thought. Kenny, I found out, was a senior. He wrote a gossip column for the school paper called "*The Snooper*." "I snoop around school and pick up bits for my column," Kenny explained. He and Jane giggled. "It's fun," said Jane.

A few days later Jane and Kenny approached me in the hall and asked me to go to a dance with them. "It's to raise money for the Junior Picnic," Jane said, swaying back and forth to imaginary dance rhythms. "It's twenty-five cents per person and seven o'clock 'til ten next Friday night. You can go with us."

"I'll have to ask Mother," I replied. I didn't want to go anywhere with Jane and Kenny, but I wanted to go to the dance, and not alone. I would talk it over with Mother. She'd probably say "no" anyway.

"Why don't you go with them?" Mother said. "If Kenny writes for the school paper he must be a nice boy, and he's probably a good driver since he's a senior. And you say that Jane is the daughter of that nice Mr. Horton at the hardware store? They sound all right to me. Why not go? But I want you home right after the dance, not a minute later."

Mother made most of my dresses, but in Fresno she had bought me a nice dress "to wear to school events." I didn't go to any school events in Fresno, so I hadn't worn my new dress yet. "This will give you an opportunity to wear that dress," Mother said.

Oh well, I thought, I was only riding to and from the dance with Jane and Kenny, so I didn't have to stick with them once I got there. I hoped the boys would dance with me. I hated the idea of being a wallflower. It was so *embarrassing.*

On the evening of the dance there was a knock on the door at 6:45. I opened the door and there stood Kenny, but no Jane. A large family car was parked in front of the house.

"Where's Jane?" I asked.

"Oh, she's in the car," Kenny answered, smiling. Later on I would remember his words.

Mother waved goodbye and reminded me to come home as soon as the dance was over. Kenny and I walked to the car and he opened the front passenger door for me. I glanced inside but didn't see Jane. "Kenny, I thought you said that Jane was in the car?"

"Oh, well, uh. . . ." Kenny stammered. "She'll be along later. She had to help her mother with something." Kenny closed the door on my side, walked around the front of the car and got into the driver's seat.

I was feeling a little uneasy. "She's coming to the dance, isn't she?"

"Oh, sure, she'll be there." Kenny started the car and drove off. He took his right hand off the steering wheel and put it down on the seat between us. I moved over as close as I could get to the door on the passenger side. Kenny's hand crept a little closer, then we came to a stop sign and he retrieved his hand to shift gears.

"Do you have a boyfriend?" he asked.

"I've only been here a couple of weeks."

"I mean in Fresno."

"No, I don't have a boyfriend in Fresno or anywhere. My parents are strict. My mother wouldn't approve of it."

"After tonight you'll probably have one." Kenny pulled

the car into the school parking lot. "Some of the boys have been asking about you. I bet you get plenty of dances."

I hoped Kenny was right. I certainly didn't want to spend the evening holding up a wall.

"How about giving me the first dance?" Kenny asked.

"What about Jane?"

"She's not here yet."

"How do you know? We'd better go see."

We each paid our twenty-five cents and entered the gymnasium. I looked around for Jane but didn't see her. The music had started. Kenny grabbed me and we danced. When the music stopped he said, "How about the next one?"

"The other girls expect you to dance with them," I replied. "I'm going to get some punch." I turned my back on Kenny hoping he wouldn't follow me. I walked over to the refreshment table and poured myself a cup of punch. Then I stood near a group of girls and watched the dancers. Kenny was dancing with Agnes Murphy. Thank goodness! At that moment I saw Jane enter the gym, glance around, and head directly for Kenny and Agnes. She grabbed Kenny's arm and gave Agnes a shove. I congratulated myself for not dancing with Kenny a second time!

A tall boy came over and asked me for the next dance. I recognized him from my English class. He was nice looking and turned out to be a fair dancer. His name was Milton. "Did you come with Kenny?" he asked.

"No. With Jane and Kenny. Only she got delayed a little bit."

I danced every dance the rest of the evening: four with Milton, the rest with others. Kenny didn't ask me for another dance. He was completely monopolized by Jane.

I danced the last dance with Milton. "I can take you home," he offered, "if you don't mind riding in a truck."

"I don't mind," I said, "but Mother would kill me. I'd better go with Jane and Kenny."

"I'll see you at school, then. Oh . . . wait a minute . . . don't let Kenny and Jane play any tricks on you."

"I won't. Goodnight, Milton. It was fun."

"Sure was." Milton hesitated, then he blurted out, "You're a swell girl!"

I managed an embarrassed smile, then said goodnight again.

What did Milton mean, "tricks"? I got into the car with Jane and Kenny. Jane sat in the middle of the front seat, next to Kenny, and I sat between Jane and the door.

"We're going to the drive-in for hamburgers and cokes," Jane said. "Wanna come?"

"No, but thanks anyway. Mother expects me home right away. Sorry you couldn't come along with Kenny and me, Jane. Thanks for the ride, Kenny."

Jane giggled, and so did Kenny. They let me out in front of my house. Kenny didn't get out of the car and open the door for me. I suppose Jane wouldn't have liked it.

"See you in the papers," Jane yelled as I walked up to my front door. I could hear Jane and Kenny giggling. A couple of nuts, I thought. I won't go anywhere with them again. They make me uncomfortable.

Mother was waiting. "Have a good time?" she asked. "Your dress looks pretty."

"I danced every dance but one," I replied, "and the one I didn't dance was because I was drinking punch."

"I guess those dancing lessons in Stockton came in handy! Did you meet any nice boys?"

"They were all nice. Especially Milton." Immediately I wished I hadn't said that. Now I was in for the third degree.

"Who's Milton?"

"He's in my English class." I might as well tell her everything I knew about Milton, because she'd get it out of me sooner or later. "Milton lives on a farm with his parents. He's sixteen. He had to stay out of school for a year to work on the farm when his father was sick. He's an amateur photographer and takes pictures for the school paper."

"Is he good looking? Not like Kenny, I hope."

"Yes, he's good looking. He's tall. And nice."

"Well, he does sound like a nice boy. A little too old for you, though. Remember, no dates until you're sixteen!"

"Mom! That's a long way off! I went out with Bobby Wilson when I was *thirteen*, and he was *sixteen*!"

"That was different. Well, we'll see what happens. No dates this year, anyway."

"No one's asked me, anyhow."

"Milton might ask you, and if he does he can come over here to visit. But no going out on a date. That's final."

When the next issue of the school paper came out it had this in "*The Snooper*" column:

> "*What new girl came to the Junior Dance with J.H.'s boyfriend, and why was J.H. late coming to the dance? Were K. and the new girl really alone in the car? The Snooper knows . . .*"

I confronted Kenny and Jane in the hall. "What was that item all about?" I asked indignantly.

Jane giggled. "Can't you guess?"

"Were you in the car, Jane? Lying on the floor in the back? Were you?" I knew it was true and I felt like a fool. Why hadn't I looked in the back of the car?

Kenny and Jane giggled. "Good thing you behaved yourself," Jane said to me.

I walked away. They were idiots! What could possibly be funny about what they did? Did they create these situations so Kenny would have something to put in his stupid column? Now I knew what Milton had meant when he used the word "tricks." From that day on I stayed as far away from Jane and Kenny as I could get. Fortunately they left me alone, too.

Milton became my friend. He came over to our house on weekends and I danced with him at the dances. Daddy drove me to the dances and picked me up afterwards. Milton seemed to understand my parents' strictness. Although he came to our house frequently and appeared to enjoy being with us, he never did ask me for a date.

I had other friends as well. There was Raymond Noritake in my Geometry class. Raymond and I were the best students in the class. We were so proud of ourselves that we cut up in the classroom by firing spitwads at each other across the room. There was Alisha Johnson and there were the sisters Suzy and Lucy. Alisha was African American and Suzy and Lucy were of Korean descent. In every school I attended in the San Joaquin Valley during my freshman and sophomore years there was a sprinkling of Asian Americans, Mexican Americans and Blacks. Even though these groups were outnumbered by whites, we all got along. I can't remember any racial incidents of any sort or any feelings whatsoever among the white kids against minority groups. We shared classrooms, teachers, books, even friendships. After school we more or less stuck with our own groups, but during school it was share and share alike.

I *loved* Delano. For our leatherwork project in art class I made a keytainer for Mother and a wallet for Daddy, which he treasured for years and years. These items were put on exhibit for Parents' Night. I had a dancing part in the Spring Festival. The teacher who supervised the choreography liked the way I used my hands and the way I pointed my toes. "Girls," said the teacher, "watch how Sunny does it and copy her." I had *friends*. I started bringing my lunch to school so I could eat with my *friends*. Kids spoke to me in the hall, and even *"The Snooper"* became kind: *"What girl—initials S.L—is artistically talented and also has a brain? The Snooper knows."*

On Sundays, when the weather was nice, Daddy took us for drives in the country. The wildflowers were abundant in April, with carpets of lupines, poppies, desert dandelions and mustard everywhere. Sometimes we would go on a picnic in the Sierra foothills, and several times Milton went with us. On the way home Mother would buy fruit and vegetables from the Japanese farmers. It was a good life in Delano. I completed my sophomore year there and was looking forward to being a junior at Delano High, but it was not to be.

Daddy expected all of us to be elated at the news. We were moving again, but this time it was different. This would be our last move. We would live in Taft, an oil town thirty-five miles southwest of Bakersfield. Daddy would be working out of the office in Fellows, near Taft. It was a good job, a promotion. We would buy a house, and changing schools was at an end. Mother seemed relieved. "Well," she sighed, "it isn't Lynwood, but at least we'll be settled. I may even start a garden."

I tried to look pleased, but I wasn't. A new school, new kids, a new town. I was happy in Delano, and I didn't want it to end. As usual Daddy had cautioned us not to get too settled, but I had settled comfortably into Delano. Now I had to face being the new girl again, taking time to make friends, getting used to things.

The sun smoldered in the western sky as we turned off highway 99 and headed toward Taft. The road shot directly west across the dry flat land.

"That's Buena Vista Lake over there," said Daddy, nodding to our left.

I had seen what looked like water beyond a fringe of

scraggly brush and tules but I thought it was probably a mirage, since the brown hills covered with black oil derricks shimmered in the blistering heat.

Mother patted her brow with a fresh white linen handkerchief. "A lake? Here?" She covered her nose with the handkerchief. "And what a smell in this God-forsaken place!"

Daddy smiled. "That's the smell of black gold, Hon. And after you've counted the churches in Taft you won't think it's God-forsaken."

The road rose and fell in gentle undulations until we reached a sloping plain among low hills and Taft appeared.

Our family, tired from cleaning, organizing and packing, said little. Daddy, however, with his usual enthusiasm for terrain, pointed to the Coast Ranges in the distance and the Sierra Madre mountains to the south. As far as we could see the derricks of the Midway Sunset oil fields bristled like quills on the back of an alarmed porcupine.

If we could have looked into the modest frame houses as we drove into town we would have seen, in some of them, luxurious Persian rugs, exquisitely carved furniture and other treasures brought back from the Middle East by people who had worked in Saudi Arabia and Iran with one of the oil companies.

In 1937 Taft had not fully outgrown its oil boom town atmosphere. A brothel, prominently located in the center of town above some shops, did a thriving business. Saloons, like The Brass Rail, prospered, and Saturday night knife fights were a regular feature in the out-of-town dance halls. In contrast to this was an excellent public school system—which included a junior college—generously financed by oil revenue and an educated section of the populace that traveled abroad and attended concerts and plays in Los Angeles.

We moved into a small two-bedroom house in Taft while Mother looked for a place to buy. Nancy and I spent several afternoons a week at the Taft Natatorium, a large swimming pool that was part of the school system. One day I met a couple of girls there who were going to be juniors in the fall. Their names were Janice and Maureen. Janice's father was in charge of an oil lease several miles out of town. Maureen's father was a geologist.

Neither of the girls had grown up in Taft. Both had moved there during the previous school year when they were sophomores.

"I know what it's like to move around a lot," Janice told me. My dad was in the army and we've lived just about everywhere."

Maureen said, "We've moved around a bit, also. Not as much as you two have, but some, so I know what it's like."

Janice exclaimed, "You'll like our school! We have oil money, so we have the best teachers, library, books, equipment, everything. Will you be taking an art class? If so, you can join our art club."

Maureen added, "We have a great drama club with trips to Los Angeles to see plays. Would you like to join?"

When Janice drove her Model A Ford into town she often dropped by our house for a visit. Then Janice and I picked up Maureen and headed for the swimming pool. Summer temperatures in Taft ranged from the high eighties to one hundred and ten or so, and frequent swims were refreshing.

"Looks as if you've found some nice girlfriends already," Mother said.

One day Milton came to visit. He drove all the way from Delano in his truck. He stayed for lunch and we talked afterwards for a couple of hours. I was glad to see him, but I didn't pine over him after he left. I liked Milton a lot, but he didn't affect me the way Bobby Wilson had.

One hot July morning a tiny, wrinkled woman with a big briefcase knocked on our front door. "I'm an artist," she said, "and a poet, too. I paint pictures of our beautiful landscape. My paintings are for sale." She rummaged in her briefcase and pulled out a framed picture.

"Just a minute," I said. "I'll have to ask Mother."

"Never mind," the woman replied, putting the picture back into her briefcase. She handed me a postcard. "Here's a reproduction of my latest painting and poem. I'll leave it with you and come back later. Show it to your mother."

Mother was sitting at her sewing machine in front of the desert cooler mending one of Daddy's khaki shirts. "Who was that?" she asked without looking up.

"A woman selling paintings. She said she'd come back later."

Mother glanced at the postcard I was holding. It showed rolling ochre hills against a bright blue sky in which an enormous black bird hovered. In the foreground a jack rabbit with long pointed pink ears and a coiled rattlesnake were juxtaposed in a field of yellow and orange poppies.

"What's that written in the right hand corner?" Mother asked, returning to her mending.

"A poem," I answered. "She says she's a poet."

"Read it."

I read the poem:

> "Oh, to be a giant bird, to soar
> High above the Valley floor,
> To swoop down canyons, over rocks and rills,
> To glide above the rolling hills
> Of Taft, my cherished home,
> Oh, never shall I roam."

Mother laughed. "All I see out there are parched brown hills, dust, oil derricks and a blinding sun. That woman has quite an imagination, I'd say!"

Nancy and I ran to the dictionary and looked up "rills." Nancy said, "None of those around here!"

Corny as it was, there was something about the picture postcard I liked. I was feeling all right about Taft. I had two new girlfriends. Now there was this strange woman who saw beauty in a barren landscape. Yes, life here would be fine after all.

It took Nancy a little longer to feel all right about Taft. Shortly after beginning the eighth grade she came down with pleurisy and was sick in bed for several weeks. After a doctor's visit which included painful extraction of fluid from Nancy's side, Mother sat by the bed holding her hand, getting up only when the mailman delivered a fat package.

"It's addressed to you, Nancy," Mother said. As Mother untied the string, more than thirty letters spilled out over the bed, get-well wishes from each member of Nancy's class.

Slowly, one by one, Nancy began reading the letters. Skippy stood by the bed and looked at each card and letter as Nancy finished. "Some of them have pictures," he marveled. "This one even has a heart."

"Give that one back to me," Nancy said, slipping it under her pillow with a smile.

I knew then that life here would be fine for her, too.

ABOUT THE AUTHORS

Dorothy Lockard Bristol holds a B.A. in English from the University of California at Berkeley, a Masters from Holy Names College in Oakland and has taught in public and private schools. Her background includes work as a geological drafter in the San Joaquin Valley oil fields. She has published articles on women in history and serves as archivist for a nonprofit organization in Santa Rosa, California.

Before her 26-year career as writer, editor and senior public relations specialist with a multinational information technology corporation, Nancy Lockard Gallop's short stories and articles appeared in a variety of publications. In her third career she has left technology behind. Now free to approach her material subjectively, she finds writing, "More fun but just as challenging."

The authors are native Californians with family connections in the state dating back to the late 1800s. They share a deep affection for California's landscape, history and people.

REFERENCES

Allen, Frederick Lewis. *Since Yesterday, The 1930s in America, September 3, 1929-September 3, 1939*. New York: Harper & Row, 1986.

Birmingham, Stephen. *California Rich*. New York: Simon and Schuster, 1980.

Brown, Joseph E., text, and Dan Guravich, photographs. *The Return of the Brown Pelican*. Baton Rouge and London: Louisiana State University Press, 1983.

California Transit Company. *Short Way to Los Angeles Via the Scenic Valley and Ridge Route*. San Francisco: C.T.C., ca. 1920.

Chandler, Lester V. *America's Greatest Depression 1929-1941*. New York: Harper & Row, 1970.

Clark, Lew and Ginny. *John Muir Trail Country*. 2d ed. Escondido: Western Trails, 1977.

Congdon, Don, ed. *The Thirties, a Time to Remember*. New York: Simon and Schuster, 1962.

Croce, Arlene. *The Fred Astaire and Ginger Rogers Book*. New York: Vintage Books, 1977.

Dillon, Richard, Thomas Moulin and Don De Nevi. *High Steel, Building the Bridges Across San Francisco Bay*. Berkeley: Celestial Arts, 1979.

Epstein, Daniel Mark. *Sister Aimee*. New York: Harcourt, Brace Jovanovich, 1993.

Evers, Anne, ed. *Discover the Californias*. San Francisco: The California Tourism Corporation, 1989.

Federal Writers' Project of the Works Progress Administration for the State of California. *The WPA Guide to California*. New York: Pantheon Books, 1939.

Green, Harvey. *The Uncertainty of Everyday Life, 1915-1945*. New York: HarperCollins Publishers, Inc., 1992.

Gregory, James N. *American Exodus, The Dust Bowl Migration and Okie Culture in California*. New York: Oxford University Press, 1989.

Gudde, Erwin G. *California Place Names, A Geographical Dictionary*. Berkeley and Los Angeles: University of California Press, 1949.

Haslam, Gerald W. *The Other California, The Great Central Valley in Life and Letters*. Santa Barbara: Capra Press, 1990.

Hutchinson, W. H. *California, Two Centuries of Man, Land, and Growth in the Golden State*. Palo Alto: American West Publishing Company, 1969.

Iacopi, Robert. *Earthquake Country*. Menlo Park: Lane Books, 1964.

Johnson, Stephen, Gerald Haslam and Robert Dawson. *The Great Central Valley, California's Heartland*. Berkeley and Los Angeles: University of California Press in association with the California Academy of Sciences, 1993.

Latta, F. F. *Black Gold in the Joaquin*. Idaho: The Caxton Printers, Ltd., 1949.

Laval, Jerome D. *As "Pop" Saw It, Volume I, The Great Central Valley of California as Seen by the Lens of a Camera*. Fresno: Graphic Technology Co., 1975.

Marshall, Richard, ed. *Great Events of the 20th Century*. New York : The Reader's Digest Association, Inc., 1977.

Mitchell, Annie R. *The Way it Was, The Colorful History of Tulare County*. Fresno: Valley Publishers, 1976.

Muir, John. *The Mountains of California*. Berkeley: Ten Speed Press, 1977.

Rintoul, William. *Oildorado, Boom Times on the West Side*. Fresno: Valley Publishers, 1978.

Rowsome, Frank Jr. *The Verse by the Side of the Road*. New York: E.P. Dutton and Co., Inc., 1966.

Scott, Elaine. *Doodlebugging, The Treasure Hunt for Oil.* New York: Frederick Warne & Co., Inc., 1982.

Shannon, David A., ed. *The Great Depression.* New Jersey: Prentice-Hall, Inc., 1960.

Smith, Wallace. *Garden of the Sun, A History of the San Joaquin Valley 1772-1939.* Los Angeles: Lymanhouse, 1939.

Stanley, Jerry. *Children of the Dust Bowl, The True Story of the School at Weedpatch Camp.* New York: Crown Publishers, Inc., 1992.

Suter, Coral. "Riding High on the Old Ridge Route." Sebastopol, California: *The Californians,* March/April 1993.

Wertheim, Arthur Frank. *Radio Comedy.* New York: Oxford University Press, 1979.